MARINERS OF THE
AMERICAN REVOLUTION

American Frigate CONFEDERACY captured by ROEBUCK and ORPHEUS, April, 1781.

Official U. S. Navy Photograph.

MARINERS OF THE AMERICAN REVOLUTION

Compiled and with an Introduction by
Marion and Jack Kaminkow

WITH AN APPENDIX OF AMERICAN SHIPS CAPTURED BY THE BRITISH
DURING THE REVOLUTIONARY WAR

CLEARFIELD

Copyright © 1967
Magna Carta Book Company
Copyright © transferred 1993 to
Genealogical Publishing Co., Inc.
All Rights Reserved.

Reprinted by Genealogical Publishing Co., Inc.
Baltimore, Maryland
1993

Library of Congress Catalogue Card Number 93-78986

Reprinted for Clearfield Company by
Genealogical Publishing Company
Baltimore, Maryland
2013

ISBN 978-0-8063-4872-8

Made in the United States of America

ACKNOWLEDGEMENTS

I should like to thank the following people for their assistance in the research for this book:

Captain F. Kent Loomis, USN (Ret.), Assistant Director of Naval History, Department of the Navy, Washington D.C.; Mr. A. W. H. Pearsall, Custodian of Mss., National Maritime Museum, Greenwich, England; H. S. Cobb, Senior Assistant Clerk of the Records, House of Lords Record Office, London, England; The Captain of H.M.S. St. Vincent, Gosport, England; Mr. M. J. W. Willis-Fear, City Archivist of Portsmouth, England; Mr. W. Best Harris, City Librarian of Plymouth, England. Also all the librarians of historical societies who have taken time to answer my letters.

M.J.K.

CONTENTS

Frontispiece	iii
Acknowledgements	vii
Introduction	xi
Notes on the Records	xix
Interpretation of the clues	xxiii
Abbreviations and explanations	xxv
Mariners of the Revolution	1
Additions and Corrections	214
Notes on the prisons	215
Appendix I. List of American ships captured by the British during the Revolutionary War.	217
Appendix II. An Act to Impower His Majesty to Secure and Detain Persons charged with or suspected of, the Crime of High Treason.	239
Appendix III. An Act for the better detaining, and more easy Exchange, of American Prisoners brought into Great Britain.	243
Bibliography	245

INTRODUCTION

It is well known that the American Navy of the Revolution was small and that most of the defense against the British at sea fell to the lot of privateers, privately owned ships which, following a general practice among maritime nations, received credentials from their government giving them permission to attack and plunder the enemies' ships without meriting the title of pirate in the eyes of their own government, though not, as we shall see in the eyes of their enemies.

The records concerning the men who manned these privateers are pathetically few and those that have been printed refer mainly to the officers, rarely to the ordinary seamen. This book tries a new approach by unravelling the records concerning those men who were captured by the enemy and is compiled from material kept by the British government of the day, together with the diaries of several of the captured seamen, which they kept while prisoners of war in England. For a more detailed description of the sources used see NOTES ON THE RECORDS, p. xix and BIBLIOGRAPHY p. 245.

When the crew of an American ship fell into British hands, they were often brought back to England, where a great deal more attention was paid to them than if they were prisoners of war overseas. For a while the British government was embarrassed to know what to do with these visitors. First an Act of Parliament had to be passed defining their exact status,* and then the Lords Commissioners of the Admiralty had to look about them and find suitable places of confinement. The chosen places were handed over to the Commissioners for taking care of sick and hurt seamen, known as the Sick and Hurt Board, with instructions as to how many officials were to be put in charge of each prison, their wages, duties, etc. and the rations for each prisoner. Old Mill Prison, near Plymouth, and Forten Prison, near Portsmouth, were the two strongholds decided upon by the Lords Commissioners of the Admiralty to hold their rebellious guests. Mill was to be fitted up for 400 men and Forten for 200. Each prison was to have a keeper or agent, a clerk, three turnkeys, a steward, cook, laborer and doctor. These facts appear in the In-letters of the Sick and Hurt Board at Greenwich, (See Bibliography No. 33). For a more detailed description of the prisons see p. 215. Military guards were also provided, as noted daily by William Widger in his diary. (Bibliography No. 10).

* *see* Appendix II

INTRODUCTION

Before confinement, a minute questionnaire was given to each prisoner by two civil magistrates, and a little later, in order to check more thoroughly, the questions were repeated and the answers compared. The motive here was to ensure that the captive was indeed an American, for whom special rules of procedure had been laid down, and not a British subject serving on an American ship, who could be brought to trial for treason. While it is true that the rebellious Americans were officially designated as pirates and traitors to His Majesty, the Act of Parliament specifically stated that persons suspected of High Treason committed in any of His Majesty's Colonies or Plantations in America or on the High Seas, were not to be brought to trial until January 1st, 1778. The sponsors of the Act perhaps expected that the conflict would be over by that time, and all the so-called traitors and pirates could be brought to trial and condemned for High Treason, which would have been logical, since the American Colonists were considered as subjects of King George III. On the other hand, if things should go wrong and the American Colonies emerge the victors from the conflict, then it would be better for all concerned if the prisoners had been treated as prisoners of war from the beginning, rather than as traitors and pirates. So the Act was renewed from time to time to defer the prisoners from being brought to trial, and the questions continued to be posed to each new prisoner to make sure that no captive who was not a genuine American escaped trial.

Some of the first prisoners to reach England included the crews of the DALTON and the CHARMING SALLEY. Since they arrived before accomadation had been prepared for them, they were passed from ship to ship in Plymouth harbor, on some of which they were treated kindly but on others cruelly. Two men have left us records of this period: Charles Herbert and Samuel Cutler, both of whom sailed in the DALTON. (See Bibliography Nos. 4 and 7). Through the winter of 1776 and the spring of 1777 they suffered cruelly from the damp and cold, from the itch and various other diseases including smallpox, which sent numbers of them ashore to the Royal Hospital before the prisons were ready to receive them. Finally in June 1777, the Old Mill Prison opened its doors and the mariners entered with mixed feelings - relief at leaving the cramped discomfort of the ships and foreboding as to what might be in store for them.

At Portsmouth a similar drama was taking place while Forten prison was being prepared for their reception. Timothy Connor of the RISING STATES was among the first to enter this prison and he has left us an account of it in his diary. (See Bibliography No. 5).

From then on the diaries are filled largely with complaints about prison life, the occupations of the men, lists of prisoners brought in and exchanged and entertaining accounts of escapes.

The In-letters of the Sick and Hurt Board at Greenwich tell us that Will-

INTRODUCTION

iam Cowdray was appointed keeper of Mill Prison and John Newsham keeper of Forten Prison on April 21, 1777. Newsham does not figure much in the diaries of the prisoners, but Cowdray, under a variety of spellings, figures quite largely in every diary that was kept at Mill. His dishonesty, vengeance and fits of ungovernable rage and drinking bouts did much to increase the hardness of the prisoners' lives. A long letter in the records at Greenwich signed "Humanitas" witnessed that Mr. Cowdray indulged in every conceivable form of corruption at the prisoners' expense; that he bought hucks and necks of beef instead of whole quarters and the meat was so tainted that maggots dropped out of it. The allowance was further reduced by boiling to get the fat out for tallow. He robbed the prisoners of their money and valuables and denied their right to work, while the greater part of the money which was collected in their charity box went into his own pocket. The beer was watered and he had made the coal place into a hog sty and had 200 hogs eating the prisoners' rations, while the prisoners were actually perishing with hunger. We do not know for sure how much of this is true, for the diarists do not mention the hogs or robberies, but it is a fact that every diary is sprinkled with complaints about the badness and inadequacy of the food, including the extremely rankling fact that the French and Dutch prisoners were allowed 1½ pounds of bread while the Americans only received one pound per day. Among the papers in the House of Lords Record Office is a document from Mill Prison, dated June 1781 and signed by about 200 prisoners, petitioning for a higher daily allowance of bread and a better allowance of clothes. According to the In-letters of the Sick and Hurt Board, the Lords Commissioners of the Admiralty did not seem to know why the American prisoners received only two thirds as much bread as the others and it was agreed that the allowance should be raised to correspond with the other prisoners' rations. But the well-fed Lords in Parliament thought otherwise and that the bread ration should remain unchanged.

The prisoners' daily rations as set out by the Admiralty Commissioners were one pound of bread, one quart of beer and three quarters of a pound of beef per day and half a pint of peas or greens five times per week. On Sunday the beef was to be replaced by cheese. The diet sounds plain but adequate and most of the prisoners were able to supplement it by their own small earnings or charities; but though the Lords Commissioners of the Admiralty proposed, Messrs. Cowdray and Newsham disposed and there is no doubt that inferior quality food, badly cooked, justified all complaints; but Cowdray was never replaced. He had the audacity to circularise a paper for the prisoners to sign at the end of hostilities, saying that he had treated them kindly. According to William Russell's diary, it was immediately torn up.

Fortunately for the prisoners, subscriptions were opened for their welfare and the amount collected was handed to them weekly in small sums, some-

INTRODUCTION

times as little as sixpence at a time, but which helped to provide them with small necessities which they would not otherwise have had. At times, however, the money ran out and they were reduced to want again, except for those who were able to make a small income by the manufacture of boxes, ladles, ship models and other wood carvings.

The prisoners were by no means idle during their confinement. Like all prisoners, their main occupation, when not engaged in handicrafts, diary writing and complaining, was attempting to escape, and this is what makes their diaries such enthralling reading. The British government, having got its rebels into prison, was now sadly pre-occupied with how to keep them there. Some went over the wall, some tunnelled under the wall, others bribed guards, some walked out dressed as officials, another tried to get into a coffin as a replacement for one of their number who had died, while several less scrupulous connived with members of the local populace who helped them escape and then brought them back to collect the five pounds reward, which they afterwards shared.

For the tunnellers, the problem of where to hide the dirt from the tunnels cropped up then, just as it did in more recent escape accounts, and one story tells how they opened a skylight and piled the dirt on the roof. Another tells of a tunneller who came up from his tunnel in the kitchen of a cottage outside the walls, much to the terror of the elderly female occupant, (see Bibliography No. 12). Those escapers who had a little money sometimes were able to make their way to London or a seaport and take ship for France but many were re-captured and brought back. Some, like Captains John Manley and Gustavus Conyngham made repeated attempts to escape and were repeatedly brought back.

Those who escaped in penniless condition could starve outside and if they reached a port could not take passage for France or Holland without money. Israel Potter, who escaped with only a few pence in his pocket, managed to subsist by casual labor and even acquired a gardening job in the Royal Gardens, once being greeted by the king himself; but becoming entangled by marriage he never did acquire sufficient funds to leave the country and remained in England thirty years before returning to his native land. (See Bibliography No. 15).

Those who escaped and were re-captured faced a term of forty days in the "black hole", a small dark cell apart from the other prisoners, on half rations, but even this threat did not deter them; in fact, a number were even found to have escaped from the black hole on several occasions. Captain Manley, an indefatigable escaper, should have spent most of his time in the black hole by rights, for although he may have been skilled as a sea captain, his attempts to escape are full of amusing blunders; but whether owing to his rank or his charm, it appears that these visits to the black hole were

INTRODUCTION

shortened or waived altogether in his case. The diaries reveal that in no case did a man serve the full forty days.

Many remedies were tried by the government. The wall was made higher, more lights were provided for the sentries but all to no avail, for as time went on the escapes became more and more numerous. Some of the most notable escapes were those of Sept. 11, 1778, when 50 escaped from Forten; and January 5, 1779 when 100 escaped from Mill, though 75 were re-captured the same day. A letter of Nov. 17, 1780, at Greenwich, complains that "213 have escaped from Mill and Forten since Dec. 1778 and 110 of that number since January last".

In 1781 it was suggested that the prisoners be moved from Forten. There were complaints of the escapes, tunnels, mutinous behaviour in spite of threats of confinement, irons, etc. and there were also rumors that the prisoners intended to sieze the guards' weapons and capture a ship. On February 18, 1782 the Sick and Hurt Board wrote to the Admiralty "We humbly conceive the vicinity of the prisons of Mill and Forten to the dockyards and harbors of Portsmouth and Plymouth and their being surrounded with public houses which may be a means of facilitating their escape, renders the removal of the said prisoners from those prisons to be a very necessary measure. (State Papers 42/57). The agent at Forten wrote in February of the same year that the prisoners were "exceedingly riotous and abusive and make their escape in such number, conniving with the population who regularly bring them back and share the five pounds reward. Some have escaped and been brough back fifteen times."

On April 29 the reward was reduced to fifteen shillings, which was the amount paid for Dutch and French prisoners.

The keeper of Kinsale prison in Ireland, which was opened much later in the war, complained "I have never had so much trouble with prisoners in my life" as well he might, considering that 100 of them escaped in February 1783. Seventy four prisoners had already been removed from Kinsale to Mill on October 9, 1781. Other measures were taken besides reducing the reward to stop the conniving. Those who escaped and were brought back automatically went to the bottom of the list for exchange and investigations were begun on a new place of confinement for the "rebels" which was proposed to be a place used by the government for deserted children at Moole Brace near Shrewsbury; but this place was never actually opened owing to the cessation of the war.

For those who did not escape the confines of the prison by their own methods, there were two avenues of exit: either join the Royal Navy or wait until they were exchanged. A number of young men, chafing at their confinement, applied to join the British Navy, thinking perhaps to increase their chances of escape, as in the case of Anthony Knapp, who, after joining the

INTRODUCTION

Royal Navy managed to make his escape and join the French ship Black Princess. Unluckily for him, this ship later fell into the hands of the British, so that he found himself once more in prison.

Having once made up his mind to join the British Navy, however, a prisoner had to wait for the Royal Pardon before he could be released, and since this was usually slow in coming, he had often changed his mind, or been talked out of the idea before it came.

The exchanging of prisoners seems to have encountered a number of snags. Benjamin Franklin, operating from France, was the chief negotiator with the British government for the exchange arrangements. By reasoning that if he produced a number of British prisoners in France, the British government would feel obliged to agree to an exchange, he set to work organizing a small number of privateers working from French ports with the object of capturing British prisoners. (See Bibliography No. 30). As soon as he had collected a sufficient number, he opened negotiations with the British government and eventually, after repeated delays and misunderstanding, an agreement was reached.

Before the exchanges could take place, however, another Act of Parliament had to be passed, giving American prisoners the status of prisoners of war, all other, etc. to the contrary. (See appendix III). Yet, oddly enough, all prisoners still had to receive the Royal Pardon before they could be exchanged. These pardons were copied out and sent to the agents of the prisons who solemnly read out the list of names to the joyous American prisoners, the main lists of pardons being issued in December 1778, February, May and December 1779, October and November 1781 and February 1782. It would seem in many cases, however, that the pardons issued by King George were pompous farces, for on many occasions the birds had already flown, and in many other cases, prisoners who were pardoned for exchange were still to be found languishing in prison in 1782. But in numerous instances all went according to plan. "Never I believe was joy equal to what I now experienced", wrote Nathaniel Fanning in his diary at Forten prison. "We began our march, which commenced about 10 o'clock, in company, or rather escorted by about forty British soldiers, and a number of black drummers and musicians who beat up the tune of Yankee doodle, which they continued playing till we arrived at the place of embarkation... On our march through the town of Gosport, the streets became crowded with people; some wishing us safe to our desired homes; others crying out that we were a set of rebels, and that if we had our deserts we should have been hanged".

For some of the prisoners who had the wisdom to make use of their enforced idleness, confinement had its compensations, and as Fanning noted in his diary, it was a blessing in disguise, for their time was employed in learning reading, writing, mathematics and navigation. "Many of these have

INTRODUCTION

since advanced to the rank of masters of vessells, otherwise, had they never seen Forten prison, they never would have been more than sailors".

William Russell, one of the diarists, is mentioned as having kept a school among the prisoners and Andrew Sherburne tells us that he learned to write in prison and acquired a literary interest that left him indifferent to gaming, the ruin of many young sailors. His fluent diary is certainly a tribute to his teachers, among whom he names Mr. Tibbitts. Captain James Brown of Kittery is mentioned also as a teacher of navigation.

Although much of the information in this book is culled from diaries which have already been printed, these sources have never before been collated with each other, and the official British records have never been printed. It is hoped that those who long to know more about a revolutionary ancestor who fought for his country by sea will find many clues which will enable him to carry his search further.

M.J.K.

NOTES ON THE RECORDS

As stated by Charles H. Lincoln in NAVAL RECORDS OF THE AMERICAN REVOLUTION, "there is no list or roster of the navy and it is only from an occasional mention that an officer or sailor can be located.

The names in this book have been collected from the records kept by the British government of the Americans whom they captured and carried back to England for imprisonment, supplemented by a number of diaries kept by the Americans during the period they were in prison in England.

The official sources are four in number. They consist of the pardons issued by the king for those men who were to be exchanged or who were to be released on condition of serving in the Royal Navy; a list of prisoners requested by the government in January 1782 and another list requested by the government in April of the same year; a petition signed by 196 prisoners on June 19, 1781 and sent to the House of Lords. If a prisoner was not exchanged or released on condition of joining the Royal Navy, he should logically be found on the lists of 1782 unless he either died or escaped. In a great many cases this assumption is verified by the diarists who mention names, such as Capt. Conyngham, who escaped or Samuel Allen, who died, which do not appear in any of the official records. If they did not escape or die, the names mentioned in the diaries should also appear in the official records, and in great many cases they do; but there are also a great many mysterious instances where they do not. Frequently this is due to the wide variety of spellings used not only by the diarists but by the government also, the signature on the petition sometimes being different again. As many of these discrepancies as possible have been tracked down and cross referenced, but it is clear that more remain to be discovered, so the reader is urged to think up every possible likely or unlikely variant of spelling. In other cases the lack of appearance in the government records could mean escape or death even though the diarists do not say so, and of course there are some such as Luke Matthewman, who appear nowhere at all except in his own diary and there are no doubt others who were captured but escaped mention anywhere.

The pardons issued by the king were taken from among the bundles of papers labelled ADM/M/404 and 405 housed in the National Maritime Museum at Greenwich, near London. These somewhat prolix documents list each prisoner's name twice.

The list of prisoners in both Forten and Mill prisons dated January 1782 appears among the State Papers at the Public Record Office in London and

NOTES ON THE RECORDS

the list dated April 1782 appears among the Home Office Papers, also in the Public Record Office. The later one includes names of prisoners at Kinsale in Ireland, and a few at Edinburgh and other places and a number not yet committed to prison. Why the government asked for these two lists to be compiled at such a short interval is not stated.

The petition sent to the House of Lords is now in the House of Lords Record Office. It was signed by 196 men, petitioning for more changes of clothes and a greater allowance of bread, and presumably all who were in Mill prison at that time signed it.

Reading through the list it is apparent that there are many situations which need explanation. Why, for instance should one man have been pardoned for exchange, then pardoned on condition of joining the Royal Navy, two evident opportunities for release, and yet remain there in the lists of 1782? There is no official explanation for these circumstances, but it is quite evident that about half of those pardoned on Dec. 11, 1779 failed to be exchanged. A number of them tired of waiting and disappointed, sought to join the Royal Navy and received a pardon for that purpose; but by the time the pardon had arrived, they had escaped and been re-captured, which sent them to the bottom of the list for exchange. Meanwhile they had changed their minds about joining the Royal Navy. It is clear that some prisoners captured in the early years remained to see many of their fellows who were captured much later exchanged before them, which must have caused great chagrin. A man who found this particularly galling must have been James Lawrence of the Dalton, the first ship whose crew was sent to Mill prison. Most were pardoned for exchange on Dec. 10, 1778, after about 18 months in prison but James Lawrence, though receiving an official pardon on Dec. 11 1779, remained until the bitter end.

The diaries which have been used to supplement the official records have all been printed (See bibliography Nos. 1-10). It is entirely possible that more diaries exist in manuscript form, either in the hands of the descendants of the compiler, or among the large collection of diaries at the Peabody Institute in Salem, for these mariners of the revolution seem to have been unusually fond of writing. It is from these diaries that the home towns of the men have been taken, for while the SP and HO records give the name of the ship on which the mariner served and the date when he was committed to prison, the pardons and petition give nothing except the name of the individual. This means that there are a number of disagreements as to the origin of some of the men, and even as to what ship they sailed on. Sometimes the controversy over ships' names is due to the fact that the mariner, though officially from one ship, was captured on an English ship which he was sailing back to an American port as a prize.

Jeremiah Colburn (See bibliography No. 3), either through ignorance or delicacy, enters a number of names in his list as having escaped, when the truth is that they joined the Royal Navy. Timothy Connor's list of men in Forten prison, is also a trifle suspect, as his entries for men who appear nowhere else are greater in number than elsewhere

All these arguments and discrepancies could be settled easily if the papers relating to the time when the men were committed to prison could be discovered. From the diaries it seems that a minute questionnaire was given to each prisoner by two civil magistrates before confinement, and a little later, in order to check more thoroughly, the questions were repeated and the answers compared, the motive being to ensure that the captive was indeed an American. The form of the questionnaire which the prisoners had to answer is described in Andrew Sherburne's diary, pp. 77-8, and it is clear that the answers to the questions could be a most valuable asset in the investigation of the mariners. Not only did the magistrates ask the prisoner's name and place of birth, but also his age, father's name and occupation and the facts relating to his capture. In the minutes of the Sick and Hurt Board in the Public Record Office in London, there is a request from the House of Lords dated Dec. 1777 for a list of the prisoners, with the magistrates' warrants, etc. These were produced and laid upon the table in the House, but they are not now to be found among the papers of the House of Lords. Neither are they to be found among the Quarter Sessions Records of Plymouth or Portsmouth. Doubtless they are still buried in the Public Record Office and will come to light eventually.

The only other known source which has not been investigated are the logs of the British ships which captured the American vessels. It is known that these logs contain lists of personnel on board in addition to the crew under the heading "supernumeries". In Appendix I can be found a list of the American ships captured, with the names of the ships that captured them in some cases, which is another possible source of investigation for those interested.

INTERPRETATION OF THE CLUES

Since there are several references given for each of the men, some of them conflicting, the following analysis of a few typical examples may prove helpful in understanding the implications of the references.

GEORGE BOOKER. Though pardoned for exchange Dec. 20, 1779 he was still to be found in prison in Jan. 1782 (SP). However, he was gone by April, 1782 as he is not in the HO list, although no further pardon is evident. Either he escaped or his later pardon is under a different spelling.

WILLIAM BLACK. Though pardoned for exchange in Dec. 1778 he was still to be found in M. Feb. 1779. But since he does not appear in the SP or HO lists it can be presumed he was exchanged shortly afterwards.

JAMES BLANEY. Pardoned for exchange Dec. 11, 1779. As there is no other mention of him anywhere, he probably went.

OFFIN BOARDMAN. Though mentioned in the diaries numerous times, this man is mentioned in none of the official records, the reason being that he escaped.

SAMUEL HUBBLE. Though pardoned for exchange Dec. 11, 1779, this poor man was still there in April, 1782, as he appears in the HO list. Naturally he signed the House of Lords Petition in June, 1781.

JOHN CHESTER of England, taken at about the same time as Hubble, was also pardoned Dec. 1779 and apparently went.

SAMUEL HARRIS of Rhode Island, committed a little later than the last two, was also pardoned for exchange Dec. 1779 but failed to go. Obviously this was because he attempted to escape and was sent to the bottom of the list.

JOHN O'HARA. Mentioned in diary No. 8 but not in any of the official records although it does not say he escaped. If he did not escape, he should appear somewhere in the official records, so he may possibly be the same person as George Ohere of the same ship who appears in SP

INTERPRETATION OF THE CLUES

and HO.

JAMES PATTERSON. Mentioned in diary No. 10 but nowhere else. It is possible that he appears in the official records under a different name, for instance, William Patterson.

JOHN ABBOT. Joined the Royal Navy according to the diarist, but there is no official pardon at Greenwich. They could not have had him down as William because the two were in different prisons. There must be a mistake somewhere.

OLIVER ARNALD. Though pardoned for Royal Navy in March, 1781 he did not go, but was still to be found in prison in April, 1782.

DAVID CLARK of Philadelphia. According to diary No. 7 and the Greenwich records, he joined the Royal Navy. Diarist No. 3, perhaps from delicacy, says he escaped.

ABBREVIATIONS AND EXPLANATIONS

Acc.	According to.
Att.	Attempted.
Comm.	Committed to.
F	Forten Prison. See p. 215 and Introduction.
G	Records at Greenwich, Bibliography No. 33.
HL	House of Lords Petition, Bibliography No. 36. Meaning he signed the petition in June, 1781.
HL (mark)	He signed the petition with his mark instead of his name. Very few were unable to sign their name.
HO	Home Office Records, Bibliography No. 35. Meaning the prisoner was still there in April, 1782.
Kinsale	Kinsale prison in Ireland. See pp. xv, xx.
M	Old Mill Prison. See p. 215 and Introduction.
Mariner	Not always stated but unless other rank is given, this can be assumed. Same as Seaman.
Pard.	Pardoned
Pembroke	A prison in Wales, not described in the records, where prisoners were sometimes kept before being transferred to Mill.
Prize	Enemy ship captured. The Grand Turk's prize, for instance, must have been an English ship captured by the American ship Grand Turk.
Seaman	See Mariner.
SP	State Papers, Bibliography No. 34. Meaning the prisoners was still there in January, 1782.
(2)	Two men of the same name listed.
*	Author of one of the diaries used, the first ten items of the Bibliography.

MARINERS OF THE AMERICAN REVOLUTION

ABBET, Francis. Steward. Rising States. Comm. F. June 14, 1777. Escaped. 5A p. 36.

ABBOT, John of Portsmouth. Dalton or Charming Polly. Comm. M. June, 1777. Sent to hospital March 23, 1777. R. N. 3 p. 75; 4 p. 184; 7 p. 244.

ABBOT, William. F. R. N. October 6, 1781. G.

ABRAHAM(S), Wood(ward) of Salem or Charlestown, N. E. Hawk's prize. Comm. M. Oct. 1778. Pard. for exchange Dec. 11, 1779 and Nov. 9, 1781. G; HL; 3 p. 137; 7 p. 252.

ACHAM, Daniel of Virginia. Reprisal's prize. Comm. M. June 29, 1777. Escaped. 7 p. 251.

ADAIR, John of Ireland. Oliver Cromwell. Comm. M. Oct. 18, 1777. Pard. for exchange Dec. 11, 1779. G; 3 p. 75; 7 p. 255.

ADAMS, (Captain). Taken in a merchantman and set at liberty October, 1777. 7 p. 53.

ADAMS, Benjamin. Seaman. Wexford. Sent from Kinsale to M. April 9, 1782. HO.

ADAMS, Charles. Seaman. Hercules. Sent from Kinsale to M. April 9, 1782. HO.

MARINERS OF THE AMERICAN REVOLUTION

ADAMS, Isaac of Boston. Mariner. Protector. Comm. M. Oct. 16 or 27, 1781. SP; HO; 3 p. 212.

ADAMS, James of Boston. Providence's prize. Comm. M. May 10, 1779. Ran away. 3 p. 138.

ADAMS, James. M. Pard. for exchange Dec. 11, 1779. G.

ADAMS, Jas. M. Attempted escapes May 13, 14 and 18, 1781. Escaped June 14, 1781. 8 p. 131; 10 v. 73 pp. 341, 342, 343; v. 74 p. 25.

ADAMS, James. HL.

ADAMS, Capt. John of Boston. Comm. M. June 1, 1777. 4 p. 186.

ADAMS, John of Marblehead. Fancy. Comm. M. Aug. 7, 1777. Exchanged. 3 p. 136; 7 p. 250.

ADAMS, John (2). M. Pard. for exchange Dec. 11, 1779. G.

ADAMS, John of England. Alliance's prize. Comm. M. March 22, 1779. R. N. July 4, 1780. G; 3 p. 138; 8 p. 125.

ADAMS, John of Boston. Protector. Comm. M. Oct. 28, 1781. 10 v. 74 p. 147.

ADAMS, John. Mariner. Mathew, prize to the Disdain. Comm. M. Dec. 7, 1781. SP; HO.

ADAMS, John. Seaman. Bienfaisant. Comm. Pembroke Jan. 17, 1782. HO.

ADAMS, John. Seaman. Hercules. Sent from Kinsale to M. April 9, 1782. HO.

ADAMS, Joseph. M. Att. escape May 8, 1781. 8 p. 131.

ADAMS, Thomas of Old York. Seaman. Hercules. Sent from Kinsale to M. April 9, 1782. Died June 17, 1782. HO; 8 p. 138.

ADAMS, William. Seaman. Hercules. Captured Oct. 15, 1781 but not committed. HO.

MARINERS OF THE AMERICAN REVOLUTION

ADDAMES, John. 10 v. 73 p. 329. (probably meant for ADAMS)

ADDISON, Wm. of Ireland. Lively. Comm. M. Dec. 27, 1780. Pard. for R. N. May, 1781. Entered June 5, 1781. G; 3 p. 140; 10 v. 74 p. 22.

ADJOLIER, Joseph. Dalton. Taken Dec. 24, 1776. M. Escaped. 3 p. 74. (Same as AGUILIER? See also ASULIER).

AGER, Henry. Franklin. Comm. M. Nov. 1781. 3 p. 212.

AGUILIER, Joseph. M. Pardoned for exchange, Dec. 11, 1779. G; (Same as ADJOLIER?)

ALBY, James. Carpenter. Jason. Captured Oct. 15, 1781 but not committed. HO.

ALCOCK, Abraham. Commerce? Comm. F. Feb. 18, 1779. Pardoned for exchange Dec. 11, 1779. G; 5A p. 39.

ALDERSON (TON), Simon of N. Carolina. Mariner. Revenge. Comm. M. May 4, 1781. SP; HO; HL; 3 p. 140.

ALDERSON, Simon, Jr. Mariner. General Nash. Comm. M. July 28, 1781. SP; HO; 3 p. 210; 10 v. 74 p. 36.

ALEXANDER, Josh. or Joseph. Mariner. Franklin. Comm. M. Dec. 6, 1781. SP; HO; 3 p. 212.

ALEXANDER, Richard. Seaman. Blossom. Comm. F. Oct. 16, 1781. SP; HO.

ALEXANDER, Saml. 1st lieutenant. Lion. Comm. M. Aug. 31 or Sept. 7, 1781. SP; HO; 3 p. 211.

ALLEN, ALLINE, Dr. Benjamin. Comm. F. Oct. 20, 1778. Pardoned for exchange Dec. 11, 1779. G; 5 v. 32 p. 168; 5A p. 38.

ALLEN, Elias. Rising States. Comm. F. June 14, 1777. Pardoned for exchange May 31, 1779. G; 5A p. 36.

ALLEN, Hooper. Seaman. Lion. Comm. M. Jan. 24, 1782. HO.

MARINERS OF THE AMERICAN REVOLUTION

ALLEN, Isaac. Seaman. Morning Star. Comm. F. Aug. 9, 1781. SP.

ALLEN, Israel. Seaman. Hercules. Sent from Kinsale to M. April 9, 1782. HO.

ALLEN, Jacob. Seaman. Newfoundland. Imprisoned at Edinburgh, June 27, 1781. HO.

ALLEN, James. Seaman. Pocahontas. Comm. F. Nov. 18, 1780. SP; HO.

ALLEN, Jno. Brig Lively. Comm. M. Dec. 27, 1780. Pard. for R.N. May, 1781. Entered. June 5, 1781. G; 3 p. 139; 10 v. 74 p. 22.

ALLEN, John. Mariner. Essex. Comm. M. July 20 or 21, 1781. In b.h. Oct. 17, 1781. SP; HO; 3 p. 210; 10 v. 74 pp. 34, 145.

ALLEN, John. Mariner. Hunter. Comm. M. July 25, 1781. SP; HO; 3 p. 210.

ALLEN, John. F. Pardoned for exchange Nov. 9, 1781. G.

ALLEN, Jonathan. Angelica. Comm. F. July 7, 1778. 5A p. 38.

ALLEN, Mayhew or Mayen of Bedford. Mariner. Tracey of Boston. Comm. M. Jan. 6, 1781. SP; HO; HL; 3 p. 140; 10 v. 73 p. 312.

ALLEN, Samuel of Manchester. Rambler. Comm. M. Feb. 16, 1780. Died. 3 p. 139.

ALLEN, William. Seaman. Bunker's Hill. Comm. F. April 7, 1780. SP; HO.

ALLIAN, William of Marblehead. In F. May 8, 1781. 10 v. 73 p. 340.

ALLINE, Benjamin. See ALLEN.

ALLOT, John. M. Pardoned for exchange Dec. 20, 1778. G.

ALMEN, ALMAN or ALMOND, Augustus of Virginia. Mariner. General Nash. Comm. M. July 27, 1781. SP; HO; 3 p. 210.

ALRIDGE, Elisha. Seaman. Adventure. Comm. M. Jan. 21, 1782. HO.

AMEN, George. See ARMON.

AMMERSON, Thos. See EMERSON.

AMSBURY, Browning of Bedford. Brig Polly. Comm. M. Sept. 10, 1778. R.N. 3 p.139.

ANDERSON, James. Seaman. Twin Sisters, privateer of Rhode Island. Comm. to Security Prison Ship at Chatham, Dec. 18, 1781. HO.

ANDERSON, John. Prize of sloop Independent. Comm. F. June 26, 1777. Escaped. 5A p.36.

ANDERSON, Robert. Seaman. Monmouth. Comm. F. Oct. 31, 1780. SP; HO.

ANDREWS, Jonathan. Seaman. Rambler. Comm. F. Dec. 30, 1779. SP; HO.

ANDREWS, William of Ireland. Charming Salley or Dalton. Captured Jan. 16, 1777. M. Still there Feb. 7, 1779. Escaped or R.N. 3 p.74; 7 p.248.

ANDRIAN, Pierre or AUDRAIN, Pier. Comm. F. July 15, 1777. Pard. for exchange May 31, 1779. G; 5A p.36.

ANNABLE, Joseph of Rye, near Portsmouth, New Hampshire. Venus from Philadelphia. Comm. F. April 2, 1778. Died Nov. 13, 1778. 5 v.32, p.281. 5A p.37.

ANSPIN, George. See ASPEN.

ANTONIO, Frank. F. Pard. for R.N. Jan. 25, 1779. G.

ANTTWOOD, John. See AUTTWOOD.

APINALL, Peter. HL. See ASPENAL.

APPLEDALE or APDALE, Jno. Stockhowes or Stackhouse of Boston. Ranger. Comm. M. July 23, 1781. Pard. for R.N. Sept. 10, 1781. G; 3 p.210; 10 v.74 p.35.

MARINERS OF THE AMERICAN REVOLUTION

APPLEGEATH, Robert. Seaman. Dolphin. Comm. F. May 24, 1781. SP; HO.

ARBUNCLE, Wm. of Marblehead. Grand Turk. Comm. M. Nov. 1781. 3 p. 212.

ARCHER, John. M. Pard. for exchange Dec. 11, 1779. G. (Same as Jonathan?)

ARCHER, Jonathan of Salem. Schooner Warren. Comm. M. June 1778. Exchanged. 3 p. 137; 7 p. 254.

ARCHER, William of Salem. Schooner Warren. Comm. M. June, 1778. Pardoned for exchange Dec. 11, 1779 and Nov. 9, 1781. R.N. according to 7. G; HL; 3 p. 137; 7 p. 255.

ARMITAGE, Shewbart, Shubert or Shawbert of Philadelphia. Lieut. of marines or mariner. Greyhound of Philadelphia. Comm. M. Jan. 9, 1781. SP; HO; HL; 3 p. 140; 10 v. 73 p. 313.

ARMON, George, alias Jonathan WOODS of Boston. Mariner. New Adventure or General Mifflin. Comm. M. Oct. 17, 1781. SP; HO; 10 v. 74 p. 145.

ARNOLD, David. Master of the Angelica. Comm. F. July 7, 1778. Pard. for exchange Dec. 11, 1779. G; 5A p. 38.

ARNOLD, Fregift. Mate or prizemaster. Alliance. Comm. F. Feb. 9, 1780. SP; HO.

ARNOLD, Joshua or Josiah. Lieut. Comm. F. Feb. 18, 1779. Pard. for exchange Dec. 11, 1779. G; 5A p. 39.

ARNOLD, Oliver. Seaman. Essex. Comm. F. March 5, 1781. Pard. for R.N. March 27, 1781. G; SP; HO.

ARNOLD, Sion. Swallow. Comm. F. Jan. 23, 1778. Pard. for exchange May 31, 1779. G; 5A p. 37.

ARNAUD, Etienne. Pard. for exchange May 31, 1779. G.

ARTHUR or ARTHER, John. Prizemaster. Comm. F. Aug. 8, 1777. Pard. for R.N. May 22, 1779. G; 5A p. 36.

MARINERS OF THE AMERICAN REVOLUTION

ASHBY or ASHBEY, Benjamin of New London. Mariner. Two Sisters. Comm. M. April 24, 1781. SP; HO; HL; 3 p. 141; 10 v. 73 p. 337.

ASHBURN, Joseph. Master. Lion. Comm. M. Aug. 31, 1781. SP; 3 p. 211.

ASHBURN or ASBURN, William of England. Charming Sally or Polly. Captured Jan. 16, 1777. M. Escaped or R. N. 3 p. 75; 7 p. 248.

ASHLEY or ASHLY, James. Revenge. Comm. F. Aug. 11, 1777. Pard. for R. N. Dec. 19, 1778. G; 5 v. 32, pp. 282-3; 5A p. 37.

ASHTON, ASHDON or ASHDOWN, John of Charleston, S. C. 2nd lieut. Comet of Philadelphia. Comm. M. Jan. 16, 1781. SP; HO; HL; 3 p. 140; 10 v. 73 p. 314.

ASHTON, Philip of Marblehead. Boy. General Glover. Comm. F. Oct. 18, 1779. SP; HO; 10 v. 73 p. 340. (Same as Philip Aston?)

ASPEN, George. Mariner. Viper. Comm. M. Dec. 7, 1781. SP; HO.

ASPANEL, ASPINAL, ASPENWAL or APINALL, Peter of Virginia. Mariner or lieut. Hero or General Sinclair (a brig from Virginia). Comm. M. Jan. 9, 1781. SP; HO; HL; 10 v. 73 p. 313; v. 74 p. 30.

ASTON, Philip. F. Pard. for exchange Dec. 11, 1779. (Same as Philip Ashton above?)

ASULIER, Joseph of Newburyport. Dalton. Comm. M. June, 1777. Escaped. 7 p. 243. (See ADJOLIER).

ATKINS, Daniel of Maryland. Reprizal's prize. Comm. M. Aug. 1777. Escaped. 3 p. 75.

ATKINS, Joseph. Son of Dudley Atkins of Newburyport. Obtained his liberty from the captain of the Thetis in Dartmouth, April, 1777. 4 p. 185.

ATKINSON, John. F. Pard. for R. N. April 20, 1781. G.

ATWOOD or ATTWOOD, Benjamin. Mariner. Resolution of Boston. Comm. M. Jan. 22, 1781. In hospital May 10, 1781. SP; HO; HL; 10 v. 73 pp. 316, 341.

ATWOOD, John. M. In hospital April, 1777. Attempted escape Aug. 27, 1777. Pard. for exchange Dec. 26, 1778. G; 4 pp. 184, 308, 395.

ATTWOOD, Nathl. Mariner. Resolution of Boston. Comm. M. Jan. 22, 1781. SP; HO; 3 p. 140; 10 v. 73 p. 316.

AUDRAIN, Pier. See ANDRIAN.

AUNCEL, William. Pard. for R. N. Sept. 25, 1778. G.

AUSTIN or OSTIN, Daniel or David of North Carolina. Mariner. Lydia or Robertson. Comm. M. April 24, 1781. SP; HO; HL; 3 p. 141; 10 v. 73 p. 337.

AUSTIN, Geo. Viper. Comm. M. Dec. 7, 1781. 3 p. 212.

AUSTIN, John. Seaman. General Mifflin. Comm. F. Aug. 9, 1781. SP; HO.

AUSTIN, Thomas of Rhode Island. Schooner Warren. Comm. M. June, 1778. Pard. for exchange Dec. 11, 1779. G; 3 p. 137; 7 p. 255.

AUTTWOOD or ANTTWOOD, John. M. Pard. for R. N. Jan. 4, 1779. G.

AVENARD, Tousaint. F. Pard. for exchange May 31, 1779. G.

AVERY, Benjamin. Seaman. Hercules. Sent from Kinsale to M. April 9, 1782. HO.

AVERY, Samuel. Seaman. Two Brothers. Comm. M. Jan. 23, 1782. HO.

AVETT, John. M. Pard. for R. N. Jan. 4, 1779. G.

AYERS, Peter. Franklin. Comm. F. Feb. 18, 1779. 5A p. 39.

AYRE, Peter. F. Pard. for exchange Dec. 11, 1779. G.

AYRES, Peter. Pard. for exchange Oct. 16, 1781 but in hospital, so Silas Talbot took his place. G.

B

BABB, Benj. of Portsmouth.   Charming Polly or Dalton.   In hospital April 1777.   Comm. M. June, 1777.   Escaped.   3 p. 75;   4 p. 184;   7 p. 244.

BABBIT, Benege.   Seaman.   Marquis de la Fayette.   Comm. M. Jan. 22, 1782.   HO.

BACK, Francis.   See BECK.

BACKER, John of Beverly.   Black Prince.   Comm. M. Oct. 20, 1781. 10 v. 74 p. 146.

BACKLYFT, Joshua.   M.   Pard. for exchange Dec. 26, 1778.

BACKSON or BANKSON, James of Baltimore.   Mariner.   Viper.   Comm. M. Dec. 7, 1781.   SP; HO;   3 p. 212.

BACON, Jacob.   Surgeon.   Jason.   Captured but not comm. Oct. 22, 1781. HO.

BACON, Nathaniel of Barnstaple.   Seaman.   Adventure.   Comm. M. Jan. 21, 1782.   HO;   3 p. 213.

BACON, Zechary.   Seaman.   Wexford.   Captured but not comm. Oct. 2, 1781.   HO.

BADAN, Stafford of Virginia.   Reprisal's prize.   Comm. M. June 29, 1777. 7 p. 251.

BADEN, Edmund of Marblehead.   Fancy.   Comm. M. Aug. 7, 1777. 7 p. 250.

BADGER? of Portsmouth, N. H.   M.   9 p. 80   (Probably same as BODGE).

BAGWELL, Isaiah.   Seaman.   Fort Stanwin.   Comm. F. June 3, 1780. SP; HO.

MARINERS OF THE AMERICAN REVOLUTION

BAILEY or BAYLEY (Capt.) Benjamin. Prize master. Revenge. Comm. F. Aug. 11, 1777. R.N. Dec. 19 or 25, 1778. G; 5 v. 30 p. 351; v. 32 p. 282; 5A p. 37.

BAILEY, Daniel. Seaman. Happy Return. Comm. F. June 27, 1781. SP; HO.

BAILEY, Nath'l of Newbury. M. Exchanged. 3 p. 75.

BAILEY, Thomas. See BAYLEY.

BAITEY or BARLEY, James. Mariner. Franklin. Comm. M. Dec. 6, 1781. SP; HO.

BAKELEY, Henry of Philadelphia. Lexington. Captured Sept. 19, 1777. M. R.N. 7 p. 253.

BAKER, Benah. F. Pard. for exchange Dec. 11, 1779. G.

BAKER, John of Beverly. Prize master. Black Princess, a French prize. Comm. M. Oct. 20, 1781. SP; HO; 3 p. 212.

BAKER, Thos. See BARKER.

BALDRIDGE, Wm. of Boston. Essex. Comm. M. July 21 or 24 1781. 3 p. 210; 10 v. 74 p. 35. See BALLRIDGE.

BALDWIN, Asa. Comm. F. April 19, 1779. Died. 5A p. 39.

BALFOUR, James. F. Pard. for R.N. Oct. 30, 1779. G.

BALL, Johannes. F. Pard. for exchange Dec. 11, 1779. G.

BALL, John. Seaman. Harlequin or American. Comm. F. Feb. 3, 1781. SP; HO; 10 v. 73 p. 340.

BALL, Thomas. Mate. Comet. Comm. M. Jan. 16, 1781. SP; HO. HL; 3 p. 140.

BALLRIDGE, William. Mariner. Essex. Comm. M. July 24, 1781. SP; HO. See BALDRIDGE.

MARINERS OF THE AMERICAN REVOLUTION

BALSH, Thomas.   Seaman.   Jason.   Captured but not comm. Oct. 15, 1781.   HO.

BANCROFT, Benj. of Stoughton.   Lyon.   Comm. M. Aug. 31, 1781. 3 p. 211.

BANGS, Joshua.   Seaman.   Ulysses.   Comm. F. June 27, 1781.   SP; HO.

BANKSON, James.   See BACKSON.

BARBER, Andrew, alias CASSIDY of Boston.   Mariner.   Essex.   Comm. M. July 21, 1781.   SP; HO; 3 p. 210; 10 v. 74 p. 34.

BARBER, George.   Seaman.   Dolphin.   Comm. F. May 24, 1781.   SP; HO.

BARD, David.   F.   Pard. for exchange Dec. 11, 1779.   G.

BARD, Robert.   See BEARD.

BARDON, William.   M.   Pard. for R.N. April 28, 1781.   G.

BARKER, David.   Seaman.   Commerce.   Comm. F. Feb. 18, 1779.   SP; HO; 5A p. 39.

BARKER or BUNKER, Francis.   Mariner.   Elijah (Prize to the Grand Turk). Comm. M. Dec. 7, 1781.   SP; HO; 3 p. 212.

BARKER, Joseph of Marblehead.   Fancy.   Comm. M. Aug. 7, 1777.   Escaped.   3 p. 136; 7 p. 249.

BARKER, Thomas of Marblehead.   Fancy.   Comm. M. Aug. 7, 1777.   Escaped.   7 p. 249.

BARKER or BAKER, Thos.   (2)   Mariner.   Essex.   Comm. M. July 21, 1781.   SP; HO; 3 p. 210; 10 v. 74 p. 34.

BARKELY?, Joseph;   Boy.   Montgomery.   Comm. F. Aug. 8, 1777.   Exchanged July 2, 1779.   Later joined the Bonhomme Richard.   5 v. 32 p. 286;   5A p. 36.

BARLEY, James.   See BAITEY.

BARNES, Charles of Ipswich. Fancy. Captured Aug. 7, 1777. M. Died. 3 p. 136; 7 p. 250.

BARNES, James. M. Pard. for R. N. April 28, 1781. G.

BARNES, James. F. Pard. for exchange Nov. 9, 1781. G.

BARNES, James. Seaman. Wexford. Sent to M. from Kinsale April 9, 1782. HO.

BARNEY, James of Pennsylvania. Mariner. Chatham. Comm. M. Aug. 23, 1781. SP; HO; 3 p. 211.

BARNEY, John. General Sullivan. Comm. F. April 26, 1779. 5A p. 39.

BARNEY, Joshua. Continental ship Saratoga. Comm. M. Jan. 16, 1781. Escaped May 18, 1781. 1; 3 p. 140; 8 p. 131; 10 v. 73 pp. 314, 336, 343.

BARNUM, Joseph. M. Sick June 29, 1778. 7 p. 140, 143.

BARRELL, Bartley of Ireland. Charming Sally. Captured Jan. 16, 1777. M. Still in M. Feb. 7, 1779. RN. 7 p. 248. (See BERRILL & BURRELL).

BARRENGER, John of Newburyport. Dalton. Comm. M. June, 1777. Escaped. 7 p. 243.

BARRETS, Benjamin. Boy. Wexford. Captured but not comm. Oct. 2, 1781. HO.

BARRETT, Henry of Ireland. Dalton. Comm. M. June 1777. Escaped. 3 p. 75; 7 p. 246.

BARRON, BAREN, BARREN or BROWN, Isaac of Chelmsford. Mariner. Betsy. Comm. M. March 22, 1779. In b. h. July 7, 1781. Out of b.h. July 8, 1781. Attempted escape, put in hospital Aug. 25, 1781. SP; HO; HL; 3 p. 137; 10 v. 74 pp. 31, 44. (An Isaac Barron was re-captured Sept. 11, 1778 after escaping, so he may have been in before. G.)

BARRY, Elisha. Seaman. Adventure. Comm. M. Jan. 21, 1782. HO; 3 p. 213.

MARINERS OF THE AMERICAN REVOLUTION

BARRY, John. M. Pard. for R. N. Jan. 4, 1779. G.

BARRY, Joshua. Lexington. Captured Sept. 19, 1777. M. Escaped. 3 p. 137. (Probably meant for John. See below).

BARRY, John. Lexington. Captured Sept. 19, 1777. M. Escaped. 7 p. 253. (See above).

BARRY or BERRY, Owen. Seaman. Adventure. Comm. M. Jan. 21, 1782. HO; 3 p. 213.

BARTER, Alex. Fancy. Captured Aug. 1777. M. Exchanged. 3 p. 136.

BARTLE, Nicks. F. Pard. for exchange Dec. 11, 1779. G.

BARTLETS, John. Seaman. Jason. Captured but not comm. Oct. 15, 1781. HO.

BARTLETT, Caesar of Ipswich. Fancy. Captured Aug. 7, 1777. Pard. for exchange Dec. 11, 1779. G; 3 p. 136; 7 p. 250.

BARTLETT, Giles. Seaman. Tom Lee. Comm. F. Aug. 9, 1781. SP; HO.

BARTLETT, James. Franklin. Comm. M. November, 1781. 3 p. 212.

BARTLETT, Jonathan of Marblehead. Fancy. Captured August 7, 1777. M. Pard. for exchange Dec. 11, 1779. G; 3 p. 136; 7 p. 249.

BARTLETT or BARTLET, Nathl. of Amesbury. Carpenter. Hannable of Newbury. Comm. M. Jan. 16 or 18, 1781. Innoculated May 29, 1781. SP; HO; 3 p. 140; 10 v. 73 pp. 314, 346.

BARTRAM, Joseph of Fairfield, Conn. Mariner. Confederacy. Comm. M. Aug. 23, 1781. SP; HO; 3 p. 211; 10 v. 74 p. 43.

BASANT or BASENT, Zacharias. Alliance. Pard. for exch. Dec. 11, 1779; G.

BASE, William. Oliver Cromwell. Comm. F. Oct. 13, 1777. Pard. Dec. 3, 1778. R. N. Dec. 19, 1778. G; 5 v. 32 p. 282-3; 5A p. 37.

BASON, Isaac. M. Pard. for exchange Dec. 11, 1779. G.

BASS, John. M. Pard. for exchange Dec. 20, 1778. G.

BASS, John of Boston. Dalton. Comm. M. June 1777. Pard. for R. N. Jan. 4, 1779. G; 3 p. 75; 4 p. 306; 7 p. 246.

BASS, Josiah or Jeriah. Mariner. Essex. Comm. M. July 21 or 27, 1781. SP; HO; 3 p. 210.

BASSETT, Zach(ariah) of Milton. Mariner. Betsy or Alliance's prize. Comm. M. March 22, 1779. Escaped, re-captured and put in b. h. July 6, 1781. Out of b. h. July 29. SP; HL; 3 p. 138; 10 v. 74 pp. 25, 31, 37.

BASTES, Wm. F. Pard. for exchange May 31, 1779. G. See BASE.

BATCHELLY, Jesse. Seaman. Rhodes. Comm. F. Nov. 18, 1780. SP; HO.

BATERAUD, Lewis. Sturdy Beggar. Comm. F. Jan. 23, 1778. 5A p. 37.

BATES, Jone? F. Pard. for exchange Dec. 11, 1779. G.

BATTA, Battis. Revenge. Comm. F. Aug. 11, 1777. Escaped. 5A p. 37.

BATTEN, Richard of Salem. Mariner. Essex. Comm. M. Aug. 25, 1781. SP; HO; 3 p. 211; 10 v. 74 p. 44.

BATTON or BATTAN, John, Senior, of Salem. Schooner Warren. Comm. M. June 1778. Pard. for exchange Dec. 11, 1779 and Nov. 9, 1781. G; 3 p. 137; 7 p. 254.

BATTON or BATTAN, John, junior of Salem. Schooner Warren. All details same as above.

BAXTER, Alexander of England. Fancy. Captured Aug. 7, 1777. M. Pard. for exchange Dec. 11, 1779. G; 7 p. 250.

BAXTER, William. Master's mate. Montgomery. Comm. F. Aug. 8, 1777. 5 v. 32 pp. 165, 167. 5A p. 36.

BAYLAND, Thos. of Ireland. Black Princess of Dunkirk. Comm. M. Oct. 20, 1781. 3 p. 212.

MARINERS OF THE AMERICAN REVOLUTION

BAYLEY, Benjamin. See BAILEY.

BAYLEY, Nathaniel of Newburyport. Dalton. Sent to Royal hospital Feb. 15, 1777; still there April, 1777. Comm. M. June 1777. Pard. for exchange Dec. 20, 1778. Went with Paul Jones. G; 4 pp. 43, 184. 7 p. 244.

BAYLEY or BAILEY, Thomas of Newburyport. All details same as Nathaniel Bayley. Extra reference 3 p. 74.

BEAL, Aaron of Salem. Seaman. Twin Sisters or Disdain's prize. Comm. M. Jan. 9, 1782. HO; 3 p. 213.

BEAL or BEALS, Nathl. Mariner. Essex. Comm. M. July 21 or 27, 1781. SP; HO; 3 p. 210.

BEALE, David. Seaman. Hercules. Sent from Kinsale to M. April 9, 1782. HO.

BEARD or BARD, Robt. Mariner. Viper. Comm. M. Dec. 7, 1781. SP; HO; 3 p. 212.

BECK, Francis, of Virginia. Petomme. Captured July 12, 1780. M. 3 p. 141.

BECK or BACK, Francis. Mate. Polonick. Comm. M. March 31, 1781. Innoculated May 29, 1781. SP; HO; HL; 10 v. 73 pp. 331, 346.

BECK, Samuel. Seaman. Happy Return or Portsmouth. Comm. F. June 27, 1781. SP; HO.

BECKBY, Henry. Pard. for R.N. Sept. 25, 1778. G.

BECKETT, Benj. Warren. Comm. M. June 4, 1778. Died. 3 p. 137.

BECKFORD, Elie. See BICKFORD.

BECKFORD, John. Fancy. Captured August, 1777. M. Exchanged. 3 p. 136.

BEEBE, Ichabid. Seaman. Bermuda. Comm. M. Jan. 22, 1782. HO.

BEEL or BEAL, Samuel of Marblehead. Fancy. Comm. M. Aug. 7, 1777. Pard. for exchange Dec. 11, 1779. G; 3 p. 136; 7 p. 247.

BEELS, William. Seaman. Protector. Comm. F. Aug. 9, 1781. SP; HO.

BEERS, Daniel. Lieut. Comm. F. Aug. 28, 1778. Pard. for exchange Dec. 11, 1779. G; 5A p. 38.

BEESBY, Henry. Seaman. Portsmouth. Comm. F. June 27, 1781. SP; HO.

BELL, John. Satisfaction. Comm. F. July 27, 1778. Pard. for R. N. Sept. 9, 1779. G; 5A p. 38.

BELL, Thomas. Seaman. Antibriton, a French ship. Confined at Edinburgh Jan. 19, 1782. HO.

BELLAMY, Anthony of Virginia. Betsey. Comm. M. July 23, 1781. SP; HO; 3 p. 210; 10 v. 74 p. 35.

BELLINGS or BILLINGS, James of New London. Chatham. Comm. M. August 23, 1781. SP; HO; 3 p. 211; 10 v. 74 p. 43.

BEMBRIDGE, BEMBERAGE or BEMBRAGE, Miles or Myles of North Carolina. Mariner. Brig Salley of N. C. Comm. M. May 11, 1781. Innoculated May 28, 1781. SP; HO; HL (mark); 3 p. 209; 10 v. 73 pp. 340, 346.

BENCROFT, Benj. Mariner. Lion. Comm. M. Aug. 31, 1781. SP; HO.

BENDOZEN, William. M. Pard. for R. N. Jan. 4, 1779. G.

BENIL, Benja. of North Carolina. Comm. M. July 28, 1781. General Nash. 10 v. 74 p. 36.

BENNETT, Arthur of Millbury. Charming Sally. Captured Feb. 7, 1777. M. Still there Feb. 7, 1779. Pard. for exchange Dec. 20, 1778. G; 7 p. 247.

BENTON, Abijah of Virginia. Brig Salley of North Carolina. Comm. M. May 11, 1781. 10 v. 73 p. 340.

BERENGER, Dominic.   Seaman.   Adventure.   Comm. M. Jan. 21, 1782. HO.

BERKLEY, Joseph.   F.   Pard. for exchange, May 31, 1779.   G.

BERRILL, Bartholomew.   M.   Pard. for R.N. Sept. 25, 1778.   G. (Probably same as B. BARRELL).

BERRY, Owen.   See BARRY.

BERRY, William.   Seaman.   Alliance.   Comm. F. Oct. 31, 1780.   SP; HO.

BERTRAND, Louis.   Pard. for exchange May 31, 1779.   Discharged.   G.

BESSELL, Hosea.   Seaman.   Centurion.   Comm. F. March 21, 1781. SP; HO.

BICKETT, Benjamin of Salem.   Schooner Warren.   Comm. M. June 1778. 7 p. 254.

BICKFORD of BECKFORD, Elie or Elia.   Seaman.   Union or Pomona. Comm. F. July 8, 1779.   Pard. for exchange Dec. 11, 1779.   G; SP; HO.

BICKFORD, Geo.   Essex.   Comm. M. July 21, 1781.   R.N.   3 p. 210.

BICKFORD, John of Newburyport.   Fancy.   Captured Aug. 7, 1777.   M. 4 p. 307; 7 p. 249.

BIGGAR or BIGGER, Moses.   Montgomery.   Comm. F. Aug. 8, 1777. Pard. for exchange May 31, 1779.   G; 5A p. 36.

BIGBY of BIGSBY, David of Middleton.   Mariner.   James and Rebecca, or prize to the Franklin.   Comm. M. Oct. 16, 1781.   SP; HO; 3 p. 211; 10 v. 74 p. 145.

BILESTON, Thomas.   Seaman.   Hercules.   Sent from Kinsale to M. April 9, 1782.   HO.

BILLINGS, James.   See BELLING.

BIRKETT, John.   Seaman.   Washington.   Comm. F. March 21, 1781. SP; HO.

BIRMINGTON, Robt.   Mariner.   Ranger.   Comm. M. July 23, 1781. SP; HO.

BLACK, Nathaniel.   Seaman.   Eagle.   Sent from Kinsale to M. April 10, 1782 "from the Stag".   HO.

BLACK, Philip.   Seaman.   Protector.   Comm. F. Aug. 9, 1781.   SP; HO.

BLACK, Richmond of Portsmouth.   General Sulivan's prize.   Comm. M. July 3, 1779.   Pard. for exchange Dec. 11, 1779 and Nov. 9, 1781. G; HL; 3 p. 138.

BLACK, William of New York.   Charming Sally.   Comm. M. Jan. 16, 1777.   Still there Feb. 7, 1779.   Pard. for exchange Dec. 20, 1778. G; 7 p. 248.

BLACKLER, BLACKLOR or BLACKLAR, William.   Mariner.   Terrible. Comm. M. Dec. 23 or 25, 1780.   SP; HO; HL; 3 p. 139; 10 v. 74 p. 40.

BLAKE, Elias.   M.   In hospital April, 1777.   Pard. for exchange Dec. 20, 1778.   G; 4 p. 184.

BLAKE, Wm. of New York.   Dalton.   Exchanged.   3 p. 74.

BLANCH, John.   F.   Pard. for R.N. April 20, 1781.   G.

BLANCH, Nicolas.   Revenge.   Comm. F. Aug. 11, 1777.   Escaped. 5A p. 37.

BLANCHARD or BLANKARD, Fredk. of North Carolina.   Success.   Comm. M. July 28, 1781.   Pard. for R.N. Oct. 25, 1781.   G; 3 p. 211; 10 v. 74 pp. 36, 147.

BLANCHARD, Jery. of Andover, Mass.   Mariner.   L'Uzerne or Ascot and John.   Comm. M. July 7 or 9, 1781.   SP; HO; 3 p. 209; 10 v. 74 p. 32.

BLANEY, James.   F.   Pard. for exchange Dec. 11, 1779.   G.

MARINERS OF THE AMERICAN REVOLUTION

BLASDELL or BLANDELL, Samuel. Prize of the Warren. Comm. F. June 26, 1777. Pard. for exchange May 31, 1779. G; 5A p. 36.

BLEE, Charles. Montgomery of Philadelphia. Comm. F. Aug. 8, 1777. Escaped. 5 v. 32 p. 165; 5A p. 36.

BLYTH, Vivian. Seaman. Fair American. Comm. F. Nov. 30, 1780. SP; HO.

BOADE or BOADY, John. Mariner. Aurora. Comm. M. July 25, 1780. SP; HO.

BOARDING, Stafford. M. Pard. for exchange Dec. 11, 1779. G. (May be the same as BORDEN and BOIDON).

BOARDMAN, Offin of Newburyport. Captain. Dalton. Comm. M. June, 1777. Escaped Feb. 1, 1778. Re-captured April 10, 1778. Out of b.h. April 27, 1778. In b.h. June 23, 1778. Escaped, re-captured and in b.h. Dec. 21, 1778. Escaped Jan. 5, 1779. 3 p. 74; 4 pp. 187 396; 7 pp. 94, 116, 138, 201, 209, 243; 11 pp. 252-3.

BODGE, Mr. from Portsmouth, New Hampshire. M. 9 pp. 85, 89. (May be the same as John BODGE. See also BADGER).

BODGE, John. Aurora. Comm. M. July 25, 1780. In hospital May 10, 1781. HL; 3 p. 139; 10 v. 73 p. 341.

BODINTON, Thomas. Seaman. Portsmouth. Comm. F. June 27, 1781. SP; HO.

BOIDON, Stafford. M. Pard. for R. N. Jan. 28, 1780. G. (May be the same as BOARDING and BORDEN).

BOISRESVAULT, Louis. F. Pard. for exchange May 31, 1779. G. (Probably same as BOUCRALT).

BOISSE, Francois. F. Pard. for exchange May 31. 1779. G. (Probably same as Francis BOSSEE.)

BOLTON or BOLTEN, James of Philadelphia. Hunter. Comm. M. July 25, 1781. Pard. for R. N. Sept. 10, 1781. G; 3 p. 210.

BOLTON, Aaron. Boy. Fair American. Comm. F. Nov. 18, 1780. SP; HO.

MARINERS OF THE AMERICAN REVOLUTION

BOMFORD, Christopher.   F.   Pard.   for R.N. Oct. 30, 1779.   G.

BONNY, Joseph.   Reprisal.   Comm. F. Aug. 9, 1777.   Pard. for R.N. May 22, 1779.   Pard. for exchange Nov. 9, 1781.   G; 5A p. 37.

BOOKER, George.   Seaman.   Nancy.   Comm. F. Oct. 14, 1779.   Pard. for exchange Dec. 20, 1779.   G; SP.

BOOTH, Robert of North Carolina?   Mariner.   Lydia (of North Carolina?) or Robertson.   Comm. M. April 24, 1781.   SP; HO; 10 v. 73 p. 337.

BORDEN, Henry.   Seaman.   Twin Sisters, a Privateer of Rhode Island. Comm. to Security Prison ship at Chatham, Dec. 18, 1781.   HO.

BORDEN, Stafford.   Reprisal's prize.   Comm. M. August, 1777. Escaped. 3 p. 75.   (May be the same as BOARDING and BOIDON.)

BOSSEE, Francis.   Revenge.   Comm. F. Aug. 11, 1777.   5A p. 37. (Probably same as Francois BOISSE).

BOSTICK, James.   F.   Pard. for exchange Dec. 11, 1779.   G.

BOSWELL, John.   F.   Pard. for R.N. Jan. 27, 1781.   G.

BOSWORTH, Ebenezer of Bristol.   Schooner Warren.   Comm. M. June, 1778.   Pard. for exchange Dec. 11, 1779.   G; 3 p. 137; 7 p. 255

BOUCRALT, Lewis.   Comm. F. July 15, 1777.   5A p. 36.   (May be same as BOISRESVAULT).

BOUNDS, James of Dartmouth.   Charming Sally or Polly.   Comm. M. Jan. 16, 1777.   Pard. for exchange Dec. 20, 1778.   Still there Feb. 7, 1779.   G; 3 p. 75; 7 p. 247.

BOUNDY, John.   Seaman.   Jason.   Captured but not comm. Oct. 15, 1781. HO.

BOURDOUX, BURDEAUX or BURDO, John.   Mariner.   Marmy.   Comm. M. July 3 or 28, 1779.   Pard. for exchange Dec. 11, 1779.   G; SP; 3 p. 138.

BOURNET, John.   F.   Pard. for exchange Dec. 11, 1779.   G.

MARINERS OF THE AMERICAN REVOLUTION

BOWDEN, Edmund. Fancy. Comm. M. August, 1777. Pard. for exchange Dec. 11, 1779. G; 3 p. 136.

BOWDEN or BOWDON, Willm. Mariner. Elijah or prize to the Grand Turk. Comm. M. Dec. 7, 1781. SP; HO.

BOWEN, Ashley. Franklin. Comm. F. Feb. 18, 1779. Pard. for exchange Dec. 11, 1779. G; 5A p. 38.

BOWEN, Elisha. Rising States. Comm. F. June 14, 1777. Pard. for exchange May 31, 1779. G; 5A p. 36.

BOWEN, Joshua. Angelica. Comm. F. July 7, 1778. Pard. for exchange Dec. 11, 1779. G; 5A p. 38.

BOWEN, Thomas. Mariner. Wexford. Comm. M. Jan. 24, 1782. HO.

BOWERS, David. Prize master. Angelica of Boston. Comm. F. July 7, 1778. Pard. for exchange Dec. 11, 1779. G; 5 vol. 32 p. 73; 5A p. 38.

BOWERS, Jacob. Seaman. Neptune. Comm. F. June 27, 1781. SP; HO.

BOWILL, Benj. of New London. General Nash. Comm. M. July 27, 1781. 3 p. 210.

BOWYER, Henry. Seaman. Retaliation. Comm. F. Oct. 31, 1780. SP; HO.

BOYCE, John of Londonderry. Mariner. Essex. Comm. M. July 24, 1781. SP; HO; 3 p. 210; 10 v. 74 p. 35.

BOYD, Adam. Seaman. Portsmouth. Comm. F. July 20, 1781. SP; HO.

BOYD, David. Seaman. Monmouth? Comm. F. Dec. 30, 1779. SP.

BOYLAND, Thoms. Black Prince. Comm. M. Oct. 20, 1781. Escaped Nov. 15, 1781. 10 v. 74 pp. 146, 153.

BRADBURY, Capt. M. 7 p. 217.

BRADBURY, Wynnard, Wym'd. or Wyman of Newburyport. Dalton. Comm. M. June, 1777. Pard. for exchange Dec. 20, 1778. G; 3 p. 74; 7 p. 243.

MARINERS OF THE AMERICAN REVOLUTION

BRADFORD, Joseph. Surgeon. Wexford. Captured but not comm. Oct. 26, 1781. HO.

BRADLEY, James. F. Pard. for exchange Dec. 11, 1779. G.

BRADLEY, Thomas of Ireland. Lexington. Comm. M. Sept. 19, 1777. Pard. for exchange Dec. 11, 1779. G; 3 p. 137; 7 p. 253.

BRAGDON, Ebenezer of Old York. Mariner. Minerva. Comm. M. Aug. 23 or 24, 1780. SP; HO; 3 p. 139.

BRAGDON, Joseph. M. Innoculated May 28, 1781. 10 v. 73 p. 346. (Probably same as Josiah).

BRAGDON, Josiah. HL. (Probably same as Joseph).

BRAMHAM or BRANUM, Francis. Prize of Sloop Independent. Comm. F. June 26, 1777. Petitioned to be released from b. h. March 25, 1778. Pardoned for R. N. Dec. 14, 1778. G; 5A p. 36.

BRANHAM or BRANON, Mathew. Lexington. Comm. M. Sept. 19, 1777. Pard. for R. N. Oct. 14, 1778. Entered or escaped. G; 3 p. 137.

BRAY, Benjamin. Beaver. Comm. M. July 23, 1781. R. N. Aug. 20, 1781. Pard. Oct. 1781. G; 3 p. 210; 10 v. 74 p. 43.

BRAY, David. Seaman. Hercules. Sent from Kinsale to M. April 9, 1782. HO.

BRAY, Ebenezer. Seaman. Two Brothers. Comm. M. Jan. 23, 1782. HO.

BRECK, Luther. Boy. Alliance. Comm. F. Feb. 9, 1780. SP; HO.

BRENNON, Nath'l of Ireland. Lexington. Comm. M. Sept. 19, 1777. R. N. 7 p. 253.

BREON, James. Doctor. Hornet. Comm. F. Oct. 13, 1777. Escaped. 5A p. 37.

BREWER, Jacob of Kittery, New Hampshire. Dalton. Comm. M. June, 1777. Pard. for exchange Dec. 20, 1778. G; 3 p. 75; 7 p. 245. (Probably same as Joseph BREWER and Joseph BREWSTER).

MARINERS OF THE AMERICAN REVOLUTION

BREWER, James. Mariner. Resolution. Comm. M. Jan. 22, 1781. SP; HO; 3 p. 140. (See James BROWER).

BREWER, John (BROWN in SP) of Boston. Mariner or carpenter. Resolution. Comm. M. Jan. 22, 1781. SP; HO; HL; 3 p. 140. (See BROWER).

BREWER, Joseph. Dalton. Captured Dec. 24, 1776. Exchanged. 3 p. 74. (Probably same as Joseph Brewster and Jacob Brewer).

BREWER, Samuel of Maryland. Mariner. Tom Lee. Comm. M. May 5, 1781. SP; HO; HL; 3 p. 141; 10 v. 73 p. 338.

BREWSTER, Joseph of Newburyport. Dalton. Comm. M. June, 1777. Later went with Paul Jones. 7 p. 243. (Probably same as Jacob BREWER and Joseph BREWER).

BREWSTER, Joshua. M. Pard. for exchange Dec. 20, 1778.

BRIANT, James. Lieutenant. Montgomery. Comm. F. Aug. 8, 1777. 5A p. 36.

BRIANT, James. Mariner. Aurora. Comm. M. July 25, 1780. SP; HO.

BRIARD, Elias. Seaman. Terrible. Comm. F. May 24, 1781. SP; HO.

BRIARD, John. HL.

BRICKELLS, Thomas. Seaman. Fair American. Comm. F. Nov. 18, 1780. SP.

BRICKFORD, John. M. Pard. for exchange Dec. 11, 1779. G.

BRIGGS, Richard. F. Pard. for exchange Dec. 11, 1779. G.

BRIGHT, Michael. Steward. Active. Comm. F. March 5, 1781. SP.

BRIGHT, William of Salem. Schooner Warren. Comm. M. June, 1778. Pard. for R. N. Sept. 25, 1778. Escaped. 3 p. 137; 7 p. 254; G.

BRIGHTMAN, Thomas of Dartmouth. Charming Sally or Polly. Captured Jan. 16, 1777. M. Still there Feb. 7, 1779. Died. 3 p. 75; 7 p. 247.

BRIGSBY, Elias.   Seaman.   Newfoundland.   Comm. to Edinburgh prison June 27, 1781. HO.

BRIMBLECORN or BRIMBLECOM, Thomas. Seaman. Terrible. Comm. F. May 24, 1781. SP; HO.

BRINNI(S)COME, BRINNICORNE or BREMBELCOM, William of Marblehead. General Glover. Comm. F. Oct. 18, 1779. Pard. for exchange Dec. 11, 1779. G; SP; HO; 10 v. 73 p. 340.

BRISTER, James of Marblehead. Boy. In F. May 8, 1781. 10 v. 73 p. 340. (Probably same as BRISTOL).

BRISTOL, James. Boy. General Glover. Comm. F. Oct. 18, 1779. Pard. for exchange Dec. 11, 1779. G; SP; HO. (Probably same as BRISTER).

BRISTOL, Thomas. Seaman. Retaliation. Comm. F. Oct. 31, 1780. SP; HO.

BRITTAIN, John. Seaman. Fair American. Comm. F. Nov. 30, 1780. SP; HO.

BROADSTRET, Sam'l. Prize master. General Sullivan. Comm. F. April 26, 1779. 5A p. 39.

BROOKE or BROOKS, Matthew of Pennsylvania? Mariner. Franklin. Comm. M. Dec. 6, 1781. SP; HO; 3 p. 212.

BROOKS, David of Stratford. Mariner. Marquis of Morbec. Comm. M. Oct. 2, 1781. SP; HO; 3 p. 211; 10 v. 74 p. 142.

BROOKS, Nathan. Imprisoned at Pembroke. Pard. for R. N. June 17, 1779. G.

BROOKS, Nehemiah. M. Pard. for exchange Dec. 11, 1779. G.

BROOKS, Skillings of Marblehead. Fancy. Comm. M. Aug. 7, 1777. Exchanged. 3 p. 136. 7 p. 250.

BROOKS, Thomas. Seaman. Marquis de la Fayette. Comm. M. Jan. 9 1782. HO; 3 p. 213.

BROONE, Benjamin. Seaman. Marquis de la Fayette. Comm. M. Jan. 9, 1782. HO. (See BROWN).

BROTHERS, James. Seaman or boy. Fair American. Comm. F. Nov. 18, 1780. SP; HO.

BROTHERS, Joseph. Seaman or boy. Fair American. Comm. F. Nov. 18, 1780. SP; HO.

BROUGHTON, James. Seaman. Susannah. Comm. F. June 27, 1781. SP; HO.

BROUGHTON, Willm. Mariner. General Sullivan's prize, Effingham or Weymouth. Comm. M. July 3, 1779. Pard. for exchange Dec. 11, 1779. G; SP; HO; HL; 3 p. 138.

BROWER, James. Resolution of Boston. Comm. M. Jan. 22, 1781. 10 v. 73 p. 316. (See James BREWER).

BROWER, Jno. Resolution of Boston. Comm. M. Jan. 22, 1781. 10 v. 73 p. 316. (See John BREWER).

BROWN, Captain of Newhaven, Conn. Charming Sally. M. Captured Jan. 30, 1777. Escaped May 27, 1777. 4 pp. 43, 185; 7 pp. 38, 41, 197.

BROWN, Benj. of Salem. Mariner. Ascott and John. Comm. M. July 7 or 9, 1781. Att. escape Nov. 14 and Nov. 21, 1781. Out of b. h. Nov. 26, 1781. SP; HO; 3 p. 209; 10 v. 74 pp. 32, 52, 155, 156.

BROWN, Benj. Marquis Lafayette. Comm. M. Jan, 1782. 3 p. 213. See BROONE.

BROWN, Capt. Dan'l of Philadelphia or New London, Conn. Hannible of Newbury or Comet. Comm. M. Jan. 9, 1781. R. N. Aug. 21, 1781. Pard. for R. N. Oct. 1781. G; HL; 3 p. 140; 10 v. 73 pp. 313, 319; v. 74 p. 43.

BROWN, Daniel. Seaman. Hercules. In M. but not comm. Oct. 15, 1781. HO.

BROWN, Ebenezer of Newburyport. Dalton. Comm. M. June, 1777. Pard. for exchange Dec. 20, 1778. Joined Alliance. G; 3 p. 74; 7 p. 244.

BROWN, Edward.   F.   Pard. for exchange Dec. 11, 1779.   G.

BROWN, Elisha.   Seaman.   Hercules.   Sent from Kinsale to M. April 9, 1782. HO.

BROWN, Francis of New Haven.   Captain.   Charming Salley or Polly. Captured Jan. 16, 1777.   M.   Escaped.   3 p. 75; 7 p. 247.

BROWN, Isaac.   See BARRON.

BROWN, Jacob.   F.   Pard. for exchange Dec. 11, 1779.   G.

BROWN, Jacob.   Seaman.   Jason.   Captured but not comm. Oct. 15, 1781. HO.

BROWN, James.   The Spy.   Comm. F. Feb. 18, 1779.   5A p. 39.

BROWN, James.   Mariner.   Aurora.   Comm. M. July 25, 1780.   Innoculated May 28, 1781.   SP; HO; 3 p. 139; 10 v. 73 p. 346.

BROWN, Capt. James of Kittery.   M.   Taught navigation, etc.   9 pp. 80, 85.

BROWN, James.   HL.

BROWN, John.   See BREWER.

BROWN, John of South Carolina.   Lieut. of Marines.   Sloop Comet of Philadelphia.   Comm. M. Jan 11, 1781.   SP; HO; 3 p. 140; 10 v. 73 p. 313.

BROWN, John.   Seaman.   Diana.   Comm. M. Jan. 23, 1782.   HO.

BROWN, John.   Seaman.   Jack.   Sent from Kinsale to M. April 10, 1782. "From the Stag". HO.

BROWN, Joseph.   Venus.   Comm. F. April 2, 1778.   Pard. for exchange May 31, 1779.   G; 5A p. 37.

BROWN, Joseph.   Seaman.   Union.   Comm. F. March 21, 1781.   SP; HO.

BROWN, Joseph of Salem.   Prize master.   Black Prince or Princess.   Comm. M. Oct. 20, 1781.   SP; HO; 3 p. 212; 10 v. 74 p. 146.

BROWN, Richard. Seaman or boy. Pocahontas. Comm. F. Nov. 8, 1780. SP; HO.

BROWN, Robert of Marblehead. Fancy. Comm. M. Aug. 7, 1777. Pard. for exchange Dec. 11, 1779. G; 3 p. 136; 7 p. 250.

BROWN, Samuel. Prize of the Warren. Comm. F. June 26, 1777. Pard. for exchange May 31, 1779 and Dec. 11, 1779. G; 5A p. 36.

BROWN, Stephan. Seaman. Two Brothers. Comm. M. Jan. 23, 1782. HO.

BROWN, Theophilus. Seaman. Hercules. Captured but not comm. Oct. 15, 1781. HO.

BROWN, Thomas of Marblehead. Freedom's prize. Comm. M. April 27, 1777. Escaped. 3 p. 75; 7 p. 251.

BROWN, Thomas. Mariner. Aurora. Comm. M. July 25, 1780. In hospital May 10, 1781. SP; HO; 3 p. 139; 10 v. 73 p. 341.

BROWN, Thomas. M. 9 p. 80.

BROWN, Thomas. M. HL.

BROWN, Wm. of Marblehead. Freedom's prize. Captured April 27, 1777. M. Pard. for exchange Feb. 2, 1779. G; 3 p. 75; 7 p. 251.

BROWN, William. Mariner. Monmouth or Rambler. Comm. M. Feb. 16, 1780. SP; HO; 3 p. 139.

BROWN, William. Saratoga's prize. Comm. M. Jan. 9, 1781. 10 v. 73 p. 313.

BROWN, Wm. M. HL.

BROWNE, Benjamin. Seaman. Hercules. Captured but not comm. Oct. 15, 1781. HO.

BROWNING, Robert of Rhode Island. Alliance of Dunkirk. Comm. M. Oct. 9, 1781. Escaped Nov. 15, 1781. 3 p. 211; 10 v. 74 pp. 143 153.

BRUNET, John. Seaman. Montgomery. Comm. F. Aug. 8, 1777. Exchanged July 2, 1779. Joined the Bonhomme Richard and was wounded in battle against Serapis. 5 v. 32 p. 286; 5A p. 36.

BRYANT, James of Philadelphia. M. R.N. July 25, 1781. 10 v. 74 pp. 35-6.

BRYER, John. Aurora. Comm. M. July 25, 1780. 3 p. 139.

BUBLER, Christopher. Phoenix. Comm. M. May 10, 1779. Escaped. 3 p. 138.

BUBROE, Thos. of New Jersey. Lyon. Comm. M. Oct. 1781. 3 p. 211.

BUCKLEY, Charles. Lieut. Alfred. Comm. F. July 18, 1778. Escaped. 5A p. 38.

BUCKLEY, John of Maryland or North Carolina. Black Snake. Comm. M. March 12, 1778. Pard. for exchange Dec. 11, 1779. G; 3 p. 137; 7 p. 255.

BUCKLEY, Henry of Philadelphia. Lexington. Comm. M. Sept. 19, 1777. Exchanged. 3 p. 137.

BUCKLIEF, Joseph. Dalton. Captured Dec. 24, 1776. M. Exchanged. 3 p. 74.

BUCKMAN, Joseph of Mystick. Mariner. Essex. Comm. M. July 21 or 24, 1781. SP; HO; 3 p. 210; 10 v. 74 p. 35.

BUCKSTONE, Abagas. see BUXTON.

BUELL, Benj. Mariner. General Nash. Comm. M. July 28, 1781. SP; HO.

BULL, Alexander. Revenge. Comm. F. Aug. 11, 1777. Escaped. 5A p. 37.

BUNKER, Benjamin. Seaman. Monmouth. Comm. F. Oct. 31, 1780. SP; HO.

BUNKER, Ebenezer. F. Pardoned for R.N. Jan. 27, 1781. G.

BUNKER, Francis. See BARKER.

BUNKER, Isiah or Isaac of Nantucket. 1st lieut. Black Prince or Princess. Comm. M. Oct. 16, 17 or 28, 1781. SP; HO; 3 p. 212; 10 v. 74 p. 147.

BUNTALL, Basset. Seaman. Hercules. Sent from Kinsale to M. April 9, 1782. HO.

BUNTEN, Capt. M. In b.h. June 23, 1778. 7 p. 138.

BUNTIN, John of Newburyport. 2nd Lieut. Dalton. Captured Dec. 24, 1776. M. Escaped Aug. 5, 1777. Re-captured Aug. 6. Pard. for exchange Dec. 26, 1778. G; 3 p. 74; 4 p. 307; 7 p. 243.

BURBANK, Jesse. Seaman. Essex. Comm. M. Dec. 4, 1780. Pard. for R.N. March 27, 1781. G; SP; HO.

BURBANK, John of Cape Porpoise. Dalton or Charming Polly. Comm. M. June, 1777. Pard. for exchange Dec. 20, 1778. Joined Paul Jones. G; 3 p. 75; 7 p. 246.

BURDENE, Joseph. F. Pard. for exchange Dec. 11, 1779. G.

BURDEAUX, John. See BOURDOUX.

BURDLETT, Richard. F. Pard. for exchange Dec. 11, 1779. G.

BURGES, Thomas. Rising States. Comm. F. June 14, 1777. Pard. for exchange May 31, 1779. G; 5A p. 36.

BURGESS, George. F. Pard. for R.N. Jan. 27, 1781. G.

BURGOYNE, Robert of Boston. Dalton. Comm. M. June 17, 1777. Swam from the Blenheim and escaped. 4 p. 187; 7 p. 246.

BURN, Thomas of Irland? Alliance of Dunkirk. Comm. M. Oct. 5 or 9, 1781. Pard. for R.N. Nov. 9, 1781. R.N. Oct. 24, 1781. G; 3 p. 211; 10 v. 74 pp. 143, 146.

BURNELL, Capt. Comm. M. June 24, 1777. Had wife and family in England. 4 pp. 188, 306, 307, 396; 7 p. 163.

BURNELL, John. M. Pard. for R.N. Sept. 25, 1778. G.

BURNET, Clement. Seaman. Newfoundland. Comm. to prison in Edinburgh June 27, 1781. HO.

BURNET, John F. Pard. for exchange May 31, 1779. G.

BURNEY, James of Pennsylvania. Chatham. Comm. M. Aug. 23, 1781. 10 v. 74 p. 43.

BURNEY, Joseph, alias Scipio GREY. M. Pard. for R.N. Nov. 22, 1780. G.

BURNHAM or BURHAM, Joseph of Block Point. Dalton or Charming Polly. In hospital April, 1777. Comm. M. August, 1777. Lost a leg. Pard. for exchange Dec. 11, 1779. G; 3 p. 75; 4 pp. 184, 306; 7 pp. 189, 246.

BURNHAM, Moses of Ipswich. 2nd captain or lieut. Marquis de Morbec. Comm. M. Oct. 2, 1781. SP; HO; 3 p. 211; 10 v. 74 p. 142.

BURNS, James. Boy or seaman. Rhodes. Comm. F. Nov. 19, 1780. SP; HO.

BURNS, Dr. Thos. Angelica. Comm. F. July 7, 1778. Escaped July 23, 1778. 5 v. 31 p. 287; 5A p. 38.

BURRELL, Bartley of Ireland. Dalton. M. Escaped. 3 p. 74. (See BARRELL).

BURRIDGE, Robert. Mariner. Sloop Comet. Comm. M. Jan. 6, 1781. SP; HO; 3 p. 140; 10 v. 73 p. 312.

BURTINGS, John. Dalton. Captured Dec. 24, 1776. M. Escaped. 3 p. 74.

BURTON, James. F. Pard. for R.N. May 28, 1781. G.

BURTON, John of Cape Ann. Mariner. General Massey or Mercer. Comm. M. Oct. 16 or 17, 1781. SP; HO; 3 p. 212; 10 v. 74 p. 145.

BUTLER, Bela. Seaman. Hercules. Sent from Kinsale to M. April 9, 1782. HO.

MARINERS OF THE AMERICAN REVOLUTION

BUTLER or BUTTLER, Dan'l. Lieut. Schooner Greyhound of Philadelphia. Comm. M. Jan. 11, 1781. Att. escape April 21, 1781. Pard. for R.N. Sept. 10, 1781. G; 10 v. 73 pp. 313, 335.

BUTLER, Denis of Boston. Greyhound. Comm. M. Jan. 1781. Escaped. 3 p. 140; 10 v. 74 pp. 28, 45, 48.

BUTLER, Edward. Seaman. Portsmouth. Comm. F. June 27, 1781. SP; HO.

BUTLER or BUTTLER, Francis of Connecticut. Mariner. Tracey of Boston. Comm. M. Jan. 11, 1781. SP; HO; 3 p. 140; 10 v. 73 pp. 48, 313.

BUTTLER, Thoms. Sloop Comet of Philadelphia. Comm. M. Jan. 16, 1781. 10 v. 73 p. 314.

BUTLEY, James. Seaman. Wexford. Comm. M. Jan. 24, 1782. HO.

BUTSMAN, Matthew. Seaman. Betsey, a merchant ship. Captured but not comm. Oct. 23, 1781. HO.

BUTTERTON, Joseph. Seaman. Tom Lee. Comm. F. Aug. 9, 1781. SP; HO.

BUTTS, Enoch. The Swallow. Comm. F. Jan. 23, 1778. Escaped. 5A p. 37.

BUXTON or BUCKSTONE, Abijah, Abagas or Abughear of Virginia. Mariner. Salley. Comm. M. May 11, 1781. SP; HO; HL; 3 p. 209.

BYLIGHT, John. Seaman. Fort Stanwin. Comm. F. April 7, 1780. SP; HO.

C

CABER, Wm. Charming Polly. M. Escaped. 3 p. 75.

CAFFINGS, Wm. F. Pard. for exchange Dec. 11, 1779. G.

CALDER, Josiah. See COLDER.

CALFE, John. Captain. Schooner Hawk. Comm. M. May 10, 1779. Escaped. 3 p. 138.

CALLAGHAN, Tho. F. Pard. for exchange Dec. 11, 1779. G.

CALLAM or CALM, David. Seaman. Oliver Cromwell. Comm. F. Aug. 7, 1779. Pard. for exchange Dec. 11, 1779. G; SP; HO.

CALLIO, John. See CILLAW.

CAMERON, Robert of Scotland. Boy. Oliver Cromwell. Comm. F. Oct. 13, 1777. Died Oct. 4, 1778. 5 v. 32 p. 167; 5A p. 37.

CAMPBELL, John. Boatswain. Angelica. Comm. F. July 7, 1778. 5A p. 38.

CAMPBELL, John. F. Pard. for R. N. Sept. 9, 1779. G.

CAMPBELL, John. Seaman. Terrible or Hetty. Comm. F. May 24, 1781. SP; HO.

CAMPBELL or CAMBOLL, Thoms. of Virginia. Comm. M. May 1 or 5, 1781. R. N. July 29, 1781. Pard. for R. N. Aug. 9, 1781. G; 3 p. 141; 10 v. 73 p. 338; 10 v. 74 p. 37.

CAMPTON, John. Boatswain. Black Snake. Comm. F. Feb. 18, 1779. 5A p. 39.

CANADA, James. Seaman. Fair American. Comm. F. Nov. 30, 1780. SP; HO.

CANADA, William. See KANADY.

CANADA, CANEDY or KANIDY, Richd. Mariner. Brig Salley. Comm. M. May 11, 1781. Innoculated May 28, 1781. SP; HO; 3 p. 209; 10 v. 73 pp. 340, 346.

CANIDY, Wm. See KANADY.

CANIES?, Alexander. Seaman. Eagle. Comm. M. Feb. 6, 1782. HO.

CANNY, Ezekial of Carolina. Warren. Comm. M. June, 1778. R.N. 7 p. 255.

CAPRON, Green. Angelica. Comm. F. July 7, 1778. 5A p. 38.

CARD, Jacob. F. Pard. for exchange Dec. 11, 1779. G.

CAREN, William. M. Pard. for R.N. Sept. 29, 1781. G.

CARIL or CARROL, Phillip of Boston. Lyon. Comm. M. Oct. 2, 1781. 3 p. 211; 10 v. 74 p. 142. (May be same as CARLTON).

CARL, Wm. F. Pard. for exchange May 31, 1779. G.

CARLTON or CARLSON, Philip. Mariner. Brune, a French prize. Comm. M. Oct. 2, 1781. SP; HO. (May be same as CARIL).

CARN(E)S, David. Rising States. Comm. F. June 14, 1777. Pard. for exchange May 31, 1779. G; 5A p. 36.

CARN(E)Y, Charles. Montgomery of Philadelphia. Comm. F. Aug. 8, 1777. Pard. Dec. 3, 1778. R.N. Dec. 19, 1778. G; 5 v. 32 pp. 165, 282-3; 5A p. 36.

CARPENTER, Caleb. Reprisal. Comm. F. Aug. 28, 1778. 5A p. 38.

CARPENTER, James. Black Prince. Comm. F. April 26, 1779. 5A p. 39.

* CARPENTER, Jonathan of Rehobeth. Reprisal. Comm. F. June 9, 1778. Pard. for exchange May 31, 1779. Exchanged July 2, 1779. Died at Randolph, Vermont, March 14, 1837. See bibliography No. 2; G.

CARPENTER, Thomas. Seaman. Fair American. Comm. F. Nov. 30, 1780. SP; HO.

CARPENTER, William of England. Charming Sally or Polly. Captured Jan. 16, 1777. M. Pard. for R.N. Sept. 25, 1778. R.N. or escaped. G; 3 p. 75; 7 p. 248.

CARR, Benjamin of Newburyport. Dalton. Comm. M. June, 1777. Pard. for exchange Dec. 20, 1778. Joined Alliance. G; 3 p. 74; 7 p. 244;

CARR, Gard(i)ner. Angelica. Comm. F. July 7, 1778. Pard. for exchange Dec. 11, 1779. G; 5A p. 38.

CARR, John. Seaman. Portsmouth. Comm. F. June 27, 1781. SP; HO.

CARR, John, born at Newburyport. Dolphin. Escaped with Capt. Johnson of the Lexington. Re-captured Feb. 18, 1778. G.

CARRANT, John. F. Pard. for R.N. May 25, 1781. G. See also CORRANT.

CARREL or CARROL, Samuel of Block Point. Dalton or Charming Polly. Comm. M. June, 1777. Pard. for exchange Dec. 20, 1778. Joined Alliance. G; 3 p. 75; 7 p. 246.

CARRICO(E), John. Seaman. Montgomery. Comm. F. Aug. 8, 1777. Pard. for exchange May 31, 1779. Exchanged July 2, 1779. Joined Bonhomme Richard. G; 5 v. 32 p. 286; 5A p. 36.

CARROL. See CARIL, Philip and CAREL, Saml.

CARTER, Gideon. Comm. F. April 19, 1779. Pard. for exchange Dec. 11, 1779 and Nov. 9, 1781. G; 5A p. 39.

CARTER, Wm. Sturdy Beggar. Comm. F. Jan. 23, 1778. Pard. for exchange May 31, 1779. G; 5A p. 37.

CARVIN, CORVIN or CURVIN, George of Philadelphia. Captain or L.M. ? General St. Clair (Sinclair?) Comm. M. Jan. 1781. Att. escape April 21, 1781. Escaped June 4, 1781 and arrived safely at Ostend, Belgium. 3 p. 140; 10 v. 73 pp. 314, 335; v. 74 pp. 22, 28.

CARVIN or CORVIN, Richard. Essex. Comm. M. Aug. 25, 1781. Att. escape May 23, 1781 and Nov. 14, 1781. Escaped Nov. 15, 1781. 3 p. 211; 10 v. 73 p. 344; v. 74 pp. 44, 152, 153.

CARWICK, Henry.   Seaman.   Harlequin.   Comm. F. May 16, 1781. SP; HO.

CARY, Wm. of Boston.   Essex.   Comm. M. July 20, 1781.   3 p. 210; 10 v. 74 p. 34.

CASCO, Francis.   Comm. F. Aug. 8, 1777.   Pard. for exchange May 31, 1779.   G; 5A p. 36.

CASE, Ebenezer.   Seaman.   Marquis de la Fayette.   Comm. M. Jan. 23, 1782.   HO.

CASEY, Ezekial of Carolina.   Warren.   Comm. M. June 4, 1778.   Escaped.   3 p. 137.

CASEY, John.   Seaman.   Twin Sisters, Privateer of Rhode Island.   Comm. to Security Prison Ship at Chatham Dec. 18, 1781.   HO.

CASHENBERRY or CASSENBIRRY, Peter of Philadelphia.   Cabot.   Comm. M. June 1777.   Pard. for exchange Dec. 11, 1779.   Pard. for R. N. Jan. 28, 1780.   G; 7 p. 256.

CASHMAN, Bartholomew.   Seaman.   Daniel.   Comm. F. Oct. 31, 1780. SP.

CASSIDY, Andrew.   See BARBER.

CASTLE, John.   Satisfaction.   Comm. F. July 27, 1778.   Pard. for R. N. Dec. 3, 1778.   R. N. Dec. 19, 1778.   G; 5 v. 32 pp. 282-3; 5A p. 38.

CASTRET, Jere.   Sturdy Beggar.   Comm. F. Jan. 23, 1778.   Escaped. 5A p. 37.

CASWELL, CASWILL or CASUAL, Joshua of Kittery.   Seaman.   Dalton or Charming Polly.   Comm. M. June, 1777.   Pard. for exchange Dec. 20, 1778.   Re-taken in Thomas merchant ship Oct. 23, 1781.   Captured but not comm.   G; HO; 3 p. 75.

CAVE, Thos.   Comm. F. Jan. 23, 1778.   Pard. for exchange May 31, 1779.   G; 5A p. 37.

CAVENDER, James.   F.   Pard. for exchange Dec. 11, 1779.   G.

CELDER, Josiah.   See COLDER.

CHACE, George.   Seaman.   Clinton or Chance.   Comm. F. May 24, 1781.   SP; HO.

CHACE, Jonathan.   Mariner.   Charming Polly.   Comm. M. Sept. 10 or 19, 1780.   In hospital May 10, 1781.   R. N. acc. 3.   SP; HO; HL; 3 p. 139; 10 v. 73 p. 341.

CHACE, Thomas.   See CHASE.

CHADWELL.   M.   10 v. 74 p. 46.

CHADWELL, Willm. of Marblehead.   Mariner.   Susanna or prize to the Oliver Cromwell.   Comm. M. July 3 or 28, 1779.   Pard. for exchange Dec. 11, 1779.   G; SP; HO; HL; 3 p. 138.

CHADWICK, Nathan.   Seaman.   Susannah.   Comm. F. June 27, 1781.   HO.

CHAISE, Nicholas.   Lexington.   Comm. M. Sept. 19, 1777.   R. N. 7 p. 253.

CHAMBERLIN, Burd.   Lieut.   Muscetor (Mosquito?)   Comm. F. Aug. 8, 1777.   Escaped.   5A p. 36.

CHAMBERLIN, George.   Lieut.   Muscetor (Mosquito?) of Virginia.   Comm. F. Aug. 8, 1777.   Escaped and re-captured Oct. 12, 1777 and sent to b. h.   Escaped.   5 v. 30 p. 345; 5A p. 36.

CHAMBERS, Mathw. of Beverly.   Mariner.   Essex.   Comm. M. July 24, 1781.   SP; HO; 10 v. 74 p. 35.

CHAMPNEY, Joshua.   Seaman.   Fame.   Comm. F. March 5, 1781.   SP; HO.

CHANDLER, Mr. (2) of Cape Ann.   Comm. M. May, 1777.   4 p. 185.

CHANDLER, John.   Mariner.   Aurora.   Comm. M. July 25 or 27, 1780.   SP; HO; HL; 3 p. 139.

CHANDLER, Saml. of Casco Bay.   Mariner.   Franklin.   At Pembroke, 1778.   Comm. M. Oct. 14 or 17, 1780.   Innoculated May 28, 1781.   SP; HO; HL; 3 p. 139; 10 v. 73 p. 348.

MARINERS OF THE AMERICAN REVOLUTION

CHAPMAN, Balam. Mariner. Confederacy. Comm. M. Aug. 23, 1781. SP; HO.

CHAPMAN, Briton of Rhode Island. Confederacy. Comm. M. Aug. 23, 1781. 3 p. 211; 10 v. 74 p. 43.

CHAPMAN, Richard. Rising States. Comm. F. June 14, 1777. Escaped Nov. 19, 1777. 5 v. 30 p. 347; 5A p. 36.

CHARD, Joseph. Seaman. Hercules. Captured but not comm. Oct. 15, 1781. HO.

CHARLES, Edward. Seaman or boy. Alliance. Comm. F. Dec. 30, 1779. SP; HO.

CHASE. M. 8 p. 130.

CHASE or CHACE, Thomas of Martha's Vineyard. Charming Sally or Polly. Captured Jan. 16, 1777. M. Pard. for exchange Dec. 20, 1778. Still there Feb. 7, 1779. G; 3 p. 75; 7 p. 248.

CHAUNCEY, Isaac or Isaacus. Aurora. Comm. M. July 25, 1780. Att. escape May 27, 1781. Out of b.h. June 6, 1781. Escaped July, 1781. HL; 3 p. 139; 10 v. 73 pp. 345, 6; v. 74 pp. 23, 30, 31.

CHERRELL, Cherlo. Revenge. Comm. F. Aug. 11, 1777. Died Nov. 7 1778. 5A p. 37.

CHESTER, John of England. Lexington. Comm. M. Sept. 19, 1777. Pard. for exchange Dec. 11, 1779. G; 7 p. 253. (See SHESTER).

CHESTER, John. Seaman. Bienfaisant, a French ship. Comm. Pembroke, Jan. 17, 1782. HO.

CHEW, Benjamin. Captain or prizemaster. Sturdy Beggar of Maryland. Comm. F. Jan. 23, 1778. Escaped July 23, 1778. Letter received from him in France Sept. 7, 1778. 5 v. 30 p. 348; v. 31 pp. 20, 212, 287; v. 32 p. 73; 5A p. 37.

CHILD, Timothy. Seaman. Wexford. Comm. M. Jan. 24, 1782. HO.

CHILTON, Littleton. Mariner. L'Uzerne. Comm. M. July 6, 1781. SP; HO; 3 p. 209; 10 v. 74 p. 31.

MARINERS OF THE AMERICAN REVOLUTION

CHIPMAN, Benjamin of Beverly or Salem. Schooner Warren. Comm. M. June, 1778. Pard. for exchange Dec. 11, 1779. Escaped. G; 3 p. 137; 7 p. 255.

CHIVRAL(L), John. Seaman. Dolphin. Comm. F. May 24, 1781. SP; HO.

CHOAT, Aaron. M. Pard. for exchange Dec. 11, 1779. G; (See Adam).

CHOAT, Ebenezer. Seaman. Bermuda. Comm. M. Jan. 22, 1782. HO.

CHOAT, Joseph of Newburyport. Dalton. In hospital April, 1777. Comm. M. June, 1777. Pard. for exchange Dec. 20, 1778. G; 4 p. 184; 7 p. 244. (Probably same as Joseph CHOVE)

CHOATE, Adam of Ipswich. Fancy. Comm. M. Aug. 7, 1777. Exchanged. 3 p. 136; 7 p. 250. (Probably same as Aaron.)

CHOULSTON, Thos. of Ireland. Lexington. Comm. M. Sept. 19, 1777. R. N. 7 p. 252. (Probably same as Colston).

CHOVE, Joseph. Dalton. Captured Dec. 26, 1776. Exchanged. 3 p. 74. (Probably same as Joseph CHOAT).

CHRISTOPHERS, Samuel. Seaman. Portsmouth. Comm. F. June 27, 1781. SP; HO.

CHUBB, Daniel of Salem. Schooner Warren. Comm. M. June, 1778. Pard. for exchange Dec. 11, 1779 and Nov. 9, 1781. G; HL; 3 p. 137; 7 p. 254.

CHURCH, Clement of Boston. Mariner. Marquis de Morbec, a French prize. Comm. M. Oct. 2, 1781. SP; HO; 3 p. 211; 10 v. 74 p. 142.

CHURCH, Jery or Jeremiah. Mariner. Franklin. Comm. M. Nov. or Dec. 6, 1781. SP; HO; 3 p. 212.

CHURCH, Silvanus of New Jersey. Mariner. Franklin. Comm. M. Nov. or Dec. 6, 1781. SP; HO; 3 p. 212.

CHURCHILL, Joseph. Seaman. Jason. Captured but not comm. Oct. 15, 1781. HO.

MARINERS OF THE AMERICAN REVOLUTION

CILLAW or CILLEY, John, alias CALLIO of North Carolina. General Nash. Comm. M. July 28, 1781. Died Oct. 1, 1781. 3 p. 210; 10 v. 74 pp. 36, 48.

CLAMPET, Abraham. Seaman. Centurion. Comm. F. March 21, 1781. SP; HO.

CLARK, Arthur of Boston. Essex. Comm. M. July 21 or 25, 1781. 3 p. 210; 10 v. 74 p. 36.

CLARK, Christopher. Carpenter. Rising States. Comm. F. June 14, 1777. Escaped, re-captured and in b. h. July 30, 1777. Pard. for exchange Dec. 1779. G; 5 v. 30 p. 344; 5A p. 36.

CLARK, David of Philadelphia. Lexington. Comm. M. Sept. 19, 1777. Pard. for R. N. Sept. 25, 1778. Entered or escaped. G; 3 p. 137; 7 p. 253.

CLARK, David. Seaman. Rambler or Jason. Comm. F. Dec. 30, 1779. SP; HO.

CLARK or CLERK, Ephraim of Kittery, N. H. Seaman and interpreter. Dalton or Charming Polly. Comm. M. June, 1777. Pard. for exchange Dec. 20, 1778. Joined Alliance. Captured in Marquis de Morbec and comm. M. Oct. 2, 1781. G; SP; HO; 3 p. 211; 7 p. 245; 9 p. 99; 10 v. 74 p. 142.

CLARK, George of Marblehead. Steward or boy. General Glover. Comm. F. Nov. 30, 1779. SP; HO; 10 v. 73 p. 340.

CLARK, Gregory of Braintree. Mariner. Essex. Comm. M. July 24, 1781. SP; HO; 3 p. 210; 10 v. 74 p. 35.

CLARK(E), James of Boston. Mariner. Sussex. Comm. M. July 21 or 24, 1781. SP; HO; 3 p. 210; 10 v. 74 p. 35.

CLARK, John. Seaman. Active. Comm. F. March 5, 1781. SP; HO.

CLARK, John of Cape Ann. Mariner. General Massey. Comm. M. Oct. 16, 1781. SP; HO; 3 p. 212; 10 v. 74 p. 145.

CLARK, John. Mariner. Elijah, prize to the Grand Turk. Comm. M. Dec. 7, 1781. SP; HO.

CLARK, Joseph of Boston. Dalton. Sent to Royal hospital Feb. 15, 1777. Comm. M. June, 1777. Pard. for R. N. Jan. 4, 1779. G; 3 p. 74; 4 p. 44; 7 p. 246.

CLARK, Joseph of Lebanon, Conn. Surgeon's mate. Protector. Comm. M. July 21 or 23, 1781. SP; HO; 3 p. 209; 10 v. 74 p. 35.

CLARK, Samuel. Seaman. Essex. Sent from Kinsale to M. April 9, 1782. HO.

CLARK, Shubal of Nantucket. Mariner. Charming Polly. Comm. M. Sept. 19, 1780. Discharged March 20, 1782. "in order that he may proceed on the Southern Whale fishery in which it is said he is well experienced." G; SP; HL; 3 p. 139; 10 v. 73 p. 346.

CLARK, Thomas. Rising States. Comm. F. June 14, 1777. Escaped Nov. 19, 1777. 5 v. 30 p. 347; 5A p. 36.

CLARK, Thos. of New York. Grand Turk's prize. Comm. M. Nov. 1781. 3 p. 212.

CLARK, Wm. of Rhode Island. Schooner Warren. Comm. M. June, 1778. Pard. for exchange Dec. 11, 1779. 3 p. 137; 7 p. 255, G.

CLARK, William. Seaman. Terrible. Comm. F. May 24, 1781. SP; HO.

CLARKE, Arthur Every or Avery. Mariner. Essex. Comm. M. July 25, 1781. SP; HO.

CLARKE, Jacob. Seaman. Hercules. Captured but not comm. Oct. 15, 1781. HO.

CLARKE, Pileg, the younger. Seaman. General Wayne. Comm. F. Aug. 9, 1781. SP; HO.

CLARKSON, John of Providence, R. I. Alliance of Dunkirk. Comm. M. Oct. 9, 1781. Pard. for R. N. Oct. 24, 1781. R. N. Nov. 9, 1781. G; 3 p. 211; 10 v. 74, pp. 143, 146.

CLAXTON, Matthias. Seaman. Terrible. Comm. F. May 24, 1781. SP; HO.

MARINERS OF THE AMERICAN REVOLUTION

CLAYPO(O)LE, John. Mariner. L'Uzerne. Comm. M. July 6, 1781. SP; HO; 3 p. 209.

CLEAR, Matthew of England. Lexington. Comm. M. Sept. 19, 1777. Pard. for R.N. Oct. 14, 1778. Entered or escaped. G; 3 p. 137; 7 p. 253.

CLEAVLAND or CLEVELAND, Seth. Prize master. Comm. F. Oct. 20, 1778. Pard. for exchange Dec. 11, 1779. G; 5A p. 38.

CLERK, Enoch of Kittery. M. 9 p. 80.

CLERK, Ephraim. See CLARK.

CLERK, Joseph. M. Pard. for exchange Dec. 20, 1778. G.

CLIFFORD, Zachariah. Seaman. Hercules. Captured but not comm. Oct. 15, 1781. HO.

CLOTHY, Josiah. Seaman. Jason. Captured but not comm. Oct. 15, 1781. HO.

CLUSTON, Thomas of Newburyport. Dalton. Comm. M. June, 1777. Escaped. 3 p. 74; 7 p. 243.

COBB, Thomas. 2nd mate. Resolution. Comm. M. Jan. 22, 1781. Innoculated May 28, 1781. SP; HO; HL; 10 v. 73 pp. 316, 346.

COCKRAN or COKRAN, John. Boatswain. Yankee. Comm. F. June 14 or 26, 1777. Escaped and re-captured, put in b.h. July 30, 1777. Escaped Dec. 1777. 5 v. 31 p. 285; 5A p. 36.

COCKSETTER or COXTER, James of New York. Mariner. Betsey. Comm. M. July 23, 1781. SP; HO; 3 p. 210.

CODNER, Christopher. Freedom's prize. Captured April 29, 1777. M. Pard. for exchange Feb. 2, 1779. G; 3 p. 75. (Probably same as next).

CODRER, Christian of Marblehead. Freedom's prize. Captured April 27, 1777. M. 7 p. 251. (Probably same as last)

COGSHALL, Matthew. The Swallow. Comm. F. Jan 23, 1778. Escaped. 5A p. 37.

COGG(E)SHALL, Michael. Seaman. Angelica. Comm. F. July 6, 1778. Pard. for exchange Dec. 11, 1779. G; SP; 5A p. 38.

COLBURN, Francis of Philadelphia. Lexington. Comm. M. Sept. 19, 1777. Pard. for R. N. Sept. 25, 1778. Entered or escaped. G; 3 p. 137; 7 p. 253.

COLDER, CELDER or CALDER, Josiah of Nantucket. Mariner. Minerva. Comm. M. Aug. 23 or 24, 1780. In hospital May 10, 1781. SP; HO; HL; 3 p. 139; 10 v. 73 pp. 341, 347.

COLDE(R), Nicholas of Philadelphia. Mariner. Franklin. Comm. M. Nov. or Dec. 6, 1781. SP; HO; 3 p. 212.

COLE, William of Marblehead. Fancy. Comm. M. Aug. 7, 1777. Pard. for exchange Dec. 11, 1779. G; 3 p. 136; 7 p. 250.

COLLIE, William. Seaman. Newfoundland. Imprisoned at Edinburgh June 27, 1781. HO.

COLLIER or COLLYER, Thomas of Marblehead. America's prize. Comm. M. March 22, 1779. Exchanged. HL; 3 p. 138.

COLLIN(G)S, Charles of Cape Ann. 2nd captain. Black Prince or Princess. Comm. M. Oct. 16, 20 or 27, 1781. SP; 3 p. 212; 10 v. 74 p. 147.

COLLINS, Isaac of Cape Ann. 2nd lieut. Black Prince or Princess. Comm. M. Oct. 20, 1781. SP; HO; 3 p. 212; 10 v. 74 p. 146.

COLLINS, John. Imprisoned at Pembroke. Petitioned to join R. N. Sept. 21, 1780. G.

COLLINS, Nathl. of Cape Ann. Mariner. Hannible of Newbury. Comm. M. Jan. 11 or 18, 1781. SP; HO; HL; 3 p. 140; 10 v. 73 p. 313.

COLLINS, Stores. F. Pard. for R. N. Jan. 12, 1781. G.

COLLINS, Thomas. M. Pard. for exchange Dec. 11, 1779 and Nov. 9, 1781. (Probably meant for Thomas Collier). G.

COLLINS, William. Seaman. Jason. Captured but not comm. Oct. 15, 1781. HO.

MARINERS OF THE AMERICAN REVOLUTION

COLLYER, Thos. See COLLIER.

COLSTON, Joseph. See COULSTON.

COLSTON or COULSON, Thos. Lexington. Comm. M. Sept. 19, 1777. Pard. for R.N. Jan. 4, 1779. Entered or escaped. G; 3 p. 137; (Probably the same as CHOULSON).

COMMOTT, Benjamin. F. Pard. for R.N. Jan. 27, 1781. G.

COMPTON, Alexander. Seaman. Tom Lee. Comm. F. Aug. 9, 1781. SP; HO.

CONDON, Jonathan. Seaman. Wexford. Captured but not comm. Feb. 8, 1782. HO.

CONNER, James. See CONNOR.

CONNER, John of Portsmouth Va? Mariner. Brig Salley of North Carolina. Comm. M. May 11, 1781. SP; HO; 3 p. 209; 10 v. 73 p. 340.

CONNER, Morris of Boston. Mariner. Essex. Comm. M. July 24, 1781. In b.h. Nov. 7, 1781. Out of b.h. Nov. 19. SP; HO; 3 p. 210; 10 v. 74 pp. 35, 150, 154.

CONNOR or CONNER, James. Carpenter. Oliver Cromwell. Comm. M. Oct. 13, 1777. Pard. for exchange May 31, 1779. Exchanged July 2, 1779. Joined Bonhomme Richard. G; 5 v. 32 p. 286; 5A p. 37.

CONNOR, John. Gunner. Angelica of Boston. Comm. F. July 7, 1778. Escaped. 5 v. 32 p. 73; 5A p. 38.

CONNOR, John of Philadelphia. Brig Hector of Philadelphia. Comm. M. Jan. 11, 1781. Pard. for R.N. March 20, 1781. Entered March 27, 1781. G; 3 p. 140; 10 v. 73 pp. 313, 330.

CONNOR, Timothy. Rising States. Comm. F. June 14, 1777. Pard. for exchange May 31, 1779. Exchanged July 2, 1779. G; 5A p. 36. See bibliography No. 5.

CONTER, James of New York. Betsey. Comm. M. July 23, 1781. 10 v. 74 p. 35.

CONYNGHAM, Gustavus. See CUNNINGHAM.

COOKE, William. Seaman. Harlequin. Comm. F. May 16, 1781. SP; HO.

COOLEDGE or COLLAGE, Augustin or Augustus. Rising States. Comm. F. June 14, 1777. Pard. for exchange May 31, 1779. G; 5A p. 36.

COOPER, John. Boy. Montgomery. Comm. F. Aug. 8, 1777. Pard. for exchange May 31, 1779. Joined Bonhomme Richard. G; 5 v. 32 p. 286; 5A p. 36.

COOPER, John of Virginia. Mariner. Lion. Comm. M. Aug. 31, 1781. In b. h. May 22, 1782. SP; HO; 3 p. 211; 8 p. 139.

COOPER, Willm. of Boston. Captain of marines. Lion. Comm. M. Nov. 21, 1781. SP; HO; 3 p. 211; 10 v. 74 p. 155.

COPP, John. Montgomery. Comm. F. Aug. 8, 1777. Escaped. 5A p. 36.

CORBETT, Robert of Wilmington. Alliance of Dunkirk. Comm. M. Oct. 9, 1781. Pard. for R. N. Nov. 9, 1781. Entered Oct. 25, 1781. G; 3 p. 211; 10 v. 74 pp. 143, 147.

CORBIN, Nathaniel. Seaman. Fame. Comm. F. March 5, 1781. SP; HO.

COREY or CORY, Philip of Rhode Island. 18 yrs. old. The Swallow. Comm. F. Jan. 23, 1778. Died Aug. 28 or 30, 1778. 5 v. 32 p. 72; 5A p. 37.

CORNISH or CORNASH, Cyprian or Sy. of Kennebeck. Mariner. Essex. Comm. M. July 21, 1781. SP; HO; 3 p. 210.

CORRANT or CARRANT, John. Seaman. Daniel. Comm. F. Oct. 31, 1780. SP; HO; See also CARRANT.

CORTER, Hammond. See COURTER.

CORVIN. See CARVIN.

CORY, Philip. See COREY.

MARINERS OF THE AMERICAN REVOLUTION

COSSAY, Ezekial. M. Pard. for R.N. Jan. 4, 1779. G.

COTES, Samuel. Seaman. Pocahontas. Comm. F. Nov. 18, 1780. SP; HO.

COTTER, Richard. F. Pard. for R.N. Oct. 30, 1779. G.

COTTLE, Dan'l of Newburyport. Dalton. Sent to Royal hospital at Plymouth, Feb. 15, 1777. Died Aug. 24, 1777. 4 pp. 44, 184; 7 pp. 57, 244. (See also Daniel CUTTING).

COTTERALL or COTTRELL, John of Rhode Island. Mariner. General Nash or Ann? Comm. M. July 28, 1781. SP; HO; 3 p. 210; 10 v. 74 p. 36.

COTTON, Joseph or Jas. Mariner. Effingham, Weymouth or General Sullivan's prize. Comm. M. July 3, 1779. Pard. for exchange Dec. 11, 1779. SP; HO; G; HL; 3 p. 138.

COULS(T)ON or COLSTON, Joseph of Ireland. Lexington. Comm. M. Sept. 19, 1777. Pard. for R.N. Jan. 4, 1779. Entered or escaped. G; 3 p. 137; 7 p. 253.

COULSON, Thomas. See COLSTON.

COURTER or CORTER, Hammon(d). Captain. Oliver Cromwell. Comm. F. Oct. 13, 1777. Escaped. 5 v. 30 p. 345; 5A p. 37.

COURTIS, Samuel. Mariner. Essex. Comm. M. July 27, 1781. SP; HO.

COVEL(L), David of Martha's Vineyard or Virginia. Cabot. Comm. M. June, 1777. Pard. for exchange May 31, 1779. Pard. for R.N. Jan. 28, 1780. Entered Dec. 11, 1779 or escaped. G; 7 p. 256; 3 p. 74.

COVELL, Joseph. Prize master or mate. Comm. F. Oct. 20, 1778. Pard. for exchange Dec. 11, 1779. G; 5A p. 38.

COVANE or COVEN, Michael or Michel. Revenge. Comm. F. Aug. 11, 1777. Pard. for exchange May 31, 1779. G; 5A p. 37.

COVENTRY, John. Mariner. Hannabal of Newbury. Comm. M. Jan. 11 or 18, 1781. In b.h. March 15, 1781. SP; HO; HL; 3 p. 140; 10 v. 73 p. 313, 328; v. 74 p. 48.

45

MARINERS OF THE AMERICAN REVOLUTION

COWARD, John of Maryland?   Tom Lee.   Comm. M. May 1, 1781.
    10 v. 73 p. 339.

COWARD, William.   Captain.   Tom Lee.   Comm. M. May 5, 1781.
    Att. escape Aug. 11, 1781.   Out of b.h. Sept. 13, 1781.   SP; HO;
    10 v. 74 pp. 40, 45.

COWES, Capt.   F.   Escaped, got to Paris and conversed with B. Franklin.
    7 p. 163.

COWIT, James.   Seaman.   Hercules.   Sent from Kinsale to M. April 9,
    1782.   HO.

COX, Bray.   Seaman.   Portsmouth.   Comm. F. June 27, 1781.   SP; HO.

COX, James.   Fancy.   Comm. M. August, 1777.   Pard. for exchange
    Dec. 11, 1779.   G;   3 p. 136.

COX, Samuel.   Fancy.   Comm. M. August, 1777.   Pard. for exchange
    Dec. 11, 1779.   G;   3 p. 136.

COX, Saml. of Dorchester.   Essex.   Comm. M. July 28, 1781.   3 p. 210.
    10 v. 74 p. 36.

COX, William.   Seaman.   Wexford.   Sent from Kinsale to M. April 9,
    1782.   HO.

COXHALL, Richard.   Seaman.   Mercury.   Comm. F. May 24, 1781.   SP.

COXTER, James.   See COCKSETTER.

CRANDAL, Lyman.   Seaman.   Fair American.   Comm. F. Nov. 18,
    1780.   SP.

CRANDALL, Joshua.   Seaman.   Hercules.   Captured but not comm.
    Oct. 15, 1781.   HO.

CRANDALL or CRANDON, William.   Seaman.   Twin Sisters.   Comm. M.
    Jan. 9, 1782.   HO;   3 p. 212.

CRANDON or CRANDOD, Thoms. of Dartmouth.   Industry.   Comm. M.
    Nov. 18, 1780.   Pard. for R.N. May 25, 1781.   Entered June 5, 1781.
    3 p. 139;   10 v. 74 p. 22.   G.

CRAW, John L.   See CROW.

CRAWFORD, Alexander.   Seaman.   Marquis de la Fayette.   Comm. M. Jan. 22, 1782.   HO.

CRAWFORD, Jacob of Philadelphia.   Lexington.   Comm. M. Sept. 19, 1777.   Pard. for exchange Dec. 11, 1779.   G; 3 p. 137; 7 p. 253.

CREAMER, Michael.   Seaman.   Morning Star.   Comm. F. Oct. 16, 1781. SP; HO.

CREAPOLE, Jno.   Luserne of Philadelphia.   Comm. M. July 6, 1781. 10 v. 74 p. 31.

CREEBE or CREPER, William of England.   Charming Sally.   Captured Jan. 16, 1777.   Pard. for R. N. Sept. 25, 1778.   G; 7 p. 248.

CRISPIN, Richard of Salem.   Schooner Warren.   Comm. M. June, 1778. Pard. for exchange Dec. 11, 1779.   Pard. for R. N. Nov. 22, 1780. Entered or escaped.   G; 3 p. 137; 7 p. 254.

CROAD, Joshua.   Mariner.   Resolution.   Comm. M. Jan. 22, 1781.   SP; HO.   (Possibly same as Jesse Crowell).

CROKER or CROCKER, John.   Mate.   Adventure.   Comm. M. July 21, 1781.   SP; HO; 3 p. 210.

CROOKEE, Jas. of Cape Cod.   Essex.   Comm. M. July 21, 1781.   10 v. 74 p. 34.

CROSS, Benjamin.   Seaman.   Newfoundland.   Imprisoned at Edinburgh June 27, 1781.   HO.

CROSS, David.   Seaman.   Montgomery.   Comm. F. Aug. 8, 1777. Pard. for exchange May 31, 1779.   Joined Bonhomme Richard.   G; 5 v. 32 p. 286; 5A p. 36.

CROSS, George.   Seaman.   Eagle.   Comm. M. Feb. 6, 1782.   HO.

CROSS, Moses of Newburyport.   Dalton.   Comm. M. June, 1777.   Pard. for exchange Dec. 20, 1778.   G; 3 p. 74; 7 p. 243.

CROSS, William. Seaman. Wexford. Captured but not comm. Oct. 2, 1781. HO.

CROW, CROWELL or CROWER, Barzelli or Barzilla of Martha's Vineyard. Charming Sally or Polly. Captured Jan. 16, 1777. M. Still in M. Feb. 7, 1779. Pard. for exchange Dec. 11, 1779. G; 3 p. 75; 7 p. 248.

CROW, James. Seaman. Jack. In F. but sent sick Jan. 14, 1781 and not comm. HO.

CROW, John. Boatswain. Oliver Cromwell. F. Escaped May 26, 1778. 5 v. 31 p. 19.

CROW or CRAW, John or John L. of Marblehead. Fancy. Comm. M. Aug. 7, 1777. Pard. for exchange Dec. 11, 1779. G; 3 p. 136; 7 p. 250.

CROWELL or CROWILL, Jesse or Josha. Resolution of Boston. Comm. M. Jan. 22, 1781. Innoculated May 28, 1781. HL (mark); 3 p. 140; 10 v. 73 pp. 316, 346. (Possibly same as Joshua Croad).

CROWELL, Sylvanus. Seaman. Adventure. Comm. M. Jan. 21, 1782. HO; 3 p. 213.

CROWNSINSHIELD or CROWNINGFIELD, Clifford of Salem. Warren. Comm. M. June, 1778. Pard. for exchange Dec. 11, 1779 and Nov. 9, 1781. G; HL; 3 p. 137; 7 p. 254.

CUFF, John. Seaman. Bienfaisant, a French ship. Imprisoned at Pembroke Jan. 17, 1782. HO.

CUFF, Wm. of Dartmouth. Charming Sally or Polly. Captured Jan. 16, 1777. M. Still in M. Feb. 7, 1779. Pard. for exchange Dec. 20, 1778. G; 3 p. 75; 7 p. 247.

CUMMINS, Thos. Boatswain. Rising States. Comm. F. June 14, 1777. Escaped. 5A p. 36.

CUNNINGHAM, CUNYNGHAM or CONYNGHAM, Gustavus of Philadelphia. Captain. Comm. M. Aug. 23, 1779. Attempted escapes April 21, May 14, May 23, May 31, 1781. Escaped June 4, 1781, in Ostend in June and in France in August. 3 p. 138; 10 v. 73 pp. 328, 335, 341, 342, 344, 345, 346; v. 74 pp. 22, 23, 28, 37. (It is believed that he previously broke out of F. on Nov. 14, 1779, according to Isaac Greenwood, (see bibliography No. 17). Colburne's date of Aug. 23, 1779 for his commitment to M. may be in error, as it is difficult to believe he was in M. nearly two years before trying to escape. Also, there is no mention of him before 1781 by other diarists who were in M.

CUNYNGHAM, Isaac. of North Carolina. General Nash. Comm. M. May 4, 1781. Pard. for R.N. Oct. 1781 but entered Aug. 20, 1781. G; HL; 3 p.141; 10 v.74 p.42.

CUNNINGHAM(E), Jacob. Angelica. Comm. F. July 7, 1778. Pard. for exchange Dec. 11, 1779. G; 5A p.38.

CUNNINGHAM, Jas. Boy. Sturdy Beggar. Comm. F. Jan. 23, 1778. Pard. for exchange May 31, 1779. Exchanged July 2, 1779. Joined Bonhomme Richard. G; 5 v.32 p.286; 5A p.37.

CUNNINGHAM, James. Seaman. Wexford. Sent from Kinsale to M. April 9, 1782. HO.

CUNNINGHAM, John. Mariner. Lion. Comm. M. Oct. 2, 1781. SP; HO; 3 p.211; 10 v.74 p.142.

CUNNINGHAM, Robert. Seaman. Pocahontas. Comm. F. Nov. 18, 1780. SP; HO.

CUNNINGHAM, Wm. of Bristol, England or Boston. Alliance of Dunkirk. Comm. M. Oct. 9, 1781. Att. escape, in b.h. Oct. 19, 1781. Att. escape Nov. 15, 1781. B.h. Nov. 18, out of b.h. Nov. 26, 1781. Pard. for R.N. Jan. 4, 1782. Entered Nov. 29, 1781. G; 10 v.74 pp. 143, 145, 153, 154, 156, 157.

CURTIS, Joseph. F. Pard. for exchange Dec. 11, 1779. G.

CURTIS, Robert. Seaman. Marquis de la Fayette. Comm. M. Jan. 22, 1782. HO.

CURTIS or CURTICE, Samuel. Mariner. Resoltuion. Comm. M. Jan. 22, 1781. SP; HO; HL; 3 p.140; 10 v.73 p.316; v.74 p.48.

CURTIS, Sam'l. Essex. Comm. M. July 21, 1781. 3 p.210.

MARINERS OF THE AMERICAN REVOLUTION

CURTIS, William.   F.   Pard. for exchange Dec. 11, 1779.   G.

CURVIN, George.   See CARVIN.

CUSHING, Peter of Philadelphia.   Cabot.   Comm. M. Jan. 1777.   3 p. 74.

CUSHING or CUSHON, John, of Haverhill.   Doctor.   Schooner Warren. Comm. M. June, 1778.   Pard. for exchange Dec. 11, 1779.   G; 3 p. 137;   7 p. 255.

CUTLAND, Francis.   M.   Pard. for R. N. Sept. 25, 1778.   G.

CUTLER, Samuel of Newburyport.   Dalton.   Comm. M. June, 1777.   Escaped Oct. 26, 1777.   See bibliography No. 4.   3 p. 74;   7 pp. 70, 243.

CUTTER, William Richard of Lexington, Mass.   Comm. F. June 14, 1777. 5 v. 30 p. 343.

CUTTING, Daniel of Newburyport.   M.   4 p. 187.   (Probably same as COTTLE).

D

DAGHAN or DOGONE, John of Holland. Charming Sally or Polly. Captured Jan. 16, 1777. M. R N. or escaped. 3 p. 75; 7 p. 248.

DAGO or DEGO, Anthony. Angelica. Comm. F. July 7, 1778. Pard. for exchange Dec. 11, 1779. G; 5A p. 38.

DAIVES, Wm. of Philadelphia. Diana. Comm. M. July 23, 1781. 10 v. 74 p. 35.

DALANY, Dennis. See DELANY.

DALTON, John. Alliance's prize. Comm. M. March 22, 1779. Escaped. 3 p. 138.

DALTON, Wm. of St. Mathias. Mosquito. Comm. M. 1778. Escaped. 3 p. 137.

DAM(E), DEM or DOM, Benj. Mariner. Aurora. Comm. M. July 25, 1780. SP; HO; HL; 3 p. 139. See also DUM.

DAME, John of Newbury. Prize master. Angelica. Comm. F. July 7, 1778. Pard. for exchange May 31, 1779. G; 5A p. 38; 7 pp. 143, 149.

DANA, Daniel. Captain's clerk. Rising States. Comm. F. June 14, 1777. 5A p. 36.

DANA, Olinda or Oriendo. Rising States. Comm. F. June 14, 1777. Pard. for exchange May 31, 1779. G; 5A p. 36.

DANANS, Shepton. 10 v. 73 p. 329.

DANIEL, William. M. Pard. for R. N. Aug. 30, 1781. G.

DANIELS, John. Seaman. South Quay. Comm. F. March 21, 1781. SP; HO.

DANNES, Stephen. M. Pard. for exchange Dec. 11, 1779. G.

MARINERS OF THE AMERICAN REVOLUTION

DANNIS, Capt.   Probably the same as DENNIS.

DARBEY, Eleazer of Boston.   Confederacy.   Comm. M. Aug. 23, 1781. 3 p. 211.

DARLING, Bonner, a negro, of Marblehead.   Dalton.   M. Pard. for exchange Dec. 20, 1778.   Died March 19, 1779.   G; 3 p. 75; 7 pp. 228, 246.

DARLING, Levi.   F.   Pard. for R.N. Sept. 9, 1779.   G.

DARREL, Thomas.   Seaman.   Peggy.   Comm. M. Feb. 27, 1782.   HO.

DATON, Wm.   See DAYTON.

DAVIES, John.   F.   Pard. for R.N. Jan. 27, 1781.   G.   (Probably the same as John Davis of the Lexington).

DAVIES, John.   See DAVIS.

DAVIES, Richard.   See DAVIS.

DAVIS, Benjamin.   Seaman.   Hydra or American.   Comm. F. Feb. 3, 1781.   SP; HO.

DAVIS or DIVIS, Elisha or Elija.   Seaman or cooper.   Franklin.   Comm. Pembroke prison 1778 and transferred to M. Oct. 17, 1780.   SP; HO; 3 p. 139.

DAVIS, Henry.   Seaman.   Wexford.   Captured but not comm. Oct. 2, 1781. HO.

DAVIS, John.   M.   Pard. for R.N. Sept. 25, 1778.   G.

DAVIS, John of North Carolina.   Mariner.   Robertson or Betsey.   Comm. M. July 28, 1781.   SP; 10 v. 74 p. 36.

DAVI(E)S, John.   Mariner.   Black Prince or Princess.   Comm. M. Oct. 20, 1781.   SP; HO; 3 p. 211; 10 v. 74 p. 146.

DAVIS, John of England.   Lexington.   Comm. M. Sept. 19, 1777.   Pard. for R.N. March 20, 1782.   Entered or escaped.   G; 3 p. 137; 7 p. 253. (Probably same as DAVIES.)

MARINERS OF THE AMERICAN REVOLUTION

DAVIS, Joshua of Boston. Essex. Comm. M. July 24, 1781. Pard. for R. N. Aug. 2, 1781. G; 3 p. 210; 10 v. 74 pp. 35, 38.

DAVI(E)S, Richard. Mariner. Lively. Comm. M. Dec. 27, 1780. Innoculated May 28, 1781. SP; HO; HL; 3 p. 140; 10 v. 73 p. 346.

DAVIS, Samuel. Seaman. Two Brothers. Comm. M. Jan. 23, 1782. HO.

DAVIS, Wm. Captain. Angelica. Comm. F. July 7, 1778. Escaped July 23, 1778. 5 v. 31 pp. 284, 287; 5A p. 38. See DANNIS and DENNIS.

DAVIS, Zebulon of New Gloucester. Seaman. Charming Polly or Dalton. Comm. M. June, 1777 or Aug. 1, 1777. Pard. for exchange Dec. 11, 1779. Joined Two Brothers. Re-taken Jan. 23, 1782. G; HO. 3 p. 75; 4 pp. 184, 306; 7 p. 244.

DAWSEY, Wm. See DORSEY.

DAWSON, John. Boy. Monmouth. Comm. F. Jan. 11, 1780. SP; HO.

DAY, Isaac. Mariner. Beaver. Comm. M. July 23 or 27, 1781. SP; HO; 3 p. 210.

DAY, James. True Blue. Comm. F. June 19, 1778. Pard. for R. N. Dec. 16, 1778. Entered Dec. 3 or 19. G; 5 v. 32 p. 282-3; 5A p. 38.

DAY, Jonathan. Seaman. Rhodes. Comm. F. Nov. 18, 1780. SP; HO.

DAY, Joshua. Mariner. Beaver. Comm. M. July 27, 1781. SP.

DAYTON or DATON, William of St. Martin's. Mosquito. M. Pard. for R. N. Sept. 25, 1778. G; 7 p. 256.

DEADHAM, John. See DEADMAN.

DEADMAN or DEADHAM, John of Salem. (Brother to William). Mariner. Hawke. Comm. M. Oct. 16 or 17, 1778. Pard. for exchange Dec. 11, 1779. G; SP; HO; HL; 3 p. 137; 7 p. 258; 9 p. 85.

DEADMAN, William. See John. 9 p. 85.

MARINERS OF THE AMERICAN REVOLUTION

DEAL, Richard.or Mr. of Virginia. Lexington. Comm. M. Sept. 19, 1777. Escaped Feb. 1, 1778. Out of b.h. April 10, 1778. Escaped Feb. 3, 1779. 3 p.137; 7 pp. 94, 110, 116, 221, 253.

DEAN, James of Hartford. Charming Sally. Captured Jan. 16, 1777. M. R.N. 7 p.248. (See below).

DEAN, James. Dalton. Captured Dec. 26, 1777. Escaped. 3 p.75. (Probably same as above in spite of discrepancies.)

DEANE, John. M. Pard. for exchange Dec. 20, 1778. G.

DEGO, Anthony. See DAGO.

DELANY or DALANEY, Dennis. Mariner. Luzerne of Philadelphia. Comm. M. July 7, 1781. SP; HO; 3 p.209; 10 v.74 p.31.

DELOCHE or DELOCK, Peter. Angelica. Comm. F. July 7, 1778. Pard. for exchange Dec. 11, 1779. G; 5A p.38.

DEM, Benj. See DAME.

DEMISE, Stephen of Marblehead. Freedom's prize. Captured April 27, 1777. M. 7 p.251.

DEMOND, John of Marblehead. Freedom's prize. Captured April 27, 1777. M. 7 p.251.

DENACHOE, James. Seaman. Antibriton, a French ship. Imprisoned at Edinburgh Jan. 19, 1782. HO.

DENNIS, Capt. Captured July 30, 1778. F. 7 p.143. (Probably Capt. Wm. DAVIS).

DENNIS, James. Seaman. Newfoundland. Imprisoned at Edinburgh June 27, 1781. HO.

DENNIS, Jonas. Newfoundland. Imprisoned at Edinburgh June 27, 1781. HO.

DENNIS, Stephen. Freedom's prize. Captured April 29, 1777. M. 3 p.75. (Probably same as DANNES).

MARINERS OF THE AMERICAN REVOLUTION

DENNIS, Thomas. Seaman. Eagle. Comm. M. Feb. 7, 1782. HO.

DERRICK, William. Seaman. Fanny. Comm. M. Jan. 23, 1782. HO.

DEVERE, Laurence. Seaman. Antibriton, a French ship. Imprisoned at Edinburgh Jan. 19, 1782. HO.

DEVERIX or DEVEREUX, Thomas of Marblehead. Seaman or boy. Rambler. Comm. F. Dec. 30, 1779. SP; HO; 10 p. 340.

DEVIR, Thomas. M. Pard. for exchange Dec. 11, 1779. G.

DEVONEUX, Thomas. Seaman. Wexford. Comm. M. Jan. 24, 1782. HO.

DEXTER, Samuel. Seaman. Thomas, a merchant ship. In M. but not comm. Oct. 23, 1781. HO.

DIAMOND, John. Freedom's prize. Captured April 29, 1777. M. Pard. for exchange Dec. 20, 1778. G; 3 p. 75.

DICK, Alexander. Capt. of marines. Muscetor (Mosquito?). Comm. F. Aug. 8, 1777. Escaped. 5A p. 36.

DICK, James of Ireland. Lexington. Comm. M. Sept. 19, 1777. Pard. for exchange Dec. 11, 1779. G; 3 p. 137; 7 p. 253.

DICKSEY or DIXEY, John of Marblehead. Boy. General Glover. Comm. F. Oct. 18, 1779. Pard. for exchange Dec. 11, 1779. G; SP; HO; 10 v. 73 p. 340.

DIGGS, Thomas. M. 10 v. 73 p. 347.

DIMINICK, Charles. Seaman. Wexford. Sent from Kinsale to M. April 9, 1782. HO

DIMON, Stephen. Seaman. Wexford. Sent from Kinsale to M. April 9, 1782. HO.

DISMORE, George. Franklin. Prize master. Comm. F. Feb. 18, 1779. Pard. for exchange Dec. 11, 1779. G; 5A p. 38.

MARINERS OF THE AMERICAN REVOLUTION

DISMORE, Thomas. Captain. Hercules. Comm. M. Feb. 7, 1782. HO.

DIXEY, John. See DICKSEY.

DOAK, Benj. of Marblehead. Still in F. May 8, 1781. 10 v. 73 p. 340.

DOAK, Michel. See DOWKE.

DOAK or DOKE, Wm. of Massachusetts. Angelica. Comm. F. July 7, 1778. Pard. for R. N. Dec. 3, 1778. G; 5A p. 38.

DOAN, Nehemiah. Comm. F. Jan. 23, 1778. 5A p. 37. (See DOES).

DODD, Nathaniel of Marblehead. Monmouth. Comm. M. Dec. 16, 1779. Pard. for R. N. Nov. 22, 1780. G; 3 p. 138.

DOES, Nehemiah. F. Pard. for exchange May 31, 1779. (See DOAN).

DOGCNE, John. See DAGHAN.

DOLFY. Samuel. F. Pard. for exchange Dec. 11, 1779 and Nov. 9, 1781. G.

DOLIBER or DOLIABER, Joseph of Marblehead. Seaman. Rhodes. Comm. F. Nov. 18, 1780. SP; HO; 10 v. 73 p. 340.

DOLIBER, Thomas. Seaman. Susannah. Comm. F. June 27, 1781. SP; HO.

DOM, Benj. See DAM(E).

DON(N) or DUNN, John of Marblehead. Seaman. Rambler. Comm. F. Dec. 30, 1779. SP; HO; HL; 10 v. 73 p. 340.

DOOR, Bowers. See DORNE.

DORITY or DOUGHARTY, John of Ireland. Oliver Cromwell. Comm. M. Oct. 18, 1777. Pard. for exchange Dec. 11, 1779. G; 3 p. 75; 7 p. 258.

DORMAN, John. Comm. F. Aug. 8, 1777. Pard. for exchange May 31, 1779. G; 5A p. 36. (Probably the same who petitioned to be released from b. h. March 25, 1778. G.)

MARINERS OF THE AMERICAN REVOLUTION

DORNE or DOOR, Bowers of Dorchester. Jason. Comm. M. Dec. 16, 1779. Died. 3 p. 138.

DORSEY, Philip. M. Pard. for R.N. July 18, 1781. G.

DORSEY or DAWSEY, Wm. of Maryland? Tom Lee. Comm. M. May 5, 1781. Innoculated May 29, 1781. Died June 26, 1781. HL; 3 p. 141; 10 v. 73 pp. 339, 346; v. 74 p. 29.

DOSSETT, Peter. Seaman. Hercules. Sent from Kinsale to M. April 9, 1782. HO.

DOUGHARTY, John. See DORITY.

DOW, John of Chelsea. Seaman. Adventure. Comm. M. Jan. 21, 1782. HO; 3 p. 213.

DOWELL, Capt. Captured by Reasonable on passage from South Carolina to France, May 10, 1777. M. 4 p. 185.

DOWKE or DOAK, Michael. Seaman. Rhodes. Comm. F. Nov. 18, 1780. Still in May 8, 1781. SP; HO; 10 v. 73 p. 340.

DOWLING, Daniel. Seaman. Centurion. Comm. F. March 21, 1781. SP; HO.

DOWN, John. See DOWNS.

DOWN, Michel of Beverly. Mariner. Rambler. Comm. M. Feb. 16, 1780. SP; HO; HL; 3 p. 139.

DOWNER, Eliphilet. Passenger on the Hornet. Comm. F. Oct. 13, 1777. Escaped. 5A p. 37.

DOWNES, James. Seaman. Wexford. Sent from Kinsale to M. April 9, 1782. HO.

DOWNS or DOWN, John of Old York, New Hampshire. Dalton or Charming Polly. Comm. M. June, 1777. Pard. for exchange Dec. 20, 1778. Went with Paul Jones. G; 3 p. 75; 7 p. 246.

57

DOWN(E)S, John.   Boy or seaman.   Black Prince.   Comm. F. April 26, 1779.   Pard. for exchange Dec. 11, 1779.   G; SP; HO; 5 v. 32 p. 286; 5A p. 39.

DOWN(S), John of Marblehead.   Mariner.   Terrible.   Comm. M. Dec. 23 or 25, 1780.   SP; HO; 3 p. 139.

DOWNS, Nathaniel.   Seaman.   Protector.   Comm. M. Feb. 7, 1782. HO.

DOWN(S), William of Philadelphia.   Capt. marines.   Diana.   Comm. M. July 23, 1781.   SP; HO; 3 p. 210.

DOW(N)SELL, Florence.   Seaman.   General Glover.   Comm. F. Oct. 18, 1779.   Pard. for exchange Dec. 11, 1779.   G; SP.

DRAGON, John.   Pard. for R. N. Oct. 14, 1778.   G.

DRAWDY, Samuel.   See DRODY.

DREER, Geo. of Pennsylvania.   Franklin or Philadelphia.   Comm. M. November, 1781.   3 p. 212.   (See Dryer).

DREW, Shadrack or Shadrick of North Carolina?   Mariner.   Ledia of North Carolina or Robertson.   Comm. M. April 24, 1781.   Innoculated May 28, 1781.   SP; HO; HL; 3 p. 141; 10 v. 73 pp. 337, 346.

DREW, William.   Mariner.   Industry.   Comm. M. Nov. 18, 1780.   SP; HO; HL; 3 p. 139.

DRIVER, John.   Quartermaster.   Jason.   Captured but not comm. Oct. 15, 1781.   HO.

DRIVER, Thomas of Ireland.   Reprisal's prize.   Comm. M. June 29, 1777. 7 p. 251.

DRODY or DRAWDY, Samuel.   Seaman.   Adventure.   Comm. M. Jan. 21, 1782.   HO; 3 p. 213.

DRUMMOND, Richard or Mr.   Schooner Mariana.   Comm. M. July 28, 1779. Pard. for exchange Dec. 11, 1779.   In b. h. Feb. 1, 1781.   Out of b. h. Feb. 2.   In b. h. April 11, 1780.   Pard. for R. N. Aug. 9, 1781.   Entered Aug. 4, 1781.   G; HL; 3 p. 138; 8 p. 125; 10 v. 73 p. 319; v. 74 p. 38.

MARINERS OF THE AMERICAN REVOLUTION

DRURY, Jotham. Gunner. Comm. F. Feb. 18, 1779. Pard. for exchange Dec. 11, 1779 and Nov. 9, 1781. G; 5A p. 39.

DRYER, George. Mariner. Franklin. Comm. M. Dec. 6, 1781. SP; HO. (See DREER).

DUFF, Daniel. Soldier taken in South Carolina. Beaver. Comm. M. Sept. 1, 1781. SP; HO; 3 p. 211.

DUFF(Y), Edwd. from Derry or Londonderry. Black Princess. Comm. M. Oct. 20, 1781. Att. escape Nov. 14, 1781. Out of b. h. Nov. 26, Taken in irons to London Nov. 28, 1781 as they said he was not an American. 3 p. 212; 10 v. 74 pp. 52, 146, 156, 157.

DUHARD, Peter. F. Pard. for exchange Dec. 11, 1779. G.

DUM, B. of Kittery. M. 9 p. 80. Probably same as DAM(E).

DUNN, John. See DON(N).

DUNN, John. Franklin. Comm. F. Jan. 18, 1779. Pard. for exchange Dec. 11, 1779. G; 5A p. 39.

DUNN, John. F. Pard. for exchange Nov. 9, 1781. G.

DUNSTONE, William. Seaman. Patty. Comm. M. Feb. 27, 1782. HO.

DUOFRY, Ezekial. See DURFEY.

DURFEY or DURPHEY, Ezekial. Angelica. Lieut. Comm. F. July 7, 1778. Escaped. 5A p. 38.

DURFEY, DUOFRY or DURBY, Ezekial of Providence. Mariner. Tracey of Boston. Comm. M. Jan. 16, 1781. SP; HO; HL; 3 p. 140; 10 v. 73 p. 314.

DURPHEY, John. Seaman. Centurion. Comm. F. Nov. 18, 1780. SP; HO.

DERRILL or DURRALL, Francis. Angelica. Comm. F. July 7, 1778. Pard. for exchange May 31, 1779. G; 5A p. 38.

DWIER, Thos.   Reprisal's prize.   Comm. M. Aug. 1777.   Exchanged. 3 p. 75.

DWYER or DWIAH.   General Sullivan.   Comm. F. April 26, 1779.   Pard. for exchange Dec. 11, 1779 and Nov. 9, 1781.   G; 5A p. 39.

DWYER, Scipio.   Seaman.   Portsmouth.   Comm. F. July 20, 1781.   SP; HO.

E

EAGLES, Benj. See INGLES.

EARL, William. Boy. Sturdy Beggar. Comm. F. Jan. 23, 1778. Exchanged July 2, 1779. Joined Bonhomme Richard. 5 v. 32 p. 286; 5A p. 37.

EATON, Daniel. Seaman. Portsmouth. Comm. F. June 27, 1781. SP.

EATON, William. Seaman. Portsmouth. Comm. F. June 27, 1781. SP; HO.

EDGAR, Thomas. Seaman. Confederacy. Comm. M. Feb. 27, 1782. HO.

EDMUNDS, Joseph. Boy. Wexford. Captured but not comm. Oct. 2, 1781. HO.

EDMUNDS, Nehemiah. Seaman. Hercules. Sent from Kinsale to M. April 9, 1782. HO.

EDWARDS, Abraham. See HAYNES.

EDWARDS, Daniel. Seaman. Morning Star. Comm. F. Aug. 9, 1781. SP.

EDWARDS, Ebenezer or Eben. of Newburyport. Dalton or Charming Polly. Comm. M. June, 1777. Pard. for exchange Dec. 20, 1778. Joined Alliance. G. 4 p. 306; 7 p. 244.

EDWARDS, James. Seaman. Eagle. Comm. M. Feb. 6, 1782. HO.

EDWARDS, Willm. Mariner. Essex. Comm. M. July 20, 1781. SP; HO. (Probably same as next).

EDWARDS, Wm. of Portsmouth. Brig Phoenix of Boston. Comm. M. July 20, 1781; 3 p. 210; 10 v. 74 p. 34. (Probably same as last.)

EIDSON, John. Seaman. Pocahontas. Comm. F. Nov. 18, 1780. SP; HO.

ELDRIDGE, Elisha of Chatham. Adventurer of Boston. M. 3 p. 213.

ELEM, George. F. Pard. for exchange Dec. 11, 1779. G.

ELIOTT, Ephraim. Seaman. Hercules. Sent from Kinsale to M. April 9, 1782. HO.

ELIOTT, John. Seaman. Hercules. Sent from Kinsale to M. April 9, 1782. HO.

ELKINS, Jonathan. Soldier taken on shore. Comm. M. Feb. 6, 1782. HO.

ELKINS, Thomas. F. Pard. for exchange Dec. 11, 1779. G.

ELLIVAL, Soloman. F. Pard. for exchange Dec. 11, 1779. G.

ELLOT, Benjamin. Seaman. Bermuda. Comm. M. Jan. 22, 1782. HO.

ELLWELL, Elias. Prize master. Comm. F. April 19, 1779. Pardoned for exchange Dec. 11, 1779. G; 5A p. 39.

ELSEY, Robert. Seaman. Somerset. Comm. M. Feb. 27, 1782. HO.

ELSWORTH or ELLSWORTH, Theophilus. Mariner. Comet. Comm. M. Jan. 11, 1781. SP; HO; HL; 3 p. 140.

ELY, Paul. Seaman. Hercules. Captured but not comm. Oct. 15, 1781. HO.

EMERSON or AMMERSON, Thos. of Reading. Mariner. James and Rebecca or prize to the Franklin. Comm. M. Oct. 16, 1781. SP; HO; 3 p. 211; 10 v. 74 p. 145.

EMMERY, John. Commerce? Comm. F. Feb. 18, 1779. Escaped. 5A p. 39.

ENDICOTT, Samuel. Seaman. Harlequin or Lark. Comm. F. May 24, 1781. SP; HO.

ENDWORTH, James. Seaman. Wexford. Captured but not comm. Oct. 2, 1781. HO.

ENGLE, John. Seaman. Nancy or Larravie. Comm. F. March 21, 1781. SP. HO.

ENGLISH, Thomas. Hawke. Comm. M. Oct. 16, 1778. Died. 3 p. 137.

ENNIS, Jn. of Boston. Essex. Comm. M. July 20, 1781. 3 p. 210; 10 v. 74 p. 34.

ENSIGN, Hervey or Harvey of Connecticut. Mariner. General Nash. Comm. M. July 28, 1781. SP; HO; 3 p. 210; 10 v. 74 p. 36.

ENSWORTH, Ephraim. Seaman. Happy Return. Comm. F. June 27, 1781. SP.

ERSKINE, Collin. Seaman. Fair American. Comm. F. Nov. 18, 1780. SP; HO.

EULIN, Benj. See YOULING.

EVANS or EVENS, Jeremiah. Boy. Montgomery. Comm. F. Aug. 8, 1777. Pard. for exchange May 31, 1779. Exchanged July 2, 1779. Joined Bonhomme Richard. G; 5A p. 36.

EVANS or EVENS, Solomon of Virginia. Mariner. Gallsey, Gatray or Gascon. Comm. M. May 4, 1781. Innoculated May 29, 1781. SP; HO; 3 p. 141; 10 v. 73 p. 346.

EVANS, William, an Englishman. Seaman. Bienfaisant, a French ship. Imprisoned at Pembroke Jan. 17, 1782. HO.

EVEREND, Jos. Comm. F. July 15, 1777. 5A p. 36.

EVERT, Mr. F. 5, vol. 32 p. 71.

F

FAGAN, Daniel of Philadelphia. Lexington. Comm. M. Oct. 19, 1777. R.N. or escaped. 3 p.137; 7 p.253.

FAILEY, Thomas. M. Pard. for R.N. Aug. 9, 1781. (Perhaps the same as FARLIS). G.

FANNING, Cyrus. The Spy. Comm. F. Feb. 18, 1779. Pard. for exchange Dec. 11, 1779 and for R.N. Nov. 6, 1780. G; 5A p.39.

* FANNING, Nathaniel. Prize master. Angelica. Born 1755. M. Pard. for exchange May 31, 1779. Exchanged June 2, 1779. Joined Bonhomme Richard and later commanded Eclipse. G; 5A p.38; 5 v.32 p.286. See bibliography No. 6.

FARLIS or FERLIS, Thomas of Salem. Rambler. Comm. M. Feb. 16, 1780. Escaped and re-captured and in b.h. July 6, 1781. Out of b.h. July 29. Pard. for R.N. Aug. 4, 1781. G; HL; 3 p.138; 10 v.74 p.31, 37, 38.

FARMER, William of Boston. Mariner. Tracey. Comm. M. May 1 or 5, 1781. SP; HO; HL; 3 p.209; 10 v.73 p.339.

FARNUM, John. Carpenter's mate. Hercules. Captured but not comm. Oct. 15, 1781. HO.

FAROW, Isaac. See PHARO.

FORO(W), Jacob. Mariner. Lydia or Robertson. Comm. M. April 24, 1781. Innoculated May 28, 1781. SP; HO; 10 v.73 pp. 337, 346.

FAROW, John. Seaman. Terrible. Comm. F. May 24, 1781. SP; HO; 3 p.141.

FARRIS, Thomas. F. Pard. for R.N. March 17, 1781. G.

FAZIR, Captain. M. Arrived safely at Ostend June 1781. 10 v.74 p.28.

FEAFFERY, John of Saredon. Dalton? Exchanged. 3 p.75.

FEATHERGAIL, Richard. See FOTHERGILL.

FEGAN, Daniel. M. Pard. for R. N. Jan. 4, 1779. G.

FELL, Joseph. M. Pard. for R. N. May 11, 1781. G.

FELT, Joseph. Mariner. William. Comm. M. Oct. 17, 1780. Innoculated May 28, 1781. SP; HO; HL; 10 v. 73 p. 346.

FELTON, John of Marblehead. Seaman. General Glover. Comm. F. Oct. 18, 1779. Pard. for exchange Dec. 11, 1779. SP; HO; 10 v. 73 p. 340.

FENTON, John of New York. Tracey of Boston. Comm. M. Jan. 6, 1781. Pard. for R. N. March 20, 1781. Entered March 27. G; 3 p. 140; 10 v. 73 pp. 312, 330.

FERLIS, Thomas. See FARLIS.

FERNALD, FIRNALD or FURNELL, Mark of Kittery. Mariner, captian or lieut. Aurora. Comm. M. July 25 or 27, 1780. SP; HO; HL; 3 p. 139; 9 pp. 80, 99.

FERNEL, George. See FURNALL.

FERRY, Jean Baptiste or Jo'n Baptist. Prize master or mate. Comm. F. July 15, 1777. Pard. for exchange May 31, 1779. G; 5A p. 36.

FERRY, John. Seaman. Hercules. Sent from Kinsale to M. April 9, 1782. HO.

FEW, Willm. M. Innoculated May 28, 1781. HL; 10 v. 73 p. 346.

FIELD, Job. Mariner. Essex. Comm. M. July 21, 1781. Pard. for exchange Feb. 6, 1782. G; SP; 3 p. 210; 10 v. 74 p. 34.

FIELD, Nichos. Black Prince or Princess. Comm. M. Oct. 20, 1781. Att. escape Nov. 18, 1781. Out of b. h. Nov. 26. Taken to London in irons Nov. 28, 1781 as they said be was not an American. 3 p. 212; 10 v. 74 pp. 146, 153, 154, 156, 157.

FIELDING, David, an Englishman. Seaman. Bienfaisant, a French ship. Imprisoned at Pembroke Jan. 17, 1782. HO.

FIELDING, John. F. Pard. for R. N. Dec. 7, 1780. G.

FINK, Daniel. Boy. Commerce. Comm. F. Feb. 18, 1779. Pard. for exchange Dec. 11, 1779. G; SP; HO; 5A p. 39.

FINNIX, William. Seaman. Portsmouth. Comm. F. June 27, 1781. SP; HO.

FIRNALD, Mark. See FERNALD.

FISH, William. Seaman. Fair American. Comm. F. Nov. 18, 1780. SP; HO.

FISH, William. F. Pard. for R. N. May 28, 1781. G.

FISHER, John. Fancy. Comm. M. August, 1777. Escaped. 3 p. 136.

FISHER, Joseph of Ipswich. Doctor. Fancy. Comm. M. Aug. 7, 1777. Escaped. 7 p. 250.

FISHER, Richard. Seaman. Wexford. Sent from Kinsale to M. April 9, 1782. HO.

FISHOW, John. See TISHAW.

FITTON, Abraham. Mate. Jason. Captured but not comm. Oct. 15, 1781. HO.

FITTS, Samuel. Seaman. Neptune. Comm. F. June 27, 1781. SP; HO.

FLETCHER, James of Philadelphia. Revenge or Ranger. Comm. M. Jan. 1781. Died. 3 p. 140; 10 v. 73 p. 312.

FLETCHER, John. M. Pard. for R. N. April 28, 1781. G.

FLETCHER, Samuel of Kittery. Dalton or Charming Polly. Comm. M. June, 1777. Pard. for exchange Dec. 20, 1778. Went with Paul Jones. G; 3 p. 75; 7 p. 245.

FLING, Philip. See KING.

FLINT, David of Marblehead. Boy. General Glover. Comm. F. Oct. 18, 1779. Pard. for exchange Dec. 11, 1779. G; SP; HO; 10 v. 73 p. 340.

FLORANCE, John of Marblehead. Boy. Comm. F. April 19, 1779. Still there May 8, 1781. Pard. for exchange Dec. 11, 1779.and Nov. 9, 1781. G; 5A p. 39; 10 v. 73 p. 340.

FLYN, John. Steward or seaman. Retaliation. Comm. F. Oct. 31, 1780. SP; HO.

FOARSIDE, Hugh. See FORSEYTH.

FOGG, David. Prize master. Comm. F. Oct. 13, 1777. Escaped. 5A p. 37.

FOGO or FOGGO, Wm. B(rown) of Boston. Saratoga. M. Escaped July 6, 1781. HL; 3 p. 140; 10 v. 74 p. 31.

FOLGER or FORGER, Cromwell or Crumwell of Nantucket. Mariner. Lydia of North Carolina or Robertson. Comm. M. April 24, 1781. In hospital May 10, 1781. SP; HO; HL; 3 p. 141; 10 v. 73 pp. 337, 341.

FOLLING, John. Seaman. Neptune. Comm. F. Dec. 30, 1779. SP; HO.

FOOT, Caleb. Prize master. Black Snake. Comm. F. Feb. 18, 1779. Pard. for exchange Dec. 11, 1779 but did not go then as a prisoner was sent over from France Aug. 19, 1780 to procure his release in exchange. G; 5A p. 39.

FOOT, Samuel of Salem. Warren. Comm. M. June, 1778. 3 p. 137; 7 p. 254.

FORD, Robert of Ireland. Lexington. Comm. M. Sept. 9, 1777. Pard. for R. N. July 13, 1779. Entered or escaped. G; 3 p. 137; 7 p. 252.

FORD, Will. of Casco Bay or Virginia. Dalton. In hospital April, 1777. Comm. M. June, 1777. Att. escape, put in b.h. Aug. 27, 1777. Put in b.h. Sept. 26, 1777. Pard. for R. N. Oct. 14, 1778. Entered or escaped. G; 3 p. 74; 4 pp. 184 308, 395, 396; 7 p. 246.

FORDHAM, George. Revenge of Philadelphia. Comm. M. Jan. 11, 1781. Petitioned to join R. N. and pardoned March, 1781. Entered May 14, 1781. G; 3 p. 140; 10 v. 73 pp. 313, 330, 342.

FOREMAN, Jacob. F. Pard. for exchange Dec. 11, 1779. G.

FORGER, Crumwell. See FOLGER.

FORNALD, Edmund. See FURNELL.

FORSEYTH, FOARSIDE or FORSIDE, Hugh. Mariner. L'Uzerne of Philadelphia. Comm. M. July 6, 1781. SP; HO; 3 p. 209; 10 v. 74 p. 31.

FORSTER, John. F. Pard. for exchange Nov. 9, 1781. (Probably same man as John FOSTER, three below). G.

FOSTER, John of Kittery, N. H. Dalton or Charming Polly. Comm. M. June, 1777. Died Feb. 1, 1779. 3 p. 75; 7 pp. 220, 245.

FOSTER, John. M. Pard. for exchange Dec. 20, 1778. G.

FOSTER, John. Prize master. Comm. F. Oct. 20, 1778. Pard. for exchange Dec. 11, 1779. G; 5A p. 38. (probably same as FORSTER).

FOSTER, John. Seaman. Harlequin or Lark. Comm. F. May 24, 1781. SP; HO.

FOSTER, Zacharias. Seaman. Diana. Comm. M. Jan. 23, 1782. HO.

FOSTICK, David. F. Pard. for exchange Dec. 11, 1779. G.

FOTHERGILL, Richd. of Harwich, Cape Cod. Mariner. Essex or Phoenix. of Boston. Comm. M. July 20, 1781. SP; HO; 3 p. 210; 10 v. 74 p. 34.

FOWER, Joseph. Dalton. Captured Dec. 26, 1776. M. Exchanged. 3 p. 74.

FOWLER, John. Fancy. Comm. M. Aug. 7, 1777. Died May 6, 1778. 3 p. 136; 7 pp. 119, 250.

FOWLER, Wm. of Casco Bay. Revenge. Comm. M. May, 1778. Pard. for exchange Dec. 11, 1779. G. 3 p. 139; 7 p. 257.

MARINERS OF THE AMERICAN REVOLUTION

FOX, James of Marblehead. Fancy. Comm. M. Aug. 7, 1777. 7 p. 249.

FOY, John of Salem or Boston. Hawk's prize. Comm. M. Oct. 1778. Died. 3 p. 137; 7 p. 252. (Perhaps the same as TOYE).

FRANCIS, Edward. Seaman. Bienfaisant, a French ship Imprisoned at Pembroke Jan. 17, 1782. HO.

FRANCIS, James. Seaman. Betsey, a merchant ship. Captured but not comm. Oct. 23, 1781. HO.

FRAZER, Alexander of New York. Charming Sally. Captured Jan, 16, 1777. M. Still there Feb. 7, 1779. Pard. for R. N. Sept. 25, 1778. G; 7 p. 248.

FRAZIER, Solomon. Captain? Brig Maryland. Comm. M. Oct. 14, 1780. Att. escape April 21, 1781. Escaped June 4, 1781. 3 p. 139; 10 v. 73 pp. 335, 336; v. 74 p. 22.

FREDERICK, Joseph of Martha's Vineyard. Charming Sally or Polly. Captured Jan. 16, 1777. M. Still there Feb. 7, 1779. Exchanged. 3 p. 75; 7 p. 248.

FREEMAN, Barney or Burney. Seaman. Adventure. Comm. M. Jan 21, 1782. HO; 3 p. 213.

FREETO, John. Black Snake. Comm. F. Feb. 18, 1779. 5A p. 39. (Probably same as FRETO).

FREFICE, Michael. Fancy. Comm. M. August, 1777. Exchanged. 3 p. 136. (probably meant for TRIFTY, q. v.).

FRENCH, Richard. Seaman. Two Brothers. Comm. M. Jan. 23, 1782. HO.

FRESON, Richard of Marblehead. Still in F. May 8, 1781. 10 v. 73 p. 340.

FRET(T)O or FRETON, John of Marblehead. Still in F. May 8, 1781. Pard. for exchange Dec. 11, 1779 and Nov. 9, 1781. G; 10 v. 73 p. 340. (Probably same as FREETO).

FRITZE, Henry. Capt. of marines. Rising States. Comm. F. June 14, 1777. Escaped June 17, 1777. 5 v. 30 p. 344 and note; 5A p. 36.

FRY, Edward. Seaman. Pocahontas. Comm. F. Nov. 18, 1780. SP; HO.

FRY, Thomas. F. Pard. for R. N. Jan. 12. 1781. G.

FULLER, James. Seaman. Happy Return. Comm. F. June 27, 1781. SP.

FULLERTON or FULLINGTON, Andrew of North Carolina. Mariner. John. Comm. M. May 4, 1781. Innoculated May 29, 1781. SP; HO; 3 p. 141; 10 v. 73 p. 346.

FULTON, Robert. Seaman. Tom Lee. Comm. F. Aug. 9, 1781. SP; HO.

FUNDAY, John. See TUNDY.

FURNALL or FERNEL, George of Kittery. Dalton or Charming Polly. Captured May, 1777. In hospital April, 1777 and August 1, 1777. Pard. for exchange Dec. 11, 1779. Escaped Nov. 21, 1781. G; 3 p. 75; 4 p. 184, 306; 7 p. 245; 10 v. 74 p. 155.

FURNELL or FORNALD, Edmnd or Edwd. of Kittery. Venus. Comm. M. Nov. 21, 1781. SP; HO; 3 p. 212; 9 p. 80; 10 v. 74 p. 155.

FURNELL, Mark. See FERNALD,

FUZE or FULZ, William. Mariner. Johns. Comm. M. May 4, 1781. SP; HO; 3 p. 141.

G

GABRIEL, Edward. Seaman. Neptune. Comm. F. June 27, 1781. SP.

GAGE, Elias, Enas, Lenus or Zenus. Mariner. Resolution of Boston. Comm. M. Jan. 22, 1781. In hospital May 10, 1781. SP; HO; HL; 3 p. 140; 10 v. 73 p. 316, 341.

GAGE, Lot(t). Mariner. Royal Louis or Effingham. Comm. M. May 10, 1779. Pard. for exchange Dec. 11, 1779. G; SP; HO; HL; 3 p. 138.

GAGE, Thomas. Seaman. Marquis de la Fayette. Comm. M. Jan. 22, 1782. HO.

GALE, Samuel. Mariner. Rambler. Comm. M. Feb. 16, 1780. SP; HO; HL; 3 p. 138.

GALLAGHAN, Fran. Mariner. Franklyn. Comm. M. Dec. 6, 1781. SP; HO. (Possibly same as next).

GALLIGHER, Patrick. Franklin of Philadelphia. Comm. M. Nov. 1781. 3 p. 212. (Possibly same as previous).

GALLAWAY, John of Bermuda. Schooner Greyhound of Philadelphia. Comm. M. Jan. 16, 1781. R. N. March 7, 1781. 10 v. 73 pp. 314, 324.

GANDON, John of Ireland. Lexington. M. Escaped. 3 p. 74.

GARBODINE or GARBODUINE, Batta. Revenge. Comm. F. Aug. 11, 1777. Pard. for exchange May 31, 1779. G; 5A p. 37.

GARDNER, Andrew of Boston. Seaman. Twin Sisters. Comm. M. Jan. 9 1782. HO; 3 p. 212.

GARDINER, Benjamin. Comm. F. Jan. 23, 1778. Pard. for exchange May 31, 1779. G; 5A p. 37.

GARD(I)NER, Benj. of Salem. Mariner. Harlequin. Comm. M. July 6, 1781. SP; HO; 3 p. 209; 10 v. 74 p. 31.

MARINERS OF THE AMERICAN REVOLUTION

GARD(I)NER, Henry. Gunner and Prize master. Angelica. Comm. F. July 7, 1778. Pard. for exchange May 31, 1779. Exchanged July 2, 1779. Joined Bonhomme Richard. G; 5 v. 32 p. 286; 5A p. 38.

GARD(I)NER, Josh. or Joseph of Boston. Mariner. Essex. Comm. M. Aug. 25, 1781. SP; HO; 3 p. 211; 10 v. 74 p. 44.

GARD(I)NER, Josh. Mariner. Little Pegey or Porgy. Comm. M. Jan. 3, 1782. SP; HO.

GARDNER, Nicholas of Marblehead. Fancy. Comm. M. Aug. 7, 1777. 7 p. 249.

GARD(I)NER, Nich. Mariner. Black Prince or Princess, a French prize. Comm. M. Oct. 20, 1781. SP; HO.

GAREY, John. Grand Turk. Comm. M. Jan. 1781. 3 p. 213.

GARISH, Joseph. See GERRISH.

GARRAWAY, John. M. Pard. for R. N. Feb. 20, 1781. G.

GARRIN, John. M. HL.

GARVIN, Rich. See CORVIN.

GAUSE, Richard. See GOSS.

GAVIN, John. Mariner. Nancy or prize to the Saratoga. Comm. M. Jan. 9, 1781. SP; HO; 3 p. 140; 10 v. 73 p. 313.

GAWIN, John. See GOWAN.

GAY, Henry of North Carolina. Brig Salley of North Carolina. Comm. M. May 11, 1781. Innoculated May 28, 1781. 10 v. 73 pp. 340, 346.

GAY, Job. Seaman. Terrible or Lion. Comm. F. Aug. 9, 1781. SP; HO.

GAY, John. Mariner. Eliza, prize to the Grand Turk. Comm. M. Jan. 3, 1782. SP; HO.

GEGHAGEN, Morris.   Master's mate.   Rising States.   Comm. F. June 14, 1777.   Escaped.   5A p. 36.

GENTLE, James.   Montgomery.   Comm. F. Aug. 8, 1777.   Escaped. 5A p. 36.

GEORGE, Isaac of Millbury or Latney.   Charming Sally or Polly.   Captured Jan. 16, 1777.   M.   Still there Feb. 7, 1779.   Pard. for exchange Dec. 20, 1778.   G; 3 p. 75; 7 p. 247.

GEORGE, John of Newburyport.   Dalton.   Comm. M.   June, 1777.   Pard. for exchange Dec. 20, 1778.   G; 3 p. 74; 7 p. 244;   (See next).

GEORGE, Joseph.   Dalton.   Captured Dec. 24, 1776.   M.   Exchanged. 3 p. 74.   (Probably intended for above).

GEORGE, Josiah of Newburyport.   Dalton.   Comm. M. June, 1777.   Escaped.   7 p. 244.

GEORGE, Wm.   Sturdy Beggar.   Comm. F. Jan. 23, 1778.   Escaped. 5A p. 37.

GEORGE, Mr.   M.   Escaped from b.h. July 12, 1777.   Taken out of b.h. Aug. 6, 1777.   4 pp. 305, 306, 307, 308.

GERRISH or GARISH, Joseph.   Thom.   Comm. M. Sept. 19, 1780.   Pard. for exchange Nov. 9, 1781.   G; HL; 3 p. 139.

GERRISH, Samuel.   Captain.   Aurora.   Comm. M. July 25, 1780.   Escaped Dec. 28, 1780.   3 p. 139; 8 p. 127.

GETTLE or GITTLE, George of Philadelphia.   Oliver Cromwell.   Comm. F. Oct. 13, 1777.   Escaped and re-captured about Nov. or Dec. 1778.   Pard. for exchange Dec. 11, 1779.   G; 5A p. 37.

GEWYER, John.   Seaman.   Hercules.   Sent from Kinsale to M. April 9, 1782.   HO.

GIBBONS, Edwd. of New York.   Mariner.   Franklin.   Comm. M. Dec. 6, 1781.   SP; HO; 3 p. 212.

GIBBS, Edward.   Mariner.   Neptune, prize to the Pilgrim.   Comm. M. July 9, 1781.   SP; HO.

GIDDINGS, Zebulon. Seaman. Susannah. Comm. F. June 27, 1781. Escaped Jan. 1782. SP. (Note at end of S.P. re escape.)

GIDDINGS, Zacharias. Seaman. Harlequin. Comm. F. May 24, 1781. SP; HO.

GIDDSON. Captain. Civil Usage. 7 p. 53.

GIDENSWORTH, James. Oliver Cromwell. Comm. F. Oct. 13, 1777. Escaped. 5A p. 37.

GIFFORD, Nicholas, Sr. of Marblehead. Seaman. General Glover. Comm. F. Oct. 18, 1779. Still there May 8, 1781. Pard. for exchange Dec. 11, 1779. SP; HO; 10 v. 73 p. 340; G.

GIFFORD, Nicholas, the younger. Boy. General Glover. Comm. F. Oct. 18, 1779. Pard. for exchange Dec. 11, 1779. Still there May 8, 1781. SP; HO; 10 v. 73 p. 340; G.

GILBERT, Caleb of Rhode Island. Hunter. Comm. M. July 25, 1781. 3 p. 210.

GILBERT, Samuel. Seaman. Bermuda. Comm. M. Jan 22, 1782. HO.

GILL, William. Seaman. Friends Adventure. Comm. F. Dec. 1780. SP; HO.

GINNELL, Wm. Lieut. Comm. F. Oct. 20, 1778. 5A p. 38.

GIRDLER or GURLER, Lewis of Marblehead. Mariner. Matthew, prize to the Disdain. Comm. M. Dec. 7, 1781. SP; HO; 3 p. 212.

GIRDLER, GIRLER or GURLER, Nicholas of Marblehead. Fancy. Comm. M. Aug. 1777. Pard. for exchange Dec. 11, 1779. Re-taken in Black Prince Oct. 20, 1781. G; 3 pp. 136, 212; 10 v. 73 p. 329; v. 74 p. 146.

GIRLER, Benjamin. Seaman. Nancy. Comm. F. Nov. 18, 1780. SP; HO.

GITTLE, George. See GETTLE.

MARINERS OF THE AMERICAN REVOLUTION

GIVET (GWET?), Stephen. Seaman. Jason. Captured but not comm. Oct. 15, 1781. HO.

GLADDING or GLADING, Carey or Carry. Commerce. Comm. F. Feb. 18, 1779. Pard. for exchange Dec. 11, 1779. Pard. for R.N. Nov. 6, 1780. G; 5A p. 39.

GLINN or GLYNN, James. Mariner. Viper. Comm. M. Dec. 7, 1781. SP; HO; 3 p. 212.

GLINN, William. Seaman. Jason. In M. but not comm. Oct. 15, 1781. HO.

GLOVER, John. F. Pard. for exchange Dec. 11, 1779. Still there May 8, 1781. G; 10 v. 73 p. 340. (See next).

GLOVER, Jonathan. F. Pard. for exchange Oct. 16, 1781. (Probably meant for John).

GLOVER, Lewis. Mariner. Essex. Comm. M. July 21 or 27, 1781. SP; HO; 3 p. 210.

GLYNN, James. See GLINN.

GODFREY. M. 10 v. 74 p. 47. (Probably Andrew).

GODFREY, Andrew of Taunton. Comm. Pembroke 1778 and M. Oct. 14, 1780. Pard. for exchange Nov. 9, 1781. HL; 3 p. 139.

GODFREY, Charles. F. Pard. for R.N. Oct. 6, 1781. G.

GODFREY, John. F. Pard. for R.N. Jan. 25, 1779. G.

GODWIN, Nath'l. The McClery. Comm. F. Aug. 28, 1778. 5A p. 38.

GOLD, William. HL. Probably same as GOULD.

GOLDING, Benjamin. Seaman. Mercury. Comm. F. March 21, 1781. HO.

GOLDSMITH, Benjamin. Seaman. Diana. Comm. M. Jan. 23, 1782. HO.

GOODHUE, Daniel of Ipswich. Fancy. Comm. M. Aug. 7, 1777. Pard. for exchange Dec. 11, 1779. G; 3 p. 136; 7 p. 250.

GOODWIN or GOODING, Aaron of Berwick or Kittery. Dalton or Charming Polly. Comm. M. June, 1777. Pard. for exchange Dec. 26, 1778. Re-captured on Marquis de Morbec. Comm. M. Oct. 2, 1781. G; SP; HO; 3 pp. 75, 211; 7 p. 245; 9 p. 80, 99; 10 v. 74 p. 142.

GOODWIN, Nehemiah. Seaman. Portsmouth. Comm. F. July 20, 1781. SP; HO.

GORDAN or GORDON, John of Ireland. Lexington's prize. Comm. M. June, 1777. Pard. for R. N. Jan. 4, 1779. G; 7 p. 249.

GORDON, Samuel. M. Died Aug. 18, 1781. 10 v. 74 p. 42.

GOREHAM, Benjamin. Seaman. Happy Return. Comm. F. June 27, 1781. SP; HO.

GOREHAM or GORHAM, Jacque. Angelica. Comm. F. July 7, 1778. Pard. for exchange Dec. 11, 1779. G; 5A p. 38.

GOSS, Joshua of Boston or Marblehead. Prize master. Comm. F. Aug. 28, 1778. Pard. for exchange Dec. 11, 1779. Still there May 8, 1781. G; SP; 5A p. 38; 10 v. 73 p. 340.

GOSS or GAUSE, Richard of Marblehead. Fancy. Comm. M. Aug. 7, 1777. In b. h. Jan. 7, 1780. Pard. for exchange Dec. 11, 1779. G; 3 p. 136; 7 p. 249; 8 p. 121.

GOSS, Samuel. M. In b. h. Jan. 7, 1780. 8 p. 121.

GOULD, Jacob. Seaman. Newfoundland. Imprisoned at Edinburgh June 27, 1781. HO.

GOULD, William. Mariner. Harlequin. Comm. M. Dec. 23 or 24, 1780. Innoculated May 28, 1781. Pard. for R. N. May 11, 1781. G; SP; HO; 3 p. 139; 10 v. 73 p. 346. (See GOULD).

GOVER, Simon. Cook. Hercules. Captured but not comm. Oct. 15, 1781. HO.

MARINERS OF THE AMERICAN REVOLUTION

GOWAN or GOWIN, Benja. of Boston.   Essex.   Comm. M. July 21, 1781. Pard. for R.N. Aug. 9, 1781.   G; 3 p. 210; 10 v. 74 p. 34.

GOWAN or GAWIN, John of Boston.   Mariner.   Protector.   Comm. M. Aug. 23, 1781.   SP; HO; 3 p. 211; 10 v. 74 p. 43.

GRACE, Andrew.   See GROSS.

GRAMNAER or GRAMMER, Joseph.   Montgomery.   Comm. F. Aug. 8, 1777.   Pard. for exchange May 31, 1779.   G; 5A p. 36.

GRAN, John.   See GREEN.

GRANBERRY, Wm.   Comm. F. Oct. 20, 1778.   Escaped.   5A p. 38.

GRANNIS, Jared or Jeard.   Seaman.   General Sullivan or Robert.   Comm. F. July 8, 1779.   Pard. for exchange Dec. 11, 1779.   G; SP; HO.

GRANT, Benjamin of Ipswich.   Mariner.   James and Rebecca, prize to the Franklin.   Comm. M. Oct. 2, 1781.   SP; HO; 3 p. 211; 10 v. 74 p. 142.

GRANT, Charles.   Phoenix.   Comm. M. May 10, 1779.   Escaped. 3 p. 138.

GRANT, William.   Seaman.   Fair American.   Comm. F. Nov. 30, 1780. SP.

GRAVES, Wm.   Rising States.   Comm. F. June 14, 1777.   Pard. for exchange May 31, 1779.   G; 5A p. 36.

GRAYBACK or GRAYSBOOK, Thoms. of North Carolina.   General Nash. Comm. M. July 28, 1781.   3 p. 210; 10 v. 74 p. 36.

GREEN, John.   Mariner.   Rambler.   Comm. M. Feb. 16, 1780.   SP; HO; HL; 3 p. 138.

GREEN or GRAN, John.   Captain.   Lion.   Comm. M. Aug. 31, 1781. SP; HO; 3 p. 211; 10 v. 74 pp. 30, 46, 148, 150, 151.

GREEN, Nehemiah.   Seaman.   Retaliation.   Comm. F. Oct. 31, 1780. SP; HO.

GREEN, Wm. Oliver Cromwell. Comm. F. Oct. 13, 1777. 5A p. 37.

GREEN, Wm. Captain. Comm. F. Feb. 18, 1779. 5A p. 39.

GREEN, Wm. of Providence. Tracey of Boston. Comm. M. Jan. 6, 1781. Escaped Nov. 14, 1781. HL; 3 p. 140; 10 v. 73 p. 312; v. 74 pp. 52, 153.

GREEN, Wm. F. Pard. for exchange May 31, 1779. G.

GREEN, Wm. F. Pard. for exchange Dec. 11, 1779. G.

GREENLEAF, Thomas. Lieut of marines. Angelica of Boston. Comm. F. July 7, 1778. Escaped. 5 v. 32 pp. 28, 71; 5A p. 38.

GREENOUGH, Peletiah. Seaman. Portsmouth. Comm. F. June 27, 1781. SP.

GREENOUGH, William. Seaman. Portsmouth. Comm. F. June 27, 1781. SP; HO.

GREGORY, William. F. Pard. for R. N. Oct. 23, 1780. G.

GREY, David of Rhode Island. Lieut. The Swallow. Comm. F. Jan. 23, 1778. Escaped. 5A p. 37.

GREY, Scipio. of Boston. General Sullivan's prize. Comm. M. July 3, 1779. Pard. for exchange Dec. 11, 1779. G; 3 p. 138. (See also Joseph BURNEY).

GREYSTOCK, Thos. Mariner. General Nash. Comm. M. July 28, 1781. SP; HO.

GRICE, Matthew. Cooper. Rising States. Comm. F. June 14, 1777. Escaped. 5A p. 36.

GRIFFIN, Joseph. Seaman. Terrible. Comm. F. May 24, 1781. SP; HO.

GRIFFIN(G), Kutland of Gilford. Charming Sally. Captured Jan. 16, 1777. M. Pard. for exchange Dec. 30, 1778. G; 3 p. 75; 7 p. 247.

MARINERS OF THE AMERICAN REVOLUTION

GRIFFIN, Lambeth. See MUFFIN.

GRIFFIN, Rossiter or Rester of New Haven. Charming Sally or Polly. Captured Jan. 16, 1777. M. Pard. for exchange Dec. 20, 1778. G; 3 p. 75; 7 p. 247.

GRIST, George. Seaman. Hetty or Hettry. Comm. F. May 24, 1781. SP.

GROSS, GROIS or GRACE, Andrew of Philadelphia. Lexington. Comm. M. Sept. 19, 1777. Pard. for R. N. Sept. 25, 1778. Entered or escaped. G; 3 p. 137; 7 p. 253.

GROSS, Benjamin. Seaman. Zephyr. Comm. F. June 27, 1781. SP; HO.

GROVE, Ebenezer, Sr. F. Pard. for exchange Dec. 11, 1779. G.

GROVE, Ebenezer, Jnr. F. Pard. for exchange Dec. 11, 1779. G.

GROW, William. Seaman. Hercules. Sent from Kinsale to M. April 9, 1782. HO.

GRUSH, Thomas. Seaman. Jason. Captured but not comm. Oct. 15, 1781. HO.

GUGLEY, Aaron. Lexington. Comm. M. Sept. 19, 1777. Escaped. 3 p. 137.

GUINES, Camp. Seaman. Newfoundland. Imprisoned at Edinburgh June 27, 1781. HO.

GUINNER, Abraham. Mariner. Rambler. Comm. M. Feb. 16, 1780. SP; HO.

GULLIVER, Rufus of Milton. Mariner. Essex. Comm. M. Sept. 1, 1781. SP; HO; 3 p. 211.

GUNNISON, Elisha. F. Pard. for R. N. Dec. 3, 1778. Entered Dec. 19, 1778. G; 5 v. 32 pp. 282-3.

GUNNISON, John of Kittery, N. H. Dalton. Comm. M. June, 1777. Pard. for exchange Dec. 20, 1778. Went with Paul Jones. G; 7 p. 245.

GUPTON or GUPTELL, Moses. General Sullivan. F   Pard. for exchange Dec. 11, 1779 and Nov. 9, 1781. G; 5A p. 39.

GURLER, Lewis. See GIRDLER.

GURLER, Nicholas. See GIRDLER.

GUTRICK, John. Comm. F. Aug. 9, 1777. Escaped. 5A p. 37.

GUY or GWY, Henry. Mariner. Salley. Comm. M. May 11, 1781. SP; HO; HL; 3 p. 309.

H

HACKET(T) or HACKER, Jno. or Mr. of Philadelphia. Saratoga's prize. Comm. M. Jan. 9, 1781. Att. escapes on April 13, 21, May 4, 23, 31. Escaped June 4, 1781. Arrived safe at Ostend in June. 3 p. 140; 10 v. 73 pp. 313, 334, 335, 342, 344, 345, 346; v. 74 pp. 22, 28.

HACKFORD, William. Dalton. Captured Dec. 26, 1776. M. Escaped. 3 p. 74.

HADDOCK, Roger of Boston. Adventure of Boston. Comm. M. March 31, 1781. Pard. for R. N. Sept. 10, 1781. G; HL; 3 p. 140; 10 v. 73 p. 331.

HAGGERMAN, Robert. Seaman. Lark. Comm. F. May 24, 1781. SP; HO.

HALA, Nathaniel. See HAYLEY.

HALE, Enoch. 11, pp. 252-3.

HALE, Jacob of Middleton. Wild Cat. Comm. M. Dec. 16, 1779. R. N. 3 p. 138.

HALEY, Thomas of England. Lexington's prize. Comm. M. June, 1777. Exchanged. 3 p. 74; 7 p. 249.

HALEY, Thos. General Sullivan. Comm. F. April 26, 1779. Died. 5A p. 39.

HALL, David. Gunner. Yankee of Boston. Comm. F. June 26, 1777. Pard. for exchange May 31, 1779. G; 5 v. 32 p. 168; 5A p. 36.

HALL, John. F. Pard. for R. N. Nov. 30, 1779.

HALL, John. Seaman. Purgey. Comm. M. Jan. 25, 1782. HO.

HALL, Joseph. Lexington. Comm. M. Sept. 19, 1777. Escaped. 3 p. 137.

MARINERS OF THE AMERICAN REVOLUTION

HALL, Prince of Dartmouth. Charming Sally. Captured Jan. 16, 1777 M. Still there Feb. 7, 1779. Pard. for R.N. Jan. 4, 1779. Entered or escaped. G; 3 p. 75; 7 p. 247.

HALL, William of New Jersey. Oliver Cromwell. Comm. M. Oct. 18, 1777. Pard. for R.N. Sept. 25, 1778. G; 7 p. 255.

HALL, Wm. of Philadelphia. Warren. Comm. M. June 4, 1778. Escaped. 3 p. 137.

HALL, William. Seaman. Fort Stanwin. Comm. F. April 7, 1780. SP; HO.

HALLADAY, Thos. Mariner. Lion. Comm. M. Dec. 7, 1781. SP; HO.

HALLEY, John. Seaman. Confederacy. Comm. M. Feb. 27, 1782. HO.

HAMBLETON or HAMILTON, Robt. of Connecticut. Betsey. Comm. M. July 23, 1781. Pard. for R.N. Aug. 18 or Aug. 30, 1781. G; 3 p. 210; 10 v. 74 pp. 35, 42.

HAMBLETON, Wm. Lieut. marines. The Alfred. Comm. F. July 18, 1778. 5A p. 38.

HAMBLIN, Jabes. Seaman. Centurion. Comm. F. Nov. 18, 1780. SP; HO.

HAMMET, Thos. See HEMMITT.

HAMMON, John. Prize master. Warren's prize. Captured Nov. 19, 1776. Comm. F. June, 26, 1777. Escaped. 5A p. 36.

HAMMOND, Benj. of Danvers. Mariner. Ship Hannable of Newbury. Comm. M. Jan. 11 or 18, 1781. SP; HO; HL; 3 p. 140; 10 v. 73 p. 313.

HAMMOND, Benjamin. Seaman. Newfoundland. Imprisoned at Edinburgh June 27, 1781. HO.

HAMMOND, Richard. Seaman. Fame. Comm. F. March 5, 1781. SP; HO.

HAMSON, John of Marblehead. Seaman. Bunker's Hill. Comm. F. April 7, 1780. SP; HO; 10 v. 73 p. 340.

HANDLEY, Benjamin. F. Pard. for R. N. Jan. 12, 1781. G.

HANES, John. Commerce? Comm. F. Feb. 19, 1779. 5A p. 39.

HANIFORD, Josiah. Seaman. Jason. Captured but not comm. Oct. 15, 1781. HO.

HANWOOD, Arans. F. Pard. for exchange Dec. 11, 1779. G.

HARDEN, John. See HARDING.

HARDEN, William of Martha's Vineyard. Charming Salley or Polly. Captured Jan. 16, 1777. Died or escaped before committed to M. 3 p. 75; 7 p. 248.

HARDING, Jesse. Prize master or mate. Sturdy Beggar. Comm. F. Jan. 23, 1778. Pard. for exchange May 31, 1779. G; 5A p. 37.

HARDING or HARDEN, John. Reprisal. Comm. F. Aug. 9, 1777. Pard. for R. N. Dec. 3 or 16, 1778. Entered Dec. 19, 1778. G; 5 v. 32 p. 282; 5A p. 37.

HARDING, Timothy. Boy. Hercules. Captured but not comm. Oct. 15, 1781. HO.

HARE(S), William of Salem. Mariner. Montgomery. Comm. M. Dec. 7, 1781. SP; HO; 3 p. 212.

HARMON, Jacob of Philadelphia. Marquis de Morbec. Comm. M. Oct. 2, 1781. 3 p. 211.

HARMON, John. F. Pard. for exchange Dec. 11, 1779. G.

HARMON, John. Mariner. Marquis de Morbec. Comm. M. Oct. 2, 1781. SP; HO; 10 v. 74 p. 142.

HARRIS, Benjamin. Mate. Twin Sisters. Comm. to Security Prison ship at Chatham, Dec. 18, 1781. HO.

HARRIS, James. Seaman. Hercules. Sent from Kinsale to M. April 9, 1782. HO.

HARRIS, John. Captain. Mosquito of Virginia. Comm. F. Aug. 8 or 9, 1777. Escaped. Prisoners still received letters from him during 1778. 5 v. 30 p. 345; 5A p. 36; 7 pp. 113, 135, 163, 173. See also Virginia Magazine of History and Biography vol. 22, pp. 160-172.

HARRIS, John. F. Pard. for exchange May 31, 1779. G.

HARRIS, John. Mariner. Little Porgy or Peggy. Comm. M. Jan. 3, 1782. SP; HO; 3 p. 213.

HARRIS, Peter of Salem. Warren. Comm. M. June, 1778. Pard. for exchange Dec. 11, 1779. G; 3 p. 137; 7 p. 254.

HARRIS, Samuel of Ipswich. Fancy. Captured Aug. 7, 1777. Pard. for exchange Dec. 11, 1779. G; 3 p. 136; 7 p. 250.

HARRIS, Samuel of Rhode Island. Mariner. Warren. Comm. M. June 9, 1778. Pard. for exchange Dec. 11, 1779. Att. escape. SP; HO; HL; 3 p. 137; 7 p. 255.

HARRIS, Samuel. M. Pard. for R. N. Dec. 7, 1780. G.

HARRIS, Saml. of Boston. Hannable. Comm. M. March 31, 1781. Pard. for R. N. Sept. 29, 1781. G; HL; 3 p. 141; 10 v. 73 p. 331; v. 74 p. 33.

HARRIS, Timo. of Old York, New Hampshire. Dalton or Charming Polly. In hospital April, 1777. Comm. M. June, 1777. Pard. for exchange Dec. 26, 1778. G; 3 p. 75; 4 p. 184; 7 p. 245.

HARRIS, William. Mariner. Lively. Comm. M. Dec. 27, 1780. SP; HO; HL; 3 p. 140.

HARRISON, Ebenezer. Seaman. Hercules. Captured but not comm. Oct. 15, 1781. HO.

HARRISON, Hiram. Seaman. Pocahontas. Comm. F. Nov. 18, 1780. SP; HO.

HARRISON, Richard. F. Pard. for R. N. May 25, 1781. G.

MARINERS OF THE AMERICAN REVOLUTION

HART, Edward of England. Lexington. Comm. M. Sept. 19, 1777. Pard. for R. N. Oct. 14, 1778. Entered or escaped. G; 3 p. 137; 7 p. 253.

HART, Elias of Marblehead. Fancy. Captured Aug. 7, 1777. M. Died Sept. 3, 1778. 3 p. 136; 7 p. 161, 250.

HART, James. M. Pard. for exchange Dec. 11, 1779. G.

HART, William. Venus. Comm. F. April 2, 1778. Pard. for exchange May 31, 1779. G; 5A p. 37.

HARTLAND, James. Charming Polly or Sally. M. Escaped. 3 p. 75.

HARVEY, John. Lexington. Comm. M. Sept. 19, 1777. Pard. for exchange Dec. 11, 1779. G; 3 p. 137.

HARVEY, Joseph. Seaman. South Quay. Comm. F. March 21, 1781. HO; SP.

HARVEY, Thomas of Philadelphia. Lexington. Comm. M. Oct. 19, 1777. 7 p. 253.

HASKELL, Adoniram. Seaman. Hercules. Captured but not comm. Oct. 15, 1781. HO.

HASKELL, John. Seaman. Hercules. Sent from Kinsale to M. April 9, 1782. HO.

HASKELL, Willm. of Beverley. Mariner. Eagle. Comm. M. July 25, 1781. SP; HO; 3 p. 210; 10 v. 74 p. 36.

HASKULL or HASKIN, Moses. Boy. Black Prince. Comm. F. April 26, 1779. Pard. for exchange Dec. 11, 1779. G; HO; 5A p. 39.

HASON, Francis. Seaman. Diana. Comm. M. Jan. 24, 1782. HO.

HATCH, Jo. of Boston. Dalton. Captured Feb. 15, 1777. In hospital at Plymouth April, 1777. Died May 5, 1777. 4 p. 184; 7 pp. 36, 246.

HATCH, Prince. Seaman or midshipman. Protector. Comm. F. Aug. 2 or 9, 1781. SP; HO.

MARINERS OF THE AMERICAN REVOLUTION

HATCH, Thos, of Boston. M. Dalton? 3 p. 75.

HATCH, Zachariah. The Spy. Comm. F. Feb. 18, 1779. 5A p. 39. (Probably same as next).

HATCH, Zephaniah. F. Pard. for exchange Nov. 9, 1781. G. (Probably same as last).

HATHAWEY or HATCHWAY, John of Dartmouth. Charming Sally. Captured Jan. 7, 1777. M. Still there Feb. 7, 1779. Pard. for exchange Dec. 20, 1778. G; 3 p. 75; 7 p. 247.

HATHAWEY, Sil(i)as of Newhaven. Charming Sally or Polly. Captured Jan. 16, 1777. M. Still there Feb. 7, 1779. Pard. for exchange Dec. 20, 1778. G; 3 p. 75; 7 p. 247.

HATTEN, John. M. In hospital April, 1777. Pard. for exchange Dec. 11, 1779. G; 4 p. 184. (Probably of the Dalton).

HAWLEY, Samuel of Marblehead. Fancy. Comm. M. Aug. 7, 1777. Pard. for exchange Dec. 11, 1779. G; 3 p. 136; 7 p. 249. (Probably same as next).

HAWLEY, Samuel. Seaman. Rhodes. Comm. F. Nov. 18, 1780. SP; HO; 10 v. 73 p. 340. (Probably same as last).

HAWLEY or HURLEY or HOWLEYS, William. Mariner. Essex. Comm. M. July 21, 1781. In b. h. Nov. 7, 1781. Out Nov. 19. SP; HO; 3 p. 210; 10 v. 74 pp. 34, 150, 154.

HAY(E)S, James of Ireland. Lexington. Comm. M. Sept. 19, 1777. Escaped. 3 p. 137, 138.

HAYLAND or HAYLARD, Thos. Mariner. Polly. Comm. M. Oct. 27, 1781. SP; HO.

HAYLEY or HALA, Nathaniel. Angelica of Boston. Comm. F. July 7, 1778. Pard. for R. N. Dec. 19, 1778. 5 v. 32 pp. 282-3. 5A p. 38.

HAYNES or EDWARDS, Abraham of Salem. Mariner. An English sloop, prize to the New Adventure. Comm. M. Oct. 16, 1781. SP; HO. 3 p. 212.

MARINERS OF THE AMERICAN REVOLUTION

HAYNES, Ebenezer.   Seaman.   Civil Usage.   Comm. M. Feb. 7, 1782. HO.

HAYNES, John of Salem.   Hawk's prize.   Comm. M. Oct. 1778.   Pard. for exchange Dec. 11, 1779.   Pard. for R. N. Nov. 4, 1780.   Entered or escaped.   G; 3 p. 137; 7 p. 252.

HAYNES, Josiah of Providence.   1st lieut.   Genl. Washington.   Comm. M. March 31, 1781.   SP; HO; 3 p. 140; 10 v. 73 p. 331; HL.

HAYS(E), Thomas.   Mariner.   Franklyn.   Comm. M. Dec. 6, 1781. SP; HO; 3 p. 212.

HAYSHAM, Wm.   M.   Pard. for exchange Dec. 11, 1779.   G.

HAYSLIP, Robert.   Seaman.   Jason.   Captured but not comm. Oct. 15, 1781.   HO.

HAYTER, Stephen.   Seaman.   Protector.   Comm. F. Aug. 9, 1781.   SP; HO.

HAYWARD, Joseph.   The Swallow.   Comm. F. Jan. 23, 1778.   Pard. for exchange May 31, 1779.   5A p. 37; G.

HAYWARD, Samuel.   Gunner.   The Swallow.   Comm. F. Jan, 23, 1778. Pard. for exchange Dec. 11, 1779.   G; 5A p. 37.

HAZE, James of Ireland.   Lexington.   Comm. M. Sept. 17, 1777.   R. N. 7 p. 252.

HAZY, Samuel.   F.   Pard. for exchange Dec. 11, 1779.   G.

HEALY, Thomas.   M.   Pard. for exchange Dec. 20, 1778.   G.

HEALYARD.   M.   10 v. 74 p. 30.

HEART, James.   M.   Pard. for R. N. Nov. 22, 1779.   G.

HEATH, Timothy.   Seaman.   Fort Stanwin.   Comm. F. Aug. 4, 1780. Escaped and re-captured Nov. 14, 1780.   Pard. for R. N. May 25, 1781. G; SP; HO.

MARINERS OF THE AMERICAN REVOLUTION

HEFFLIN, William. Seaman. Wexford. Sent from Kinsale to M. April 9, 1782. HO.

HEILY, Daniel. F. Pard. for R. N. Dec. 3, 1778. G.

HELBRAND, Daniel. Seaman. Aurora. Comm. F. Nov. 18, 1780. SP; HO.

HELLER, HELLIER or HILLER, Edwd. (Senior). Mariner. Rambler. Comm. M. May 20, 1780. SP; HO; HL; 3 p. 138.

HELLIER or HILLER, Edward Junior. Mariner. Rambler. Comm. M. May 20, 1780. SP; HO; HL; 3 p. 138.

HEMMENWAY, Jon'n. Carpenter. Comm. F. Sept. 24, 1778. 5A p. 38. (Probably same as next).

HEMMENY, John. F. Pard. for exchange Dec. 11, 1779. (Probably same as last). G.

HEMMITT or HAMMET, Thomas of Berwick, New Hampshire. Dalton. Comm. M. June, 1777. Pard. for exchange Dec. 20, 1778. Went with Paul Jones. G; 7 p. 245; (See also Thos. HERMIT).

HENFIELD or MANFIELD, Gid(d)eon. Captain. Roebuck of Salem. Comm. M. Jan. 16, 1781. SP; HO; 3 p. 140; 10 v. 73 p. 314; 10 v. 74 pp. 33, 143.

HENRICK, Richard. Seaman. Eagle. Comm. F. March 5, 1781. SP; HO.

HENRY, Caleb Carpenter. F. Pard. for exchange Dec. 11, 1779. G.

HENSDELL, Thos. Master's mate. Comm. F. June 19, 1778. 5A p. 38.

HERBERT, Charles of Newburyport. Born Nov. 17, 1757. Dalton. Comm. M. June 5, 1777. Pard. for exchange Dec. 20, 1778. Exchanged March 16, 1779. See bibliography No. 7. 3 p. 74; 4 pp. 184, 187.

HERCULES, George. Boy. Jason. Captured but not comm. Oct. 25, 1781. HO.

MARINERS OF THE AMERICAN REVOLUTION

HERMIT, Thos. Charming Polly. Comm. M. May, 1777. Exchanged. (Probably meant for Thos. HEMMITT, q.v.). 3 p. 75.

HESSAM or HESSMAN, William of Philadelphia. Revenge. Comm. M. May, 1778. 3 p. 139; 7 p. 257.

HEWIT, Robert. P.M. mate. Sturdy Beggar. Comm. F. Jan. 23, 1778. Escaped. 5A p. 37.

HEYLAND, Benjamin. Pembroke prison. Pard. for R.N. June 17, 1779. G.

HICHBORN, Joseph. Seaman. Morning Star. Comm. F. Aug. 9, 1781. SP; HO.

HICKS, Barney. Mate or seaman. Fame or Morning Star. Comm. F. Aug. 9, 1781. SP; HO.

HICKS, Benjamin. Master's mate. The Swallow. Comm. F. Jan. 23, 1778. Pard. for exchange Dec. 11, 1779. G; 5A p. 37; (Probably same as next).

HICKS, Benjamin. F. Pard. for R.N. March 3, 1781. (Probably same as last). G.

HIDDEN, Adoniran of Rowley. Pilgrim's prize. Comm. M. July 9, 1781. Died Aug. 8, 1781. 10 v. 74 p. 39.

HIGGANS or RIGGINS, Eleazer. Mariner. Resolution of Boston. Comm. M. Jan. 22, 1781. SP; HO; HL; 3 p. 140; 10 v. 73 p. 316.

HIGGENSON, John. Seaman. Salley and Beckey. Comm. F. Dec. 30, 1779. SP; HO.

HIGGINS, John of Berwick, New Hampshire. Dalton or Charming Polly. Comm. M. Dec. 20, 1778. Pard. for exchange Dec. 20, 1778. G; 3 p. 75; 7 p. 245.

HILL, Benjamin of Massachusetts. Captain. Montgomery. Comm. F. Aug. 9, 1777. Escaped. 5 v. 30 p. 345; 5A p. 36.

HILLER. See HELLER.

HILLMAN, John of Martha's Vineyard.　Boatswain.　Genl. Washington. Comm. M. Sept. 7, 1781.　SP; HO; 3 p. 211.

HILTON, Isaac of Casco Bay.　Effingham.　Comm. M. May 10, 1779. In b.h. July 7, 1781.　Out of b.h. July 8.　Pard. for exchange Dec. 11, 1779 and Nov. 9, 1781.　G; HL; 3 p. 138; 10 v. 74 p. 31.

HILTON, Stilton.　Seaman.　American.　Comm. F. June 27, 1781.　SP; HO.

HINDMAN, Dr.　See information on Wm. Richardson, whom he accompanied.

HINDMAN, Samuel.　Soldier taken on shore.　Comm. M. Feb. 6, 1782. HO.

HINDS, Caldwel.　Soldier taken on shore.　Comm. M. Feb. 6, 1782. HO.

HINES, Francis.　F.　Pard. for R.N. Oct. 24, 1781.　G.

HINES, Willm. (Senior) of Marblehead.　In F. May 8, 1781.　Pard. for exchange Dec. 11, 1779.　G; 10 v. 73 p. 340.

HINES, Willm. Junior.　Still in F. May 8, 1781.　Pard. for exchange Dec. 11, 1779.　G; 10 v. 73 p. 340.

HINES, Wm.　Master's mate.　The Black Snake.　Comm. F. Feb. 18, 1779.　5A p. 39.

HINES, Wm.　F.　Pard. for R.N. Oct. 24, 1781.　G.

HINMAN or INMAN, Elisha.　Captain.　Alfred.　Comm. F. July 18, 1778. Escaped July 23, 1778.　5 v. 31 pp. 286, 287; 5A p. 38.

HINSDALE, Thomas.　2nd mate.　Comm. F. June 19, 1778.　5 v. 32 p. 286.

HIRNDON, Joseph.　Seaman.　Pocahontas.　Comm. F. Nov. 18, 1780. SP; HO.

HOBBELL or HOBBLE, Saml. of New London.　Lexington.　Comm. M. Sept. 19, 1777.　Escaped, re-taken and in b.h. July 6, 1781.　Out of b.h. July 29.　10 v. 74 pp. 31, 37.　(See HUBBLE).

MARINERS OF THE AMERICAN REVOLUTION

HOBBS, John. Seaman. Tom Lee. Comm. F. Aug. 9, 1781. SP; HO.

HOCKET(T), John. Seaman. Nancy or Larravie. Comm. F. March 21, 1781. SP; HO. (Probably same as HACKETT)

HODGCARE, Jonathan. See HOTCKISS.

HODGE, George. M. Pard. for R. N. April 28, 1781. G.

HODGE, Robert. Angelica. Comm. F. July 7, 1778. Pard. for exchange May 31, 1779. G; 5A p. 38.

HODGES, Ebenezer. Seaman. Hercules. Sent from Kinsale to M. April 9, 1782. HO.

HOFFIN. See HOSSIN, Daniel.

HOGEEASE, Jona. Charming Polly. M. 3 p. 75. (Probably meant for HOTCHKISS, q. v.).

HOGG, Ebenezer. Stuard. Angelica. Comm. F. July 7, 1778. Escaped. 5A p. 38.

HOLBROOK, James. Seaman. Portsmouth. Comm. F. July 20, 1781. SP; HO.

HOL(L)IDAY, John. Boy. Rattlesnake. Comm. F. Jan. 23, 1778. Pard. for exchange May 31, 1779. Joined Bonhomme Richard and later wounded in fight against Serapis. G; 5 v. 32 p. 286; 5A p. 37.

HOLLAND, Thomas of Maryland. General Washington. Comm. M. Oct. 1781. 3 p. 212.

HOLLAND, Thomas of Newbury. Lion. Comm. M. October, 1781. 3 p. 211.

HOLLAND, William. Mariner. Little Porgy or Pegey. Comm. M. Jan. 3, 1782. SP; HO; 3 p. 213.

HOLMES, Thomas. Imprisoned at Pembroke. Pard. for R. N. June, 17, 1779. G.

HOLT, Joseph. Pard. for R.N. Sept. 25, 1778. G.

HOLTON, James. Rising States. Comm. F. June 14, 1777. Pard. for exchange May 31, 1779. G; 5A p. 36.

HOLTON, John. F. Pard. for exchange Dec. 11, 1779. G.

HOMER, Chapman of Cape Cod. Mariner. Jolly Tar. Comm. M. Oct. 17, 1780. Innoculated May 28, 1781. SP; HO; HL; 3 p. 139; 10 v. 73 p. 346.

HOMER (Jacob). Midshipman. Protector. Comm. M. July 21, 1781. SP; HO; 3 p. 209; 10 v. 74 p. 34.

HOMES, William. Seaman. Wexford. Sent from Kinsale to M. April 9, 1782. HO.

HOOD, John. M. Att. escape Nov. 21, 1781. Out of b.h. Nov. 26, 1781. 10 v. 74 pp. 155, 156.

HOOK, Jacob. Seaman. Retaliation. Comm. F. Oct. 31, 1780. SP; HO.

HOOKER, Michael of Portsmouth, New Hampshire. M. 9 p. 80. (Probably meant for HOOPER, q.v.).

HOOPER, James of Kittery. Mariner. Aurora. Comm. M. July 25 or 27, 1780. In hospital May 10, 1781. SP; HO; HL; 3 p. 139; 9 pp. 80, 89; 10 v. 73 p. 34.

HOOPER, Michael. Seaman. Bermuda. Comm. M. Jan. 22, 1782. HO. (See also HOOKER).

HOOPER, Thomas. Seaman. Marquis de la Fayette. Comm. M. Jan. 22, 1782. HO.

HOOTHAM, John. Seaman. Lion. Comm. M. Jan. 25, 1782. HO.

HOPES, John of Ireland. Lexington. Comm. M. Sept. 19, 1777. Pard. for exchange Dec. 11, 1779. G; 3 p. 137; 7 p. 252.

HOPKINS, Alexander. Carpenter. Daniel. Comm. F. Oct. 31, 1780. SP.

MARINERS OF THE AMERICAN REVOLUTION

HOPPING, Nicholas. Seaman. Harlequin. Comm. F. May 24, 1781. SP; HO.

HORKE-, Saml. F. Pard. for exchange Dec. 11, 1779. G.

HORN, William. Seaman. Hercules. Sent from Kinsale to M. April 9, 1782. HO.

HORNER, Will. of Ireland. Dalton. Sent to Royal hospital[7] at Plymouth Feb. 17, 1777. Still there April, 1777. R.N. 4 pp. 43, 184, 187; 7 p. 246.

HORSEWELL, Pearce or Pierce. Mariner. Minerva. Comm. M. Aug. 23, 1780. SP; HO; HL; 3 p. 139.

HORSHIN, Samuel. Seaman. Genl. Glover. Comm. F. Oct. 18, 1779. SP; HO.

HORTON, James of Casco Bay. Sweet Lucretia. Comm. M. Oct. 16, 1778. Pard. for exchange Dec. 11, 1779 and Nov. 9, 1781. G; HL; 3 p. 137; 7 p. 256.

HORTON, Thomas of Marblehead. Fancy. Comm. M. Aug. 7, 1777. Pard. for exchange Dec. 11, 1779. G; 3 p. 136; 7 p. 250.

HORTON, William of Milton. Mariner. Essex. Comm. M. July 21 or 28, 1781. SP; HO; 3 p. 210; 10 v. 74 p. 36.

HOSFIN, Daniel. See HOSSIN.

HOSSIN, Hosfin or HOFFIN, Daniel. Seaman. Hercules. Captured but not comm. Oct. 15, 1781. HO.

HOTCKISS or HODGCARE, Jonathan of New Haven. Charming Sally. Captured Jan. 16, 1777. M. Pard. for exchange Dec. 20, 1778. G; 7 p. 247.

HOVER, John. Seaman. Hercules. Sent from Kinsale to M. April 9, 1782. HO.

HOW, David of Scotland. Alliance's prize. Comm. M. March 22, 1779. Pard. for R.N. July 13, 1779. G; 3 p. 138.

HOW, Samuel. Seaman. Wexford. Captured but not comm. Oct. 2, 1781. HO.

HOWARD, Clement. Seaman. Flying Fish. Comm. F. May 24, 1781. SP; HO.

HOWARD, John. Lexington. Comm. M. Sept. 19, 1777. R. N. or escaped. 3 p. 137; 7 p. 253.

HOWARD, Richard. M. Pard. for R. N. Sept. 25, 1778. G.

HOWARD, Simon of North Carolina? Mariner. Lydia or Robertson. Comm. M. April 24, 1781. Innoculated May 28, 1781. SP; HO; HL; 3 p. 141; 10 v. 73 pp. 337, 346.

HOWARD, Wm. Prize master. Angelica. Comm. F. July 7, 1778. Escaped. 5A p. 38.

HOWE, John. M. R.N. 7 p. 192.

HOWELL, Nathl. of Southampton, Long Island. Mariner. Marquis de Moulbank or Countess of Marlboro. SP; HO; 3 p. 212; 10 v. 74 p. 155.

HOWLEYS, Willm. See HAWLEY.

HOWSER or HOWFER, Jno of Pennsylvania. Luzerne of Philadelphia. Comm. M. July 7, 1781. Pard. for R. N. Nov. 9, 1781. Entered Oct. 24, 1781. G; 3 p. 209; 10 v. 74 pp. 31, 146.

HOYDFORD, William. See LLOYDFORD.

HUBBARD, Charles. Seaman. Pocahontas. Comm. F. Nov. 18, 1780. SP; HO.

HUBBARD, Jesse. Seaman. Pocahontas. Comm. F. Nov. 18, 1780. SP; HO.

HUBBARD, John. Seaman. Pocahontas. Comm. F. Nov. 18, 1780. SP.

HUBBARD, Philip. Seaman. Portsmouth. Comm. F. June 27, 1781. SP; HO.

HUBBARD, Samuel. Seaman. Wexford. Comm. M. Jan. 24, 1782. HO.

HUBBERT, Charles. F. Pard. for R. N. April 20, 1781. G.

HUBBLE, Samuel of Connecticut. Comm. M. Oct. 1, 1777. Pard. for exchange Dec. 11, 1779. SP; HO; HL; 3 p. 137. (See HOBBLE).

HUDSON, Mr. M. 9 p. 85. (Probably Benjamin).

HUDSON, Benjamin. Seaman. Prize of the Mars privateer. Comm. M. July 3, 1779. Pard. for exchange Dec. 11, 1779. HO; 4 p. 396.

HUDSON, William. Seaman. Hercules. Sent from Kinsale to M. April 9, 1782. HO.

HUGGINS, William. Quartermaster. Wexford. Captured but not comm. Oct. 2, 1781. HO.

HULING, Edwd. of Salem. Warren. Comm. M. June 4, 1778. Exchanged. Re-captured as prize master of the Diligence, prize to the Black Princess or Duc de Coigne. Comm. M. July 18, 1780. SP; HO; HL; 3 pp. 137, 139.

HULIN, Richard. M. Pard. for exchange Dec. 11, 1779. G.

HULL, John of Rhode Island. Franklin. Comm. Pembroke 1778. Comm. M. Oct. 14 or 17, 1780. In hospital May 10, 1781. SP; HO; HL; 3 p. 139; 10 v. 73 p. 341.

HUMBER, William. Rising States. Comm. F. June 14, 1777. Att. escape Nov. 18, 1777. In b. h. Escaped Feb. 15, 1778. 5 v. 30 pp. 347, 348; 5A p. 36.

HUMPHREY. M. 10 v. 74 p. 47.

HUMPHREY, Annaziah. Seaman. Taken on shore. Comm. M. Feb. 6, 1782. HO.

HUMPHREY, George. Comm. Pembroke 1778. Comm. M. Oct. 14, 1780. R. N. 3 p. 139.

HUMPHREYS, George. M. Pard. for exchange Nov. 9, 1781. G; HL.

MARINERS OF THE AMERICAN REVOLUTION

HUNT, Abijah of New Jersey. Mariner. L'Uzerne. SP; HO; 3 p. 209.

HUNT, Benjamin of Braintree. Mariner. Royal Louis. Comm. M. May 10 or July 3, 1779. Pard. for exchange Dec. 11, 1779. G; SP; HO; HL; 3 p. 138; 8 p. 92.

HUNT, Daniel of Portsmouth. Mariner. Venus. Comm. M. Nov. 21, 1781. SP; HO; 3 p. 212; 10 v. 74 p. 155.

HUNT, Ebenezer of Newburyport. Dalton or Charming Polly. Sent to Royal hospital at Plymouth, Feb. 15, 1777. Died Feb. 20, 1777. 4 p. 43, 44. 7 pp. 27, 244; 3 p. 75.

HUNT, James of New Jersey. Mariner. L'Uzerne. Comm. M. July 7, 1781. SP; HO; 3 p. 209; 10 v. 74 p. 31.

HUNT, John of New Jersey. Luzerne. Comm. M. July, 1781. 10 v. 74 p. 31.

HUNT, Thomas. Comm. Pembroke, 1778. Comm. M. Oct. 14, 1780. Pard. for R. N. May, 1781. Entered June 5, 1781. 3 p. 139; 10 v. 74 p. 22.

HUNT, William. Mariner. Essex. Comm. M. July 27, 1781. SP; HO; 3 p. 210.

HUNTER, Alex. of Nantucket. Mariner. Protector. Comm. M. Aug. 23, 1781. SP; HO; 3 p. 211; 10 v. 74 p. 43.

HUNTRESS, Daniel of Portsmouth, New Hampshire. M. 9 p. 80.

HURLEY, William. See HAWLEY.

HUTCHIN(G)S, Saml. of Malden. James and Rebecca, prize to the Franklin. Comm. M. Oct. 17, 1781. SP; HO; 3 p. 211; 10 v. 74 p. 145.

HYAM, Richard. F. Pard. for exchange Dec. 11, 1779. G.

HYFIELD, Mr. M. Escaped Dec. 13, 1778. 7 p. 196, 198.

HYLLARD, Thoms. of Virginia. General Washington. Comm. M. Oct. 28, 1781. 10 v. 74 p. 147.

HYSER or KYSER, Thomas. Seaman. Mercury. Comm. F. March 21, 1781. SP; HO.

I

INGLES, INGELLS or EAGLES, Benjamin of Lynn. Mariner. Ascott and John. Comm. M. July 23, 1781. SP; HO; 3 p. 210; 10 v. 74 p. 35.

INGERSOL(L), Joseph of Cape Ann. Warren. M. Pard. for R. N. Oct. 14, 1778. Entered or escaped. G; 3 p. 137; 7 p. 255.

INGERSOL, Joseph. F. Pard. for exchange Dec. 11, 1779. G.

INGERSOL, Joseph. F. Pard. for R. N. Nov. 6, 1780. G.

INGRAM, William. Seaman. Fair American. Comm. F. Nov. 18, 1780. HO; SP.

INMAN, Elisha. See HINMAN.

IREME or IREMY, Thos. of Salem. Mariner. Susanna, prize to the Oliver Cromwell. Comm. M. July 3 or 28, 1779. Pard. for exchange Dec. 11, 1779. SP; HO; HL; 3 p. 138.

IRESON or IVERSON, Richard. Seaman. General Glover. Comm. F. Oct. 18, 1779. Pard. for exchange Dec. 11, 1779. G; SP; HO.

ISNE, John. See JENNE.

IVORY, Benjamin. Angelica. Comm. F. July 7, 1778. Pard. for exchange Dec. 11, 1779.and Oct. 16, 1781. G; 5A p. 38.

J

JABOR. See JEBOE.

JACKSON, Capt. M. 10 v. 74 p. 33.

JACKSON, Bennet. Seaman. Portsmouth. Comm. F. July 20, 1781. SP; HO.

JACKSON, Elezor. Seaman. Hercules. Sent from Kinsale to M. April 9, 1782. HO.

JACKSON, John. F. Pard. for R. N. May 25, 1781. G.

JACKSON, Thomas. Seaman. Huntingdon. Comm. F. May 24, 1781. SP; HO.

JAGER or YAGGER, Henry. Mariner. Franklin. Comm. M. Dec. 6, 1781. SP; HO.

JAMES, Wm. of Marblehead. Roebuck of Salem. Comm. M. Jan. 9, 1781. Exchanged. HL; 3 p. 140; 10 v. 73 p. 313.

JAMES, William F. Pard. for exchange Oct. 16, 1781. G.

JANDILL, Alixander of Philadelphia. Pilgrim's prize. Comm. M. July 9, 1781. 10 v. 74 p. 32.

JANES, Peter of Marblehead. True Blue. Comm. M. Aug. 20, 1778. 7 p. 256.

JARVAS or JARVIS, Robert of Virginia. Mariner. Marmy or Mariana. Comm. M. July 3 or 28, 1779. Pard. for exchange Dec. 11, 1779. G; SP; HL; 3 p. 138.

JASPER, Selan or Selden of North Carolina. Mariner. Nancey. Comm. M. July 28, 1781. SP; HO; 10 v. 74 p. 36.

JASPER, Wm. Rising States. Comm. F. June 14, 1777. Pard. for exchange May 31, 1779. G; 5A p. 36.

MARINERS OF THE AMERICAN REVOLUTION

JEBOE, JABOR or JIBB, Edward of Marblehead. Pilgrim's prize. Comm. M. July 9, 1781. 3 p. 209; 10 v. 74 pp. 32, 40.

JEFFERYS, JEFFERES or JEFFROYS, James. Seaman. McCleary or Hambden. Comm. F. Jan. 19, 1779. Pard. for exchange Dec. 11, 1779. G; SP; HO; 5A p. 39.

JEFFERY, Josh or Joseph. Mariner. Betsey. Comm. M. July 23, 1781. SP; HO; 3 p. 210; 10 v. 74 p. 35.

JENKINS, Capt. In hospital at Plymouth, April, 1777. 4 p. 184.

JENKINS, Benj. Mariner. Lion. Comm. M. Aug. 31, 1781. SP; HO; 3 p. 211.

JENKINS, Charles. Seaman. Fair American. Comm. F. Nov. 30, 1780. SP.

JANKINSON, John. Seaman. Franklin. Comm. M. Feb. 27, 1782. HO.

JENNE or ISNE, John. M. Pard. for R. N. Aug. 9, 1781. G.

JENNER, Saml. Mariner. Jason. Comm. M. Dec. 16 or 18, 1779. SP; HO; HL; 3 p. 138.

JENNINGS, James. F. Pard. for R. N. April 20, 1781. G.

JENNY, Langhorn. Seaman. Marquis de la Fayette. Comm. M. Jan. 22, 1782. HO.

JERVES or JERVIS, Boston. Seaman. Union or Pomona. Comm. F. Aug. 7 or 9, 1779. Pard. for exchange Dec. 11, 1779. G; SP; HO.

JIBB, Edward. See JEBOE.

JILLSON, Oliver. Seaman. General Miflin. Comm. F. Aug. 9, 1781. SP; HO.

JOANES, Oliver. F. Pard. for exchange May 31, 1779. G. (Possibly same as JOHNNOT).

JOHN, Jack. Cook. Hercules. Captured but not comm. Oct. 15, 1782. HO.

JOHNNOT, John. Boy. Betsey, a merchant ship. Captured but not comm. Oct. 23, 1781. HO.

JOHNS, Jacob. See JONES.

JOHNSON, Charles. Seaman. Wexford. Sent from Kinsale to M. April 9, 1782. HO.

JOHNS(T)ON, Eleazer of Newburyport. Captain. Dalton. Comm. M. June 2, 1777. Escaped Feb. 1, 1778. 3 p. 74; 4 p. 186; 7 pp. 94, 243.

JOHNS(T)ON, Elisha of Hampton. Dalton. Comm. M. June, 1777. Pard. for exchange Dec. 20, 1778. G; 7 p. 246.

JOHNS(T)ON, Henry of Marblehead. Mariner. Rambler. Comm. M. Feb. 16, 1780. SP; HO; HL; 3 p. 138.

JOHNSON, Henry of Boston. Captain. Lexington. Comm. M. Sept. 26, 1777. Escaped Feb. 1, 1778. 3 p. 137; 4 p. 396; 7 pp. 64, 87, 94, 252.

JOHNSON, James. Oliver Cromwell. Comm. F. Oct. 13, 1777. Escaped. 5A p. 37.

JOHNS(T)ONE, Jas. of Salem. Essex. Comm. M. July 21, 1781. Pard. for R. N. Aug. 9, 1781. G; 3 p. 210; 10 v. 74 p. 34.

JOHNS(T)ON, Josh. or Joseph of Boston. Mariner. Essex. Comm. M. July 21, 1781. SP; HO; 3 p. 210; 10 v. 74 p. 34.

JOHNSON, Thomas. Seaman. Thomas, a merchant ship. Captured but not comm. Oct. 23, 1781. HO.

JOHNSON, Wm. Comm. F. April 19, 1779. Pard. for exchange Dec. 11, 1779. G; 5A p. 39.

JOHNSON, William. Seaman. Confederacy. Comm. M. Feb. 27, 1782. HO.

JOHNSTON. See JOHNSON.

JOHONOT, Oliver. Rising States. Comm. F. June 14, 1777. 5A p. 36. (Possibly same as JOANES).

JONES, Abraham. M. HL.

JONES, Elisha or Elijah of Cape Cod. Mariner. Resolution of Boston. Comm. M. Jan. 22, 1781. SP; HO; HL; 10 v. 73 p. 316.

JONES, Ephram or Ephreham of North Carolina. Mariner. Salley. Comm. M. May 11, 1781. Innoculated May 28, 1781. Pard. for R. N. May, 1781. G; SP; HO; 3 p. 209; 10 v. 73 pp. 340, 346.

JONES, Evan. Seaman. Jason. Captured but not comm. Oct. 15, 1781. HO.

JONES, Faunel of Marblehead.. Captain. True Blue. Comm. M. Jan. 1778. Exchanged. 3 p. 137.

JONES, Francis. Prize to the Warren. Comm. F. June 26, 1777. Petitioned to be released from b. h. March 25, 1778. Pard. for exchange May 31, 1779. G; 5A p. 36.

JONES, Griffith of Philadelphia. 2nd lieut. Alliance. Comm. M. Nov. 21, 1781. SP; HO; 3 p. 212; 10 v. 74 p. 155.

JONES or JOHNS, Jacob. Mariner. Essex. Comm. M. July 21 or 24, 1781. SP; HO; 3 p. 210; 10 v. 74 p. 35.

JONES, John. Rising States. Comm. F. June 14, 1777. Escaped. 5A p. 36.

JONES, John of Salem. Warren. Comm. M. June 4, 1778. Pard. for exchange Dec. 11, 1779. Escaped. 3 p. 137; 7 p. 254; G.

JONES, John. Seaman. Franklin or Fair American. Comm. F. Nov. 30, 1780. SP; HO.

JONES, John of Virginia. Friendship. Comm. M. May 15, 1781. 3 p. 209. (Probably same as next).

JONES, John. Mariner. Lydia. Comm. M. May 11 or 15, 1781. SP; HO. (Probably same as last).

JONES, John. Seaman. Confederacy. Comm. M. Feb. 27, 1782. HO.

JONES, John. F. Pard. for exchange Dec. 11, 1779. G.

JONES, John. M. Pard. for R. N. Nov. 4, 1780. G.

JONES, Jno. M. HL.

JONES, Nathaniel of Ipswich. Fancy. Comm. M. Aug. 7, 1777. Pard. for exchange Dec. 11, 1779. G; 3 p. 136; 7 p. 250.

JORDAN, Isaiah or Josiah of Salem. Warren. Comm. M. June, 1778. Exchanged. 3 p. 137; 7 p. 254. (Probably same as next).

JORDAN, Isaak. M. Pard. for exchange Dec. 11, 1779. (Probably same as last). G.

JORDAN, Simon of Casco Bay. Beaver. Comm. M. July 23, 1781. Died. 3 p. 210.

JOY, Elisha. Imprisoned at Pembroke. Pard. for R. N. June 17, 1779. G.

JUSTICE, Thomas. 1st lieut. Hector. Comm. M. March 31, 1781. SP; HO; HL; 3 p. 141; 10 v. 73 p. 331.

JUTSON or JUDSON, James. Charming Sally. Captured Jan. 16, 1777. M. Died May 26, 1777. 7 pp. 41, 248.

K

KANIDY, Richd.   See CANEDY.

KANADY, KENNEDY, CANADA or CANIDY, Willm. of North Carolina. Mariner. Lydia or Robertson. Comm. M. April 24, 1781. SP; HO; HL; 3 p. 141, 210; 10 v. 73 p. 337.

KASHIN, Moses.   Seaman.   Black Prince.   Comm. F. April 26, 1779. SP.

KEATH, George.   M.   Pard. for exchange Dec. 11, 1779.   G.

KEATON or KEETON, John of Virginia.   Mariner.   Susanna.   Comm. M. Nov. 21, 1781.   SP; HO; 3 p. 212; 10 v. 74 p. 155.

KEENAN, Michl. of Boston.   Essex.   Comm. M. July 21 or 24, 1781. 3 p. 210; 10 v. 74 p. 35.   (Probably same as Michel KELLY).

KELDER, George.   Boy.   Thomas, a merchant ship.   Captured but not comm. Oct. 23, 1781.   HO.

KELLY, John.   Prize master.   Antibriton.   Imprisoned at Edinburgh Jan. 19, 1782.   HO.

KELLY, Michel.   Mariner.   Essex.   Comm. M. July 24, 1781. SP; HO; (Probably same as Michl. KEENAN).

KELLY, Silvester.   Seaman.   Antibriton.   Imprisoned at Edinburgh Jan. 19, 1782.   HO.

KELLY, Thomas.   Brig Thom.   Comm. M. Sept. 19, 1780.   Pard. for exchange Nov. 9, 1781.   G; HL; 3 p. 139.

KELLY, Timothy of Boston.   Mariner.   Marquis de Morbec.   Comm. M. Oct. 2, 1781.   SP; HO; 3 p. 211; 10 v. 74 p. 142.

KELLY, Wm.   Lexington.   Comm. F. Sept. 19, 1777.   Pard. for exchange Dec. 11, 1779. and Oct. 16, 1781.   G; 3 p. 137.

MARINERS OF THE AMERICAN REVOLUTION

KELLY, Wm.   Angelica of Boston.   Comm. F. July 7, 1778.   5A p. 38.

KELSICK, Richard.   Seaman.   Polly.   Comm. F. June 27, 1781.   SP; HO.

KELTON or KILTON, John.   Reprisal.   Comm. F. Aug. 28, 1778.   Pard. for exchange Dec. 11, 1779.and Nov. 9, 1781.   G; 5A p. 38.

KEMP(E), John of Maryland.   Captain.   Greyhound of Philadelphia.   Comm. M. Jan. 6, 1781.   Escaped and re-taken June 9, 1781.   Escaped and re-taken June 29, 1781.   Out of b.h. July 19, 1781.   SP; HL; 3 p. 140; 10 v. 73 p. 312; v. 74 pp. 24, 29, 33, 151.   (Probably escaped as not in HO).

KEMP(E), Willm.   Mariner.   L'Uzerne.   Comm. M. July 7, 1781.   SP; HO; 3 p. 209; 10 v. 74 p. 31.

KEMPER, John.   Brig Hector.   Comm. M. Jan. 11, 1781.   Petitioned to go R.N. March 27, 1781.   Pard. for R.N. March 20, 1781.   Entered April 25, 1781.   G; 3 p. 140; 10 v. 73 pp. 313, 337.

KEMPTON, Joseph.   Seaman.   Gates.   Comm. F. Feb. 18, 1779.   Pard. for exchange Dec. 11, 1779.   G; SP.

KENDALL, Smith.   Seaman.   Wexford.   Sent from Kinsale to M. April 9, 1782.   HO.

KENDLEY, James.   See KENNERLY.

KENEDY, Willm.   See KENNEDA.

KENNARD, Nathl, of Kittery or Portsmouth.   Dalton or Charming Polly.   Comm. M. June, 1777.   Pard. for exchange Dec. 20, 1778.   Went with Paul Jones.   G; 3 p. 75; 7 p. 245; 9 p. 80.   (Probably same as below).

KENNARD, Nathl. of Kittery.   Mariner.   Venus.   Comm. M. Nov. 21, 1781.   SP; HO; 3 p. 212; 10 v. 74 p. 155.   (Probably same as above).

KENNEDA or KENEDY, Willm. of Salem.   Mate.   Essex or Ulysses.   Comm. M. July 21, 1781.   SP; HO; 10 v. 74 p. 34.

MARINERS OF THE AMERICAN REVOLUTION

KENNEDY, John of Ireland. Lexington. Comm. M. Sept. 17, 1777. R. N. or escaped. 3 p. 137; 7 p. 252.

KENNEDY, Wm. See KANADY.

KENNEL, Francis. Seaman. Terrible. Comm. F. May 24, 1781. SP; HO.

KENNEL, George. Boy. Jason. Captured but not comm. Oct. 15, 1781. HO.

KENNERLY, KENNELBY or KENDLEY, James. Soldier taken in South Carolina. (Black Princess). Comm. M. Oct. 2, 1781. SP; HO; 3 p. 211; 10 v. 74 p. 142.

KENNINGTON or KENNISON, Hugh of Kittery. Dalton or Charming Polly. Comm. M. June, 1777. Pard. for exchange Dec. 20, 1778. Escaped. G; 3 p. 75; 7 p. 245.

KENNINGTON, Joseph of Scotland. Lexington. Comm. M. Sept. 19, 1777. Died. 7 p. 253.

KENNINGTON, Simon. Seaman. Purgey. Comm. M. Jan. 24, 1782. HO.

KENNISON, Hugh. See KENNINGTON.

KENNY, Benjamin of New Hampshire. Prize master. Black Prince. Comm. F. April 26, 1779. Pard. for exchange Dec. 11, 1779. G; 5A p. 39.

KENSINGTON, Joseph. Lexington. M. Died May 14, 1778. 7 p. 121.

KENSOL, William. Seaman. Neptune. Comm. F. June 27, 1781. SP.

KENT, Edward. Seaman or midshipman. Lion. Comm. F. Aug. 2, 1781. SP; HO.

KEY, John of Newburyport. Dalton. In hospital April, 1777. Comm. M. June, 1777. Escaped or exchanged. 3 p. 74; 4 p. 184; 7 p. 243.

KEYS, William or Mr. of Long Island. 2nd lieut. Charming Sally or Polly. Captured Jan. 16, 1777. M. 3 p. 75; 4 p. 307; 7 p. 247.

KILBY or KILBEE, John. Boy. Sturdy Beggar. Comm. F. Jan. 23, 1778. Pard. for exchange May 21, 1779. Joined Bonhomme Richard. G; 5 v. 32 p. 286; 5A p. 37.

KILTON, John. See KELTON.

KINDALL, Joseph. Seaman. Wexford. Captured but not comm. Oct. 2, 1781. HO.

KINDALL, Joshua. Seaman. Wexford. Sent from Kinsale to M. April 9, 1782. HO.

KING, Edwd. of Virginia. Mariner. Success, Bellona or Two Brothers. Comm. M. July 20, 1781. SP; HO; 3 p. 211; 10 v. 74 p. 34.

KING, Henry. Seaman. South Quay. Comm. F. March 21, 1781. SP; HO.

KING, John. Seaman. Venus. Comm. F. Dec. 30, 1779. SP; HO.

KING, John. Seaman. Marquis de la Fayette. Comm. M. Jan. 23, 1782. HO.

KING or FLING, Philip of Boston. Mariner. Essex. Comm. M. July 21 or 24, 1781. SP; HO; 3 p. 210; 10 v. 74 p. 35.

KINGINGROW, Joshua. Lexington. Comm. M. Sept. 19, 1777. Died. 3 p. 137.

KINSDALE, Thos. F. Pard. for exchange May 31, 1779. G.

KIRK, Arthur, Archer W. or Mr. of Ireland. Lexington. M. Escaped Oct. 1, 1778. 3 p. 137; 7 pp. 170, 252.

KINSEY, Thomas. Seaman. Mary and Elizabeth. Comm. F. Dec. 30, 1779. SP; HO.

KINSEY, Thomas. F. Pard. for R. N. March 17, 1781. G.

KIRTLAND, Francis of England. Charming Sally. Captured Jan. 16, 1777. M. R.N. 7 p. 248.

KITTS, John of Philadelphia. Marboys of Philadelphia. Comm. M. Jan. 9, 1781. Att. escape April 13, 1781. Escaped May 24, 1781. 3 p. 140; 10 v. 73 pp. 313, 334, 344.

KNAPP, Anty. of Newburyport. 1st lieut. Dalton. Comm. M. June 5, 1777. Escaped Aug. 5, 1777. Re-captured Oct. 13, 1777. Finally escaped. 3 p. 74; 4 pp. 187, 307; 7 pp. 67, 243. (Appears in no official list but mentioned in G as having escaped using the name of Anthony HART).

KNAPP, Enoch. Alfred. Comm. F. July 18, 1778. Pard. for R.N. Sept. 9, 1779. G; 5A p. 38.

KNAPP, Samuel of Salem. Warren. Comm. M. June, 1778. Pard. for exchange Dec. 11, 1779. Pard. for R.N. Nov. 22, 1780. Re-taken on Black Prince. Comm. M. Oct. 20, 1781. G; 3 pp. 137, 212; 7 p. 254; 10 v. 74 pp. 146, 148, 155. (The story is clarified in a letter in the G. records. He joined the R.N., ran away and embarked on a French ship, the Black Princess. Afterwards he was re-taken and tried as a deserter. Colburn says he escaped as usual when a prisoner joined the R.N.)

KNAST, Samuel of Dartmouth. Charming Sally. Captured Jan. 16, 1777. M. Still there Feb. 7, 1779. 7 p. 247.

KNEELAND, John of Braintree. Essex. Comm. M. Aug. 25, 1781. 3 p. 211.

KNEET, Charles of Baltimore. Reprisal's prize. Comm. M. June 29, 1777. 7 p. 251.

KNELL, NEAL or NEIL, Alex. of Virginia. Reprisal's prize. Comm. M. June 29, 1777, or Aug. 1777. Pard. for R.N. Oct. 14, 1778. Entered or escaped. G; 3 p. 75; 7 p. 251.

KNIGHT, Mr. In b.h. April 9, 1780. M. 8 p. 125.

KNIGHT, Danl. of Kittery. Dalton. In hospital April, 1777. Comm. M. June, 1777. Pard. for exchange Dec. 26, 1778. Joined Alliance. G; 3 p. 75; 4 p. 184; 7 p. 245.

KNIGHT, John of Newbury. Hawk. Comm. M. May 10, 1779. Pard. for exchange Dec. 11, 1779. Escaped. G; 3 p. 138. (Probably could not wait for the exchange).

KNIGHT, Richard. Seaman. Susannah. Comm. F. June 27, 1781. SP; HO.

KNIGHT, Thos. Pard. for exchange Dec. 20, 1778. G.

KNODLE, Frederick. Seaman. Hercules. Sent from Kinsale to M. April 9, 1782. HO.

KNOWLES, James. Seaman. General Mifflin. Comm. F. Aug. 9, 1781. SP; HO.

KNOWLTON, KNOLTON or NOLTON, John of Newburyport. Cashr. of the Dalton. In hospital at Plymouth May, 1777. Escaped from hospital July 2, 1777. Re-captured on Black Prince. Comm. F. April 26, 1779. Pard. for exchange Nov. 9, 1781. G; 3 p. 74; 4 pp. 185, 305; 5A p. 39; 7 p. 243.

KNOWLTON, Thomas of Marblehead or Manchester. Hawk's prize. M. Pard. for exchange Dec. 11, 1779. G; 3 p. 136-7; 7 p. 252. (Probably same as next).

KNOWLTON, Thomas of Bridgewater. Twin Sisters. Comm. M. Jan. 9, 1782. HO. (Probably same as previous).

KNOX, Alexander. Seaman. Wexford. Captured but not comm. March 30, 1782. HO.

KNOX, Willm. Seaman. Lion. Comm. M. Aug. 31, 1781. SP; HO; 3 p. 211.

KUSE, William. M. Pard. for exchange Dec. 20, 1778. G.

KYZER, Thomas. See HYSER.

L

LA CACHAUX or CACHEUX, Francis or Francois. Sturdy Beggar. Comm. F. Jan. 23, 1778. Pard. for exchange May 31, 1779. G; 5A p. 37.

LACONTA, Lewis or Louis. Revenge. Comm. F. Aug. 11, 1777. Pard. for exchange May 31, 1779. G; 5A p. 37.

LADEN, John. F. Pard. for R.N. Dec. 13, 1778. G. (See LEADAN).

LADLEY, Adam of Scotland or England. Dalton. Comm. M. June, 1777. Escaped. 3 p. 74; 7 p. 246.

LAFDELL, Israel of Cape Pursue. Charming Polly. Captured May, 1777. Exchanged. 3 p. 75.

LAGEAR, Edward. See LASHIRE.

LAIRD, Wm. A letter in G. dated Sept. 2, 1782 states that he escaped from Plymouth and was impressed aboard the Nightingale (a British warship). Orders were given to return him to prison. Since there is no other mention of him, he probably escaped again.

LAKEMAN, Samuel. M. Pard. for exchange Dec. 11, 1779. G. (Same as LATHAM?)

LAMBARD, Samuel. M. Pard. for R.N. Oct. 30, 1781. G. (Same as Samuel LAMBERT of the Chatham and Simon LAMBERT?)

LAMBERT, Benjamin of Massachusetts. Rising States. F. Put in b.h. June 23, 1777. 5 p. 344 and note; 5A p. 36.

LAMBERT, John. Seaman. Daniel. Comm. F. Oct. 31, 1780. SP; HO.

LAMBERT or LAMBETH, Joseph. Warren. Comm. M. June, 1778. Pard. for exchange Dec. 11, 1779. G; HL; 3 p. 137; 7 p. 254.

LAMBERT, Samuel of Martha's Vineyard. Charming Sally or Polly. Captured Jan. 16, 1777. M. Pard. for exchange Dec. 20, 1778. Still there Feb. 7, 1779. G; 3 p. 75; 4 p. 307; 7 p. 248.

MARINERS OF THE AMERICAN REVOLUTION

LAMBERT, Sam'l. Chatham. Comm. M. Aug. 23, 1781. 3 p. 211. See Samuel LAMBARD.

LAMBERT, Samuel. Seaman. Antibriton. Imprisoned at Edinburgh Jan. 19, 1782. HO.

LAMBERT or LOMBART, Simon of Cape Cod. Chatham. Comm. M. Aug. 23, 1781. R.N. Oct. 16, 1781. 10 v. 74 pp. 43, 145. See Samuel LAMBARD.

LAMBERT, William. M. R.N. May 25, 1781. G. (See below).

LAMBERT, Wm. M. Pard. for exchange Dec. 11, 1779. (See below). G.

LAMBERT, Wm. M. Pard. for exchange Nov. 9, 1781. G. (Three separate men or all the same?)

LAMBETH, Jos. See LAMBERT.

LAMPRELL, Saml. F. Pard. for exchange Dec. 11, 1779. G.

LANDELL, John. Mate. Wexford. Captured but not comm. Oct. 2, 1781. HO.

LANDER, John of Salem. Warren. Comm. F. June, 1778. Pard. for exchange Dec. 11, 1779. G; 3 p. 137; 7 p. 254.

LANDER, John. Black Prince. Comm. F. April 26, 1779. 5A p. 39.

LANE, Caleb. Alfred. Comm. F. July 8, 1778. Escaped. 5A p. 38.

LANE, Charles. Mariner. Franklin. Comm. M. Dec. 6, 1781. SP; HO; 3 p. 212.

LANE, Dan'l. of New Gloucester. Dalton or Charming Polly. Sent to Royal hospital at Plymouth Feb. 15, 1777. Still there April, 1777. Escaped. 3 p. 75; 4 pp. 44, 184, 307; 7 p. 244.

LANE, Daniel. Comm. F. April 19, 1779. Pard. for exchange Dec. 11, 1779. G; 5A p. 39.

LANE, Daniel of Newburyport. Fancy. Comm. M. Aug. 7, 1777. Pard. for exchange Dec. 11, 1779. G; 3 p. 136; 7 p. 249.

LANE, Wm. of Philadelphia. Lexington's prize. Comm. M. June, 1777. Pard. for exchange Dec. 20, 1778. G; 3 p. 74; 7 p. 249.

LANGWORTHY or LONGWORTHY, John of Pennsylvania. Betsey. Comm. M. July 23, 1781. In b. h. Oct. 17, 1781. SP; HO; 3 p. 210; 10 v. 74 pp. 35, 145.

LANGWORTHY or LONGWORTHY, Jonathan. Seaman. Angelica. Comm. F. July 6 or 7, 1778. Pard. for R. N. May 25, 1781. Pard. for exchange Dec. 11, 1779. G; HO; 5A p. 38.

LANNIER, John. See LAUNIER.

LAPARA, Jos. Comm. F. July 15, 1777. Escaped. 5A p. 36.

LAPTHORN(E), John. America's prize. Comm. M. March 22, 1779. Pard. for exchange Dec. 11, 1779. Pard. for R. N. Nov. 4, 1780. Entered or escaped. G; 3 p. 138.

LARAMON, John Baptist of France. Mariana. Comm. M. July 28, 1779. 3 p. 138.

LARKEN or LARKINS, Peter. Comm. F. Oct. 20, 1778. Pard. for exchange Dec. 11, 1779. G; 5A p. 38.

LARKMAN, LARCOMB or LASCOMBE, Luke of England. Fancy. Comm. M. Aug. 7, 1777. Pard. for exchange Dec. 11, 1779. G; 3 p. 136; 7 p. 250.

LARKMAN, Saml. Fancy. Comm. M. Aug. 1777. Exchanged. 3 p. 136.

LASEDEL, Israel. See LEARSELL.

LASHIRE, LEGEAR or LAGEAR, Edward or Mr. Lieut. Hornet. Comm. F. Oct. 13, 1777. Escaped July 23, 1778. 5 v. 31 pp. 18, 20, 287; 5A p. 37.

LASKEY, Thomas. Boy. Hercules. Captured but not comm. Oct. 15, 1781. HO.

LASKEY, William of Marblehead.   Fancy.   Comm. M. Aug. 7, 1777. Pard. for exchange Dec. 11, 1779.   G; 3 p. 136; 7 p. 249.

LASSALL, George.   See LEASELLS.

LATHAM, Samuel of Ipswich.   Fancy.   Comm. M. Aug. 7, 1777.   7 p. 250.   (Same as LAKEMAN?)

LATTIMORE or LETIMORE, William.   Revenge.   Comm. M. Jan. 1781. In b. h. July 12, 1781.   Out of b. h. July 18.   Pard. for R. N. Sept. 10, 1781.   G; HL; 3 p. 140;   10 v. 74 pp. 32, 33.

LATTIMORE, Zachariah of Philadelphia.   Angelica.   Comm. F. July 7, 1778.   Died.   5A p. 38.

LAUGHTON or LEIGHTON, James of Swansey.   Twin Sisters.   Comm. M. Jan. 9, 1782.   HO; 3 p. 212.

LAUNDER, Jonathan.   M.   Pard. for exchange Dec. 11, 1779.   G.

LAUNIER or LANNIER, John.   F.   Pard. for R. N. May 28, 1781.   G.

LAUNIERERS? Joseph.   F.   Pard. for exchange Dec. 11, 1779.   G.

LAURENCE, William.   Seaman.   Fame.   Comm. M. Feb. 27, 1782.   HO.

LAURENS, Henry of South Carolina (appointed minister to Holland).   Put in Tower of London Sept. 10, 1780.   Exchanged for Lord Cornwallis in 1782.   Letters in G.   8 p. 126, 136.

LAWFORD, John.   Mariner.   Eliza, prize to the Grand Turk.   Comm. M. Jan. 3, 1782.   SP; HO.

LAWLEY, Stephen of Kittery.   Dalton.   Comm. M. June, 1777.   Pard. for exchange Dec. 20, 1778.   G; 7 p. 245.

LAWNY, James of Ireland.   Oliver Cromwell.   Comm. M. Oct. 18, 1777. 7 p. 255.

LAWRENCE, Henry of Virginia.   Lexington.   Comm. M. Sept. 19, 1777. Pard. for exchange Dec. 11, 1779.   G; 3 p. 137; 7 p. 253.

MARINERS OF THE AMERICAN REVOLUTION

LAWRENCE, James of Salem. Mariner. Dalton. Comm. M. June 21, 1777. Pard. for exchange Dec. 11, 1779. G; SP; HO; HL; 3 p. 74; 7 p. 246.

LAWRENCE, Joshua. Mariana. Comm. M. July 28, 1779. Pard. for R. N. Oct. 21, 1779. G; 3 p. 138.

LAWSON, Richard. Boy. Sturdy Beggar. Comm. F. Jan. 23, 1778. Pard. for exchange May 31, 1779. Exchanged July 2, 1779. Joined Bonhomme Richard. G; 5 v. 32 p. 286; 5A p. 37.

LAYCOCK, Daniel. Seaman. Polly. Comm. F. June 27, 1781. SP; HO.

LAYCOCK, Thomas. Seaman. Polly. Comm. F. June 27, 1781. SP; HO.

LAYDEN, John. See LEADAN.

LAYER, Jacob. Freedom. M. Escaped. 3 p. 75.

LAYWARD, Jonathan. Seaman. General Sullivan. Comm. F. April 26, 1779. SP.

LEA, James. F. Pard. for exchange May 31, 1779. G.

LEACH, John. See LEECH.

LEACH or LEECH, Jos. of Beverly. Comm. Pembroke 1778. Comm. M. Oct. 14, 1780. Pard. for R. N. May, 1781. Entered June 5, 1781. G; 3 p. 138; 10 v. 74 p. 22.

LEACH, Wm. of Maryland. Luzerne of Philadelphia. Comm. M. July 6, 1781. Pard. for R. N. July, 1781. Entered July 29. G; 3 p. 209; 10 v. 74 pp. 31, 37.

LEADAN or LAYDEN, John. Angelica of Boston. Comm. F. July 7, 1778. R N. Dec. 19, 1778. 5 v. 32 p. 282; 5A p. 38. (See LADEN).

LEAJOR, Isaac of Casco Bay. Dalton. Comm. M. June, 1777. 7 p. 246. (Possibly same as LEASON).

MARINERS OF THE AMERICAN REVOLUTION

LEARSELL or LASEDEL, Israel of Cape Porpoise.   Dalton.   Comm. M. June, 1777.   Pard. for exchange Dec. 20, 1778.   G; 7 p. 246.

LEASELLS or LASSALL, George of Salem.   Ascott and John.   Comm. M. July 9, 1781.   3 p. 209; 10 v. 74 p. 32.   (See LESSAL).

LEASON or LEESON, Isaac.   Dalton.   M.   Pard. for R. N. July 13, 1779. G; 3 p. 75.   (Possibly same as LEAJOR).

LE CRAW, William of Marblehead.   Captain.   Black Snake.   Comm. M. Aug. 1777.   Pard. for exchange Dec. 11, 1779.   Escaped.   G; (SEE   (See LUCRAN).

LEE, Abial.   Hawk's prize.   Comm. M. Oct. 16, 1777.   Exchanged. 3 p. 136; 7 p. 252.

LEE, Adam of Virginia, Jersey or Staten Island.   General St. Clair (Sinclair?) M.   Pard, for R. N. Nov. 26, 1781.   Entered Nov. 10.   G; HL; 10 v. 74 p. 151.

LEE, Andrew.   Seaman.   Jason.   Captured but not comm. Oct. 15, 1781. HO.

LEE, Asia.   M.   Pard. for exchange Dec. 11, 1779.   G.

LEE, Charles.   Hector of Philadelphia.   Comm. M. Jan. 9, 1781.   10 v. 73 p. 313.

LEE, James.   Prize master.   Montgomery.   Comm. F. Aug. 8, 1777. 5A p. 36.

LEE, James.   Seaman.   Pocahontas.   Comm. F. Nov. 18, 1780.   SP; HO.

LEE, John of Newburyport.   Captain.   Fancy.   Comm. M. Aug. 7 or 12, 1777.   Out of b. h. July 31, 1778.   Escaped Oct. 14, 1778.   Arrived in Bilboa Jan., 1779.   3 p. 136; 4 pp. 307, 396; 7 pp. 55, 56, 66, 74, 80, 100, 115, 143, 150, 158, 159, 164, 175, 217, 249.

LEE, John.   Seaman.   Wexford.   Captured but not comm. Oct. 2, 1781. HO.

LEE, Robert.   Seaman.   Harlequin.   Comm. F. Feb. 3, 1781.   SP; HO.

LEE, Thoms. of Marblehead. Franklin's prize. Comm. M. Oct. 2, 1781. 10 v. 74 p. 142.

LEE, Wm. of Ireland. Lexington. Comm. M. Sept. 19, 1777. Pard. for exchange Dec. 11, 1779. G; 3 p. 137; 7 p. 252.

LEECH, Benjamin of Manchester. Hawk's prize. Comm. M. Oct. 16, 1777. Pard. for exchange Dec. 11, 1779. G; 3 p. 136; 7 p. 252.

LEECH or LEACH, John. Seaman. Eagle. Comm. F. March 5, 1781. SP; HO.

LEECH, Joseph. See LEACH.

LEESON, Isaac. See LEASON.

LEGEAR, Edward. See LASHIRE.

LEGGETT, Thos. Commerce? Comm. F. Feb. 18, 1779. Escaped. 5A p. 39.

LE GROVE or LEGRO, Ebenezer the younger of Marblehead. Boy. General Glover. Comm. F. Oct. 18, 1779. SP; HO; 10 v. 73 p. 340.

LEIGHTON, James. See LAUGHTON.

LENNARD, Robert. Seaman. Wexford. Sent from Kinsale to M. April 9, 1782. HO.

LEO, Jeremiah. See LEV.

LEPEAR, Andrew. Midshipman. Lion. Comm. F. Aug. 2, 1781. SP.

LESSAL, George. Mariner. Ascott and John. Comm. M. July 7, 1781. SP; HO. (See LEASELLS).

LESTER, Elisha. Seaman. Happy return. Comm. F. June 27, 1781. SP; HO.

LETIMORE, Wm. See LATTIMORE.

LEV or LEO, Jeremiah. Seaman. Terrible. Comm. F. Aug. 9, 1781. SP; HO.

LEVELL, James. Black Prince. Comm. M. Oct. 20, 1781. 10 v. 74 p. 146.

LEVERETT or LIVERETT, (Dr.) Thomas. Surgeon. Protector. Comm. M. July 21, 1781. SP; HO; 3 p. 209; 10 v. 74 p. 34.

LEVERING, William. M. Pard. for R.N. Oct. 1781. G. Probably same as LOVERIN.

LEVING(S)TON(E), Saml. of Virginia. Mariner. Chatham. Comm. M. Aug. 23, 1781. SP; HO; 3 p. 211; 10 v. 74 p. 43.

LEWIS, David of Lynn. Essex. Comm. M. July 21, 1781. 3 p. 210; 10 v. 74 p. 34.

LEWIS, Edward of Philadelphia. Reprisal's prize. Comm. M. Aug., 1777. Pard. for R.N. Sept. 25, 1778. Entered or escaped. G; 3 p. 75; 7 p. 251.

LEWIS, Henry of New York. Mariner. Black Prince or Princess. Comm. M. Oct. 20, 1781. SP; HO; 3 p. 212; 10 v. 74 p. 146.

LEWIS, John. Mariner. Terrible. Comm. M. Dec. 23 or 25, 1780. SP; HO; HL; 3 p. 139.

LEWIS, John. Prize master. Hercules. Captured but not comm. Oct. 15, 1781. HO.

LEWIS, John. Seaman. Antibriton. Imprisoned at Edinburgh Jan. 19, 1782. HO.

LEWIS, Samuel of Boston. Sweet Lucretia. Comm. M. Oct. 16, 1778. Escaped. 3 p. 137; 7 p. 256.

LEWIS, Will of Kittery. Dalton or Charming Polly. Comm. M. June, 1777. Pard. for exchange Dec. 11, 1779. G; 3 p. 75; 4 p. 184. 7 p. 245.

LEWITT, Joshua. Carpenter. Portsmouth. Comm. F. June 27, 1781. SP.

LIBBEY, Ebenezer of Berwick, New Hampshire. Dalton or Charming Polly. Comm. M. June, 1777. Pard. for exchange Feb. 2, 1779. G; 3 p. 75; 7 p. 245.

MARINERS OF THE AMERICAN REVOLUTION

LILLIBRIDGE, Jonathan. The Swallow. Comm. F. Jan. 23, 1778. Pard. for exchange Dec. 11, 1779. G; 5A p. 37.

LINES, Thomas of England. Lexington. Comm. M. Sept. 19, 1777. R. N. 7 p. 253.

LINN, Charles. See LYNN.

LINN, Wm. of Sweden. Fancy. Comm. M. Aug. 1777. Exchanged. 3 p. 136. (Probably same as Wm. LIR).

LINNIKIN or LINEKIN, Benj. of Salem. Mariner. Jason. Comm. M. Dec. 16 or 18, 1779. SP; HO; 3 p. 138.

LIO, John of Marblehead. Fancy. Comm. M. Aug. 7, 1777. 3 p. 136; 7 p. 249.

LIR, William of Sweden or Ipswich. Fancy. Comm. M. Aug. 7, 1777. 7 p. 250. (Probably same as LINN).

LITTLE, Francis or Mr. of Newburyport. Dalton. Sent to hospital March 23, 1777. Still there in April. M. Escaped July 12, 1777, recaptured and in b.h. July 21, 1777. Pard. for exchange Dec. 26, 1778. 3 p. 74; 4 pp. 184, 188, 305, 306, 307, 395; 7 p. 243; G.

LITTLEHALE or LITTLEALE, Joseph. Comm. F. April 19, 1779. Pard. for R. N. Sept. 9, 1779. G; 5A p. 39.

LIVERETT, Thomas. See LEVERETT.

LIVINGSTON, Sam'l. See LEVING(S)TON(E).

LLOYDFORD or HOYDFORD, William. Seaman. Fair American. Comm. F. Nov. 30, 1780. SP.

LOCK, Reuben. Rising States. Comm. F. June 14, 1777. Pard. for exchange May 31, 1779. G; 5 v. 32 pp. 168, 286; 5A p. 36.

LOCKART or LOCKET, Benjamin of England. Lexington's prize. Comm. M. June, 1777. Pard. for R. N. Sept. 25, 1778. Entered or escaped. G; 3 p. 74; 7 p. 249.

LOCKHART, John. Seaman. Fair American. Comm. F. Nov. 30, 1780. SP.

LOCKHART, Thomas. Seaman. Fair American. Comm. F. Nov. 30, 1780. SP.

LOLLY, Stephen. Charming Polly or Dalton. Comm. M. May ? 1777. 3 p. 75.

LOMBART, Simon. See LAMBERT.

LOMAS, LOMIS or LUMMIS, George of Connecticut. Mariner. Industry. Comm. M. Nov. 18, 1780. SP; HO; HL; 3 p. 139.

LONGFELLOW, William of Ipswich. Fancy. Comm. M. Aug. 7, 1777. Pard. for exchange Dec. 11, 1779. G; 3 p. 136; 7 p. 250.

LONGWORTHY. See LANGWORTHY.

LORD, Ichabod of Berwick, New Hampshire. Dalton or Charming Polly. Comm. M. June, 1777. Pard. for exchange Dec. 20, 1778. Went with Paul Jones. G; 3 p. 75; 7 p. 245.

LORD, Jacob of Marblehead. Freedom's prize. Captured April 27, 1777. M. Escaped. 7 p. 251.

LORD, Moses. F. Pard. for R. N. Dec. 3, 1778. Entered Dec. 19. G; 5 v. 32 pp. 282-3.

LORIMAN, Bapta. Mariner. Marmy. Comm. M. July 3, 1779. Pard. for exchange Dec. 11, 1779. G; SP; HO.

LOTT, John of Martha's Vineyard, an Indian. Charming Sally or Polly. Captured Jan. 16, 1777. M. Died Dec. 15, 1778. 3 p. 75; 7 pp. 197, 248.

LOUGHBOROUGH, John. Seaman. Mercury. Comm. F. March 21, 1781. SP; HO.

LOUIS, David. Mariner. Essex. Comm. M. July 21, 1781. SP; HO.

LOV-, Thomas. F. Pard. for exchange Dec. 11, 1779. G. (Probably LOW, q. v.)

LOVATT or LOVERING, Nehemiah. Seaman. Adventure. Comm. M. Jan. 21, 1782. HO; 3 p. 213.

LOVELL or LOWELL, William. Commerce? Comm. F. Feb. 18, 1779. Pard. for R. N. June 17, 1779. G; 5A p. 39.

LOVERIN, Wm. of Boston. Pilgrim's prize. Comm. M. July 9, 1781. R. N. Aug. 23, 1781. 10 v. 74 pp. 32, 33, 43.

LOVERING, Nehemiah. See LOVATT.

LOVET, Benja. of Beverly. Essex. Comm. M. Aug. 25, 1781. 10 v. 74 p. 44.

LOVETT, James. 2nd lieut. Essex. Comm. M. Aug. 25, 1781. SP; HO; 3 p. 211.

LOVIS, Thomas of Marblehead. Boy. General Glover. Comm. F. Oct. 18, 1779. SP; HO; 10 v. 73 p. 340.

LOW, Asa. Seaman. Pilgrim or Oliver Cromwell. Comm. F. Aug. 7, 1779. Pard. for exchange Dec. 26, 1779. G; SP; HO.

LOW, Thos. Prize master. Comm. F. Feb. 18, 1779. 5A p. 39. See LOV.

LOW(E), Thos. Mariner. James and Rebecca, prize to the Franklin. Comm. M. Oct. 2, 1781. SP; HO; 3 p. 211.

LOWE, Daniel. Seaman. Two Brothers. Comm. M. Jan. 23, 1782. HO.

LOWELL, Wm. See LOVELL.

LOWING, Richard. Seaman. Huntingdon. Comm. F. May 24, 1781. SP; HO.

LOWRIE, James. Oliver Cromwell. Comm. M. May 17, 1777. Pard. for R. N. Sept. 25, 1778. Entered or escaped. G; 3 p. 75.

LOWREY, Robert. Seaman. Fame. Comm. F. Aug. 9, 1781. SP; HO.

LUCE, Elijah or Elisha. Captain. Comm. F. Oct. 20, 1778. Pard. for exchange Dec. 11, 1779. G; 5A p. 38.

LUCE, Jeremiah of Martha's Vineyard. Charming Salley or Polly. Captured Jan. 16, 1777. M. Still there Feb. 7, 1779. Pard. for exchange Dec. 11, 1779. G; 3 p. 75; 7 p. 248.

LUCE, Thomas of Martha's Vineyard. Charming Salley. Captured Jan. 16, 1777. M. Still there Feb. 7, 1779. Pard. for exchange Feb. 2, 1779. G; 7 p. 248.

LUCRAN, William of Marblehead. Captain. Black Snake. Comm. M. March 12, 1778. 7 p. 255. (See LECRAW).

LUMBER, Wm. of Cape Cod. Effingham. Comm. M. May 10, 1779. R. N. 3 p. 138; 10 v. 74 p. 22.

LUMMIS, George. See LOMAS.

LUNNER, Jos. A passenger. Comm. F. July 15, 1777. 5A p. 36.

LUNT, Cutting of Newburyport. Dalton. Comm. M. June, 1777. Pard. for exchange Dec. 20, 1778 and Dec. 11, 1779. Went with Paul Jones. G; 4 p. 187; 7 p. 243; 11 pp. 252-3.

LUNT, Daniel of Newburyport. Dalton. Comm. M. June 5, 1777. Escaped. 3 p. 74; 4 p. 187; 7 p. 243.

LUNT, Henry of Newburyport. Dalton. Comm. M. June, 1777. Escaped July 12, 1777. Re-captured July 25. Taken out b.h. Aug. 6, Pardoned for exchange Dec. 20, 1778. Went with Paul Jones. G; 3 p. 74; 4 pp. 187, 305, 306, 307, 395; 7 p. 243.

LUNT, Johnson. Rising States. F. 5A p. 36; 11 pp. 252-3.

LUNT, Joseph. Lieut. or seaman. Rising States. Comm. F. June 14, 1777. Pard. for exchange May 31, 1779. G; 5 v. 30 p. 345; 5A p. 36.

LUNT, Joshua. F. Pard. for exchange May 31, 1779. G.

LUNT, Richard of Newburyport. Dalton. Comm. M. June, 1777. Pard. for exchange Dec. 26, 1778. Joined Alliance. G; 3 p. 74; 4 p. 187; 7 p. 244.

LUTHER, Abner. Angelica. Comm. F. July 7, 1778. Pard. for exchange Dec. 11, 1779. G; 5A p. 38.

LUTHER, Amos. Angelica. Comm. F. July 7, 1778. Pard. for exchange Dec. 11, 1779. G; 5A p. 38. (Probably same as next).

LUTHER, Emos. Seaman. Thomas, a merchant ship. Captured but not comm. Oct. 23, 1781. HO. (Probably same as last).

LUTHER, Israel. Angelica. Comm. F. July 7, 1778. Pard. for exchange Dec. 11, 1779. Pard. for R. N. Nov. 6, 1780. G; 5A p. 38.

LYE, Robert. F. Pard. for R. N. Oct. 10, 1780. G.

LYNCH, George. M. Pard. for R. N. Sept. 10, 1781. G.

LYNN or LINN, Charles. Hector. Comm. M. Jan. 1781. Escaped July 12, 1781. HL; 3 p. 140; 10 v. 73 p. 328; v. 74 p. 32.

LYNE or LYON, Thomas. Lexington. Comm. M. Sept. 19, 1777. Pard. for R. N. Oct. 14, 1778. Entered or escaped. G; 3 p. 137.

LYON(S), James of Marblehead. Freedom's prize. Captured April 27, 1777. M. Pard. for exchange Feb. 2, 1779. G; 3 p. 75; 7 p. 250.

LYON(S), Robert. Sturdy Beggar. Comm. F. Jan. 23, 1778. Pard. for exchange May 31, 1779. Exchanged July 2, 1779. Joined Bonhomme Richard. G; 5 v. 32 p. 286; 5A p. 37.

M

MACARTY, Laurence. M. Pard. for R.N. April 28, 1781. G.

McCAFFREY, Matthew. Seaman. Fame. Comm. F. Aug. 9, 1781. SP; HO.

McCANN, Patrick of Ireland. Oliver Cromwell. Comm. M. Oct. 18, 1777. Pard. for R.N. July 13, 1779. G; 7 p. 255.

McCANNIGOAL, Benjamin. Seaman. Huntingdon. Comm. F. May 24, 1781. SP; HO.

McCARTNEY, Henry. Seaman. Essex. Comm. F. Dec. 4, 1780. SP; HO.

M'CARTY, Edwd. Captain. Black Prince or Princess. Comm. M. Oct. 28, 1781. Taken in irons to London Nov. 28, 1781 as they said he was not an American. 3 p. 212; 10 v. 74 pp. 147, 157.

McCLENNAN, John. Seaman. Hercules. Sent from Kinsale to M. April 9, 1782. HO.

McCLERRY or McCLEARY, Robert. Warren. Comm. M. June, 1778. Pard. for R.N. Sept. 25, 1778. Entered or escaped. G; 3 p. 137; 7 p. 255.

McCLEUER, William. Captain or mate. Morning Star. Comm. F. Aug. 9, 1781. SP; HO.

McCLOUGHLIN, McCOCKLIN or McLAUGHLIN, Philip of Ireland. Lexington. Comm. M. Sept. 19, 1777. Pard. for R.N. Oct. 14, 1778. Pard. for exchange Dec. 11, 1779. G; 3 p. 137; 7 p. 252.

McCLURE, James. See McLURE.

McCOCKLIN, Philip. See McCLOUGHLIN.

McCOLLOM, Allen. Seaman. Hetty. Comm. F. March 21, 1781. SP; HO.

McCOMBE, Josh. F. Pard. for R. N. Oct. 6, 1781. G.

McCORD or McCAUD, Patrick. Oliver Cromwell. Captured May 17, 1777. F. Pard. for R. N. March 27, 1781. G; 3 p. 75.

McCRAFFEE or McCOFFREY, John of Casco Bay. Dalton. Comm. M. June, 1777. Pard. for exchange Dec. 20, 1778. G; 7 p. 246.

McCRAY, Wm. Oliver Cromwell. Comm. F. Oct. 13, 1777. Pard. for exchange May 31, 1779. G; 5A p. 37.

McCULLOCK, Edward. Captain. Comm. F. April 15, 1778. Escaped. 5 p. 352; 5A p. 37.

McCULLOCK, William. Boy. Oliver Cromwell. Comm. F. Oct. 13, 1777. Pard. for exchange May 31, 1779. Exchanged July 2, 1779. Joined Bonhomme Richard. G; 5 v. 32 p. 286; 5A p. 37.

McDONALD(S), Wm. of Wenham. Essex. Comm. M. July 21, 1781. R. N. Aug. 18, 1781. 3 p. 210; 10 v. 74 pp. 34, 42.

MACE, Abraham. Alfred. Comm. F. July 18, 1778. Pard. for exchange Dec. 11, 1779. Pard. for R. N. Nov. 6, 1780. G; 5A p. 38.

McELENNY or M'CLANY, Willm. Soldier taken in South Carolina. Beaver? Comm. M. Sept. 1, 1781. SP; HO; 3 p. 211.

McGRAW, Edward. Angelica. Comm. F. July 7, 1778. Pard. for exchange Dec. 11, 1779. G; 5A p. 38.

McGRAW, Moses of Boston. Essex. Comm. M. July 21, 1781. Pard. for R. N. Aug. 9, 1781. G; 3 p. 210; 10 v. 74 p. 34.

MACGUIRE, Loughlan. F. Pard. for exchange Dec. 11, 1779. G.

McINHAM, Nich. Viper. Comm. M. Dec. 7, 1781. 3 p. 212.

MACK, Thomas of Marblehead. Fancy. Comm. M. Aug. 7, 1777. Escaped. 7 p. 249.

McKENNY, James of Philadelphia. Lion. Comm. M. Aug. 31, 1781. Pard. for R. N. Sept. 29, 1781. G; 3 p. 211.

McKENNIE or McKINNEY, Thos. of Massachusetts. Comm. F. Oct. 13, 1777. Pard. for exchange May 31, 1779. G; 5A p. 37.

McKOWN or McKOWL, Robert. Born in Boston and lives in Norwich. Master. Hibernia of Connecticut. Comm. M. March 31, 1781. SP; HO; 3 p. 141; 10 v. 73 p. 331. (Probably same as MIKOWN).

McLAIN or McLEAN, Alen or Alexander of Boston. Essex. Comm. M. July 20, 1781. Pard. for R. N. Oct. 30, 1781. Entered Oct. 17, G; 3 p. 210; 10 v. 74 pp. 34, 145.

McLAIN or McLEAN, Hector. Angelica. Comm. F. July 7, 1778. Pard. for exchange Dec. 11, 1779 and Oct. 16, 1781. G; 5A p. 38.

McLAMER or McLEMER, Michael. Tom Lee. Comm. M. May 5, 1781. Escaped. 3 p. 141; 10 v. 74 p. 30.

M'CLANY. See McELENNY.

McLAUGHLIN, Philip. See McCLOUGHLIN.

McLENNAN, Michael of Maryland. Tom Lee. Comm. M. May 1, 1781. 10 v. 73 p. 339.

McLEVER, Robert. Prize master. Reprisal. Comm. F. Aug. 9, 1777. Escaped. 5A p. 37.

McLURE, James. Seaman. Tom Lee. Comm. F. Aug. 9, 1781. SP; HO.

McMAHON, James. F. Pard. for exchange May 31, 1779. G.

McMEKEN, James. Boy. Montgomery. Comm. F. Aug. 8, 1777. Exchanged July 2, 1779. Joined Bonhomme Richard. 5 v. 32 p. 286; 5A p. 36.

McMELLEN, Collen of Pennsylvania. Lion. Comm. M. Aug. 31, 1781. 3 p. 211. (Probably same as Colin MILLAN).

McMULLEN or McMULLING, Joseph of Ireland or England. Reprisal's prize. Comm. M. June 29, 1777. Pard. for exchange Dec. 11, 1779. G; 3 p. 75; 7 p. 251.

MARINERS OF THE AMERICAN REVOLUTION

McMULLAN or McMILLAN, Wm. Mariner. L'Uzerne of Philadelphia.
   Comm. M. July 7, 1781. SP; HO; 3 p. 209; 10 v. 74 p. 31.

McNAMARA or McNAIRS, Michel or Nicholas. Mariner. Viper. Comm.
   M. Dec. 7, 1781. SP; HO; HL.

McNAIRS, Nicholas. See McNAMARA.

McNEAL or McNIEL, Arch. of Charleston, South Carolina. In Pembroke
   1778. Comm. M. Oct. 14, 1780. Pard. for exchange with Manley,
   Talbot and 6 others Oct. 16, 1781. G; HL; 3 p. 139; 10 v. 74 p. 47.

McNEAL, Capt. of the Genl. Whipples? Letter in G. states: "He is about
   5'6" or 7", pock marked with the small pox and has a long nose".

McNICKLE, Archibald. Doctor. Muscetor (Mosquito?) Comm. F. Aug.
   8, 1777. Escaped. 5A p. 36.

MACON, William. See MASON.

MADDEN, MADDIN or MADDON, John of Block Point. Dalton or Charming
   Polly. Comm. M. June, 1777. Pard. for exchange Dec. 20, 1778.
   Went with Paul Jones. G; 3 p. 55; 7 p. 246.

MADDOCKS, Caleb. Seaman. Portsmouth. Comm. F. June 27, 1781.
   SP; HO.

MADDOX, William. M. Pard. for R. N. May 25, 1781. G.

MADDY, Willm. of Philadelphia. Medley of North Carolina. Comm. M.
   May 5 or 11, 1781. R. N. June 2, 1781. 10 v. 73 p. 340, 347.

MAGEE, Paul of Rhode Island. Cabot. Comm. M. June, 1777. 7 p. 256.

MAGERY, MAJORY or MARGERY, Joseph of Marblehead. Freedom's prize.
   Comm. M. April 27, 1777. Pard. for exchange Dec. 20, 1778. G;
   3 p. 75; 7 p. 251.

MAHONY, Silvester. Seaman. French Bermuda. Comm. M. Jan. 9,
   1782. HO.

MAHONY or MEHANEY, Thos. of Kittery. Dalton or Charming Polly.
   In hospital April, 1777. Comm. M. June, 1777. Pard. for exchange
   Dec. 20, 1778. Went with Paul Jones. G; 3 p. 75; 4 p. 184; 7 p. 245.

MARINERS OF THE AMERICAN REVOLUTION

MAHONEY or MAHANEY, Thomas. F. Pard. for exchange Dec. 11, 1779. G.

MAIN, William. Boy or seaman. Terrible. Comm. F. Feb. 3, 1781. SP; HO.

MAINS, Tapley. Seaman. Pocahontas. Comm. F. Nov. 18, 1780. SP; HO.

MAJOR(Y), Jonathan of Salem. Harlequin. Comm. M. Dec. 24, 1780. Pard. for R. N. May 11, 1781. Entered June 5. G; 10 v. 74 p. 22.

MAJORY, Joseph. See MAGERY.

MAJOR(Y), Thomas of Salem. Warren. Comm. M. June, 1778. Pard. for exchange Dec. 11, 1779 and Nov. 9, 1781. G; 7 p. 254.

MALEY, Thomas. N. Pard. for R. N. Sept. 25, 1778. G.

MALL, Jacob. M. Pard. for R. N. Nov. 4, 1780. G.

MALONEY, Jonathan. F. Pard. for exchange Dec. 11, 1779. G.

MALONEY, Michael. Seaman. Wexford. In M. but not comm. Oct. 2, 1781. HO.

MALOON, Timothy of Boston. Essex. Comm. M. July 21 or 24, 1781. 3 p. 210; 10 v. 74 p. 35.

MALTON or MOLTON, Barthy or Bartholomew of Danvers, Massachusetts. Ascott and John. Comm. M. July 7, 1781. SP; HO; 10 v. 74 p. 31.

MANCHESTER, Danl. Angelica. Comm. F. July 7, 1778. Pard. for exchange Dec. 11, 1779. G; 5A p. 38.

MANCHESTER, Thaddeus or Thades. The Swallow. Comm. F. Jan. 23, 1778. Pard. for exchange May 31, 1779. G; 5A p. 37.

MANFIELD, Gideon. See HENFIELD.

MANION, Gabriel. Seaman. Jason. Captured but not comm. Oct. 15, 1781. HO.

MANLEY, John. Captain. Jason. Comm. M. Dec. 16, 1779. Att. escapes May 11, 1780, April 21, April 24, May 8, May 31, July 31, Sept. 13, 1781. Out of b.h. Sept. 19, 1781. Pard. for exchange Oct. 16, 1781. G; 3 p. 138; 7 p. 53; 8 pp. 121, 122, 124, 125, 128, 129, 131; 10 v. 73 pp. 319, 335, 337, 341; v. 74 pp. 24, 30, 33, 37, 40, 44, 45, 46, 47, 143. (Capt. Manley was exchanged in place of one prisoner who had escaped, when it was requested that eight American prisoners should be exchanged for Mr. Dillon and seven others. His numerous attempts to escape should have sent him to the bottom of the exchange list but he seems to have been treated with indulgence as there is only one mention of the b.h. and that only for six days. For other adventures see bibliography No. 17 and introduction to No. 8.

MANNING, Edward. Rising States. Comm. F. June 14, 1777. Escaped and re-captured March 7, 1778. Escaped March 8. Re-captured and put in b.h. April 20, 1778. Out of b.h. May 7. Pard. for exchange May 31, 1779. G; 5 v. 30 pp. 348-9, 351-2; v. 31 pp. 18, 19, 20. 5A p. 36.

MANNING, James of Salem. Brig Polly. Comm. M. Sept. 10, 1780. 3 p. 139.

MANNING, John. Mariner. Beaver. Comm. M. Sept. 1, 1781. SP; HO; 3 p. 211.

MANNING, Thomas of Salem. Warren. Comm. M. June, 1778. Died. 3 p. 137; 7 p. 254.

MARBLE, Benjamin. Seaman. Twin Sisters. Comm. M. Jan. 9, 1782. HO.

MARGERY, Joseph. See MAGERY.

MARGAN, Andrew. See MORGAN.

MARIENE. Hannable of Newbury. Comm. M. Jan. 9, 1781. 10 v. 73 p. 313.

MARKHAM, James. Mariner. Taken at South Carolina? Essex. Comm. M. Aug. 31, 1781. SP; HO; 3 p. 211.

MARLEY or MARLIN, Thomas of Ireland. Lexington. Comm. M. Sept. 19, 1777. R.N. or escaped. 3 p. 137; 7 p. 253.

MARSH, John. Seaman. Fearnought. Comm. M. March 26, 1782. HO.

MARSHALL or MERSHALL, John of Plymouth. Mariner. Beaver or Dennis. Comm. M. July 28, 1781. SP; HO; 3 p. 211; 10 v. 74 p. 36.

MARSHALL, Joseph. Mariner. Essex. Comm. M. July 27, 1781. SP; HO; 3 p. 210

MARSHALL or MARSHELL, Josiah of Baltimore. Tom Lee. Comm. M. May 1, 1781. Pard. for R. N. May, 1781. Entered June 5. G; 3 p. 141; 10 v. 73 p. 338; v. 74 p. 22.

MARSHALL, Nathaniel of Portsmouth. Dalton or Charming Polly. Comm. M. June, 1777. Pard. for exchange Dec. 29, 1778. G; 3 p. 75; 7 p. 244.

MA(R)STON, Benjamin of Marblehead. Fancy. Comm. M. Aug. 7, 1777. Pard. for exchange Dec. 11, 1779. G; 3 p. 136; 7 p. 250.

MARTIN, Isaac. Seaman. Jason. Captured but not comm. Oct. 15, 1781. HO.

MARTIN, John of England. Captain. Mosquito. M. R. N. 7 p. 256.

MARTIN, John. Mariner. L'Uzerne of Philadelphia. Comm. M. July 6, 1781. SP; HO; 3 p. 209; 10 v. 74 p. 31.

MARTIN, Josiah or Mr. Rising States. Comm. F. June 14, 1777. In b. h. June 23, 1777. Out of hospital Sept. 9, 1778. Pard. for exchange May 31, 1779. G; 5 v. 30 pp. 177, 344; v. 32 p. 165; 5A p. 32.

MARTIN, Thomas of Marblehead. Hannible of Newbury. Comm. M. Jan. 18, 1781. Died Sept. 27, 1781. HL; 3 p. 140; 10 v. 73 p. 313; v. 74 pp. 74, 149.

MARTION, Wm. of Maryland. Betsey. Comm. M. July 23, 1781. 3 p. 210; 10 v. 74 p. 35.

MARVEL, Benj. Twin Sisters. Comm. M. June 11, 1781. 3 p. 212.

MASHBURY, Thos. Warren. Comm. M. June 4, 1778. Exchanged. 3 p. 137.

MARINERS OF THE AMERICAN REVOLUTION

MASKELL, Street.   M.   R.N.

MASKFIELD, Wm.   Charming Polly.   Captured May, 1777.   M.   Escaped.   3 p. 75.

MASON, David.   F.   Pard. for exchange Dec. 11, 1779.   G.

MASON, Joseph.   Black Prince.   Comm. F. April 26, 1779.   Pard. for exchange Dec. 11, 1779.   G; 5A p. 39.

MASON or MACON, William of Maryland.   Mariner.   Franklin.   Comm. M. Dec. 6, 1781.   SP; HO; 3 p. 212.

MASSEY, Alexander.   Mariner.   Franklin.   Comm. M. Dec. 6, 1781. SP; HO.

MASSEY, Peter.   M.   HL.   Same as MERCEY or MERRY?

MATTHEWMAN, Luke.   Lieut.   F.   Escaped.   12.

MATHEWS, Joseph.   Mariner.   L'Uzerne of Philadelphia.   Comm. M. July 6, 1781.   SP; HO; 10 v. 74 p. 31.

MATTHIAS or MATHEWS, William of Salem.   Mariner.   Ascot and John. Comm. M. July 23, 1781.   In b. h. Nov. 7, 1781.   Out of b. h. Nov. 19.   SP; HO; 3 p. 210; 10 v. 74 pp. 35, 150, 154.

MATTHEWS, Israel of England.   Fancy.   Comm. M. Aug. 7, 1777.   Escaped.   3 p. 136; 7 p. 250.

MAXWELL, John.   Seaman.   Confederacy.   Comm. M. Feb. 27, 1782. HO.

MAXWELL, William of Block Point.   Dalton.   Comm. M. June, 1777. Pard. for exchange Dec. 20, 1778.   7 p. 246; G.

MAXWELL, Wm.   Commerce?   Comm. F. Feb. 18, 1779.   Pard. for exchange Dec. 11, 1779.   G; 5A p. 39.

MAYES, Paul.   M.   Pard. for exchange Dec. 11, 1779.   G.

MAYO.   M.   8 p. 130; 10 v. 73 p. 338.

MARINERS OF THE AMERICAN REVOLUTION

MAY(O), Edmon. or Edmd. of Cape Cod.   Mariner.   Minerva or Mulbury or Marlborough.   Comm. M. Aug. 23, 1780.   In hospital May 10, 1781.   SP; HO; 3 p. 139; 10 v. 73 p. 341.

MAYO, Gideon.   Seaman.   Hercules.   Captured but not comm. Oct. 15, 1781.   HO.

MAYO, Thomas.   Seaman.   Hercules.   Captured but not comm. Oct. 15, 1781.   HO.

MEAD(S), Joseph.   General Sullivan's prize.   Comm. M. July 3, 1779.   Pard. for exchange Dec. 11, 1779. and Nov. 9, 1781.   G; 3 p. 138.

MEAGE, Paul of Rhode Island.   Cabot.   Comm. M. June, 1777.   Exchanged.   3 p. 74.

MEARS, Daniel.   Seaman.   Wexford.   Sent from Kinsale to M. April 9, 1782.   HO.

MEDIA, James.   Seaman.   Hercules.   Sent from Kinsale to M. April 9, 1782.   HO.

MEEK, Thomas.   Fancy.   Comm. M. Aug. 7, 1777.   Escaped.   3 p. 136.

MEHANEY, Thomas.   See MAHONEY.

MELBERRY, William.   Seaman.   Hercules.   Captured but not comm. Oct. 15, 1781.   HO.

MELLUS, Henry.   See MULLUS.

MERCHANT, Cornelius.   Quar. Mastr.   Hercules.   Captured but not comm. Oct. 15, 1781.   HO.

MERCY, Alex of Maryland?   Franklin of Philadelphia.   Comm. M. Nov. 1781.   3 p. 212.

MERCEY or MERRY, Peter of Philadelphia.   Mariner.   Warren.   Comm. M. June 9, 1778.   In b. h. May 27, 1781.   Out of b. h. June 3.   Pard. for exchange Dec. 11, 1779.   SP; HO; 3 p. 137; 7 p. 255; 10 v. 73 p. 345; v. 74 p. 22; G.   (See also Peter MASSEY).

MARINERS OF THE AMERICAN REVOLUTION

MERRIDIFF, John. Captain. (Philadelphia). Comm. F. April 2, 1778. Escaped. 5A p. 37.

MERRILL, Moses of Newburyport. Dalton. Comm. M. June, 1777. Exchanged. 3 p. 74; 7 p. 244.

MERRITT, Samuel. Seaman. Susannah or Harlequin. Comm. F. June 27, 1781. SP; HO.

MERRY, Peter. See MERCEY.

MERRY, Wm. See MURRY.

MERSHALL, John. See MARSHALL.

MESERVE(Y), Amos. P. M. Mate. Franklin. Comm. F. Feb. 18, 1779. Pard. for exchange Dec. 11, 1779. G; 5A p. 38.

MESERVEY, Francis. America's prize. Comm. M. March 22, 1779. Escaped. 3 p. 138.

MESERVEY, Philip of Marblehead. Sturdy Beggar. Comm. M. June, 1777. 3 p. 74.

METER, Peter of Danvers. Essex. Comm. M. July 25, 1781. Died Aug. 27, 1781. 10 v. 74 pp. 36, 44.

MICHEL. See also MITCHELL.

MICHELL or MITCHEER, Philip of Maryland. Mariner. Franklin. Comm. M. Dec. 6, 1781. SP; HO; 3 p. 212.

MICHEL, Samuel. Satisfaction. Comm. F. July 27, 1778. 5A p. 38.

MICHEL, Wm. Satisfaction. Comm. F. July 27, 1778. Pard. for exchange Dec. 11, 1779. G; 5A p. 38.

MIDDLETON, William. Captain. Dolphin. Comm. F. May 24, 1781. SP.

MIKOWN, Robert. M. HL. See McKOWN.

MILES, George.   F.   Pard, for R. N. Nov. 22, 1780.   G.

MILES, Levi of Newburyport.   Little Porgy.   Comm. M. Jan. 3, 1782. 3 p. 213.

MILES, Willm.   Mariner.   Lion.   Comm. M. Aug. 31, 1781.   SP; HO; 3 p. 211.

MILLAN, Colin.   Mariner.   Lion.   Comm. M. Aug. 31, 1781.   SP; HO. See McMELLEN.

MILLARD, Nathaniel.   Soldier.   Taken on shore.   Comm. M. Feb. 6, 1782.   HO.

MILLEE, Francis.   Revenge.   Comm. F. Aug. 11, 1777.   Escaped. 5A p. 37.

MILLER, Nathl. of Long Island.   Mariner.   Industry.   Comm. M. Nov. 18, 1780.   SP; HO; HL; 3 p. 139.

MILLER, Patrick of Portsmouth.   Mariner.   Marquis de Morbec.   Comm. M. Oct. 2, 1781.   SP; HO; 3 p. 211; 10 v. 74 p. 142.

MILLER, Richey of Philadelphia.   Jolly Tar.   Comm. M. Oct. 1780. 3 p. 139.

MILLER, Reily.   M.   Pard. for R. N. Nov. 4, 1780.   G.

MILLER, Robert.   Seaman.   Hercules.   Captured but not comr'. Oct. 15, 1781.   HO.

MILLER, Thomas.   Seaman.   Wexford.   Sent from Kinsale to M. April 9, 1782.   HO.

MILLER, Wm. of Boston.   Essex.   Comm. M. Aug. 25, 1781.   Pard. for R. N. Oct 30, 1781.   Entered Oct. 17.   G; 3 p. 211; 10 v. 74 pp. 44, 145.

MILLES, Leviah.   Mariner.   Little Pegey.   Comm. M. Jan. 3, 1782. SP; HO.

MILLETT, Thomas.   F.   Pard. for exchange Dec. 11, 1779.   G.

MILLIGAN, William.   Angelica.   Comm. F. July 7, 1778.   Pard. for R. N. Dec. 3, 1778 and Dec. 16, 1778.   G; 5A p. 38.

MILTON or NULTON, Benjamin.   F.   Pard. for exchange Dec. 11, 1779. G.

MILTON, John.   Seaman.   Wexford.   Sent from Kinsale to M. April 9, 1782   HO.

MILVANNY, Thos.   F.   Pard. for exchange Dec. 11, 1779.   G.

MINER, Nathnal of New London.   Chatham.   Comm. M. Aug. 23, 1781. 3 p. 211; 10 v. 74 p. 43.

MINSEY, Thos.   Angelica.   Comm. F. July 7, 1778.   Pard. for exchange Dec. 11, 1778 and Oct. 16, 1781.   G; 5A p. 38.

MIRICK or MYRICK, Joseph of Nantucket.   Captain.   American Union. Comm. M. Sept. 19, 1780.   Pard. for R. N. Sept. 10, 1781.   G; HL; 3 p. 139.

MISSEROY, Philip of Marblehead.   Sturdy Beggar.   Comm. M. June, 1777. 7 p. 257.

MITCHELL, George.   Adventure.   Comm. M. March 31, 1781.   Out of b. h. June, 6, 1781.   Escaped.   3 p. 140; 10 v. 73 p. 331; v. 74 p. 23.

MI(T)CHELL, George of Pennsylvania.   Commander.   Friendsgoodwill. Comm. M. July 23, 1781.   Att. escape April 21, 1781.and May 27, 1781.   Pard. for R. N. Sept. 10, 1781.   G; SP; HO; 10 v. 73 pp. 345, 355; v. 74 pp. 35, 45.

MITCHELL, Gregory.   F.   Pard. for R. N. Jan. 12, 1781.   C.

MITCHELL, James.   Seaman.   Hercules.   Sent from Kinsale to M. April 9, 1782.   HO.

MITCHEL(L), Robert.   Steward.   Hercules.   Captured but not comm. March 30, 1782.   HO.

MITCHELL, Samuel.   F.   Pard. for exchange Dec. 11, 1779.   G.

MARINERS OF THE AMERICAN REVOLUTION

MITCHELL, Thomas. M. Pard. for R.N. April 28, 1781. G.

MI(T)CHELL, Willm. Mariner. Venus. Comm. M. Nov. 21, 1781. SP; HO; 3 p. 212; 10 v. 74 p. 155.

MOLINEAUX or MOURLYNEAUX or MOLENON, Fredk. Mariner. Comet. of Philadelphia. Comm. M. Jan. 6, 1781. SP; HO; HL; 3 p. 140; 10 v. 73 p. 312.

MOLONE, Timothy. Mariner. Essex. Comm. M. July 24, 1781. SP; HO.

MONGO, Peter. Revenge. Comm. F. Aug. 11, 1777. 5A p. 37. (Same as below?)

MONGOME, Pierre. F. Pard. for exchange May 31, 1779. G. (Same as above?)

MONSTONE, William. Seaman. Mercury. Comm. M. Feb. 7, 1782. HO.

MONTGOMERY, Allen. Seaman. Morning Star. Comm. F. Aug. 9, 1781. SP; HO.

MONTGOMERY, Andrew. F. Pard. for R.N. Nov. 22, 1780. G.

MOORE, Alexander. Midshipman or prizemaster. Muscator (Mosquito?) of Virginia. Comm. F. Aug. 8, 1777. Pard. for exchange May 31, 1779. G; 5 v. 32 p. 286; 5A p. 36.

MOORE, Benj. of Kittery. Mariner. Venus. Comm. M. Nov. 21, 1781. SP; HO; 3 p. 212; 9 pp. 80, 89; 10 v. 74 p. 155.

MOORE, Francis. M. Pard. for R.N. April 28, 1781. G.

MOORE, George. Mariner. L'Uzerne of Philadelphia. Comm. M. July 7, 1781. SP; HO; 3 p. 209; 10 v. 74 p. 31.

MOORE, Isaac. Seaman. Bermuda. Comm. M. Jan. 22, 1782. HO.

MOORE, John. Seaman. Fair American. Comm. F. Nov. 30, 1780. SP; HO.

MARINERS OF THE AMERICAN REVOLUTION

MOORE, Ralph. Captain. Comm. F. April 2, 1778. Escaped. 5A p. 37.

MOORE, William. Seaman. Monmouth. Comm. F. Dec. 30, 1779. SP.

MOORE, Woodman. Mate. Hercules. Captured but not comm. Oct. 15, 1781. HO.

MOORHEAD, Samuel. Seaman. Hercules. Captured but not comm. Oct. 15, 1781. HO.

MOOTRY, James. Oliver Cromwell. Comm. F. Oct. 13, 1777. Escaped. 5A p. 37.

MORANN, Wm. Lieut. Hornet. Comm. F. Oct. 13, 1777. Escaped. 5A p. 37.

MORGAN, Andrew. Seaman. Disdain. Comm. M. Jan. 9, 1782. HO; 3 p. 213.

MORGAN, Benjamin. Seaman. Rambler. Comm. F. Dec. 30, 1779. SP.

MORGAN, George. Seaman. South Quay. Comm. F. March 21, 1781. SP; HO.

MORRIS, Mr. Capt. Burnell's Lieut. Sent to hospital at Plymouth July 17, 1777. 4 pp. 306, 307. (Probably Wm.)

MORRIS, Unathan or Elnathan. Mariner. Chatham. Comm. M. Aug. 23, 1781. SP; HO.

MORRIS, Malachi. See NORRIS.

MORRIS, William of England. (Nephew of Benjamin West, celebrated artist in London). Mosquito. M. Escaped Oct. 26, 1777. 4 p. 397; 7 pp. 70, 256. (See also MORRIS, Mr.)

MORRISON, George of Scotland or Maryland. Lexington. Comm. M. Sept. 19, 1777. Escaped. 3 p. 137; 7 p. 253.

MORRISON, John of Boston. Mariner. Essex. Comm. M. July 20, 1781. SP; HO; 3 p. 210; 10 v. 74 p. 34. (Probably same as NORRISON).

MORRISON, John. Mariner. Medley. Comm. M. July 21, 1781. SP; HO.

MORRISON, Jonathan. Surgeon. Civil Usage. Comm. M. Feb. 7, 1782. HO.

MORROW, William. M. HL. (Perhaps same as MURRY).

MORSLANDER, Zeneus. Seaman. Daniel. Comm. F. Oct. 31, 1780. SP; HO.

MORTON, James. L'Uzerne. Comm. M. July 6, 1781. 3 p. 209.

MORTON, Thomas. Seaman. Fair American. Comm. F. Nov. 18, 1780. SP.

MORTON, William. Seaman. Fort Stanwin. Comm. F. April 7, 1780. SP; HO.

MORTON, William. M. Pard. for R. N. Sept. 29, 1781. G.

MOUGHAN, George. Seaman. Pocahontas. Comm. F. Nov. 18, 1780. SP; HO.

MOULTON, Barth. of Danvers. Ascot and John. Comm. M. July 7, 1781. 3 p. 209.

MOULTON, Job. Seaman. Wexford. Sent from Kinsale to M. April 9, 1782. HO.

MOURLYNEAUX, Fredk. See MOLINEUX.

MUFFIN, Lambeth. See MURPHY.

MULL or MULE, William of Baltimore. Mariner. Duke of Leinster or General Nash. Comm. M. May 4, 1781. Innoculated May 28, 1781. SP; HO; 3 p. 141; 10 v. 73 p. 346.

MULLIGAN, Francis. P.M.'s mate. Revenge. Comm. F. Aug. 11, 1777. Escaped. 5A p. 37.

MULLIN, James. Reprisal. Comm. F. Aug. 9, 1777. Pard. for exchange May 31, 1779. G; 5A p. 37.

MARINERS OF THE AMERICAN REVOLUTION

MULLUS or MELLUS, Henry.   3rd lieut or mariner.   Lion.   Comm. M. Aug. 31, 1781.   SP; HO; 3 p. 211.

MUNNION, James.   See MUNSEN.

MUNRO(E), William.   Angelica.   Comm. F. July 7, 1778.   Pard. for exchange Dec. 11, 1779.   G; 5A p. 38.

MUNSEN or MUNNION, James.   Mariner.   Charming Polly.   Comm. M. Sept. 19, 1780.   SP; HO.

MURFEY, Lamberth.   See MURPHY.

MURISON, Hathcoat.   Capt. Marines.   Angelica.   Comm. F. July 7, 1778.   Escaped.   5A p. 38.

MURPH(E)Y, John of Rhode Island.   Captain.   The Swallow of Rhode Island.   Comm. F. Jan. 23, 1778.   Escaped July 23, 1778.   5 v. 30 p. 348; v. 31 pp. 20, 287; 5A p. 37.

MURPHY, Lambeth or Lambirth.   F.   Pard. for exchange Dec. 11, 1779.   G.   (See also below).

MURPHY, MURFEY, MUFFIN, GRIFFIN, Lambeth.   M.   Pard. for R. N. Aug. 30, 1781.   Entered Aug. 18, 1781.   G; HL; 10 v. 74 p. 42. (See above and also MUSSEY).

MURPHY, Peter.   Seaman.   Roebuck.   Comm. M. Jan. 25, 1782.   HO.

MURPH(E)Y, William.   Boy.   Montgomery.   Comm. F. Aug. 8, 1777.   Exchanged July 2, 1779.   Joined Bonhomme Richard.   G; 5 v. 32 p. 286; 5A p. 36.

MURRAY, John.   Seaman.   Jack.   Comm. F. June 27, 1781.   SP; HO.

MURRAY, John.   Mariner.   Franklin.   Comm. M. Dec. 6, 1781.   SP; HO; 3 p. 212.

MURRY, MURRAY, MERRY, William of Philadelphia.   Washington.   Comm. M. Jan. 9, 1781.   In b. h. July 6, 1781.   Pard. for R. N. Sept. 10, 1781.   G; 3 p. 140; 10 v. 73 p. 313; v. 74 p. 31.

MURREY, James of Ireland. Alliance. Comm. M. Oct. 9, 1781. Pard. for R.N. Nov. 9, 1781. Entered Oct. 25, 1781. G; 3 p. 211; 10 v. 74 pp. 143, 147.

MURRY, John. Montgomery of Philadelphia. Comm. F. Aug. 8, 1777. Pard. for R.N. Dec. 3, 1778. Entered Dec. 19, 1778. G; 5 v. 32 pp. 282-3; 5A p. 36.

MUSSEY, Lambert of Marblehead. Duke de Coigny. Comm. M. July 17, 1780. R.N. 3 p. 139. (Probably same as MURPHY).

MYRICK, Joseph. See MIRICK.

N

NAGERS, Bennet. See NEGUS.

NAGLE, Richard. M. Pard. for R.N. Nov. 22, 1780. G.

NAPP, Peter. Boy. General Glover. Comm. F. Nov. 30, 1779. SP; HO.

NASH, Samuel. Charming Polly. M. Pard. for exchange Dec. 20, 1778. G; 3 p. 75.

NAZRO, or NEAZRO, Nathl. of Boston. Mariner. Hannable of Newbury. Comm. M. Jan. 9 or 18, 1781. Att. excape April 27. Out of b.h. June 6. In b.h. Nov. 9. Att. escape Nov. 16. Out of b.h. Nov.19. SP; HO; HL; 3 p.140. 10 v. 73 pp. 313, 345; v. 74 pp. 23, 150, 154.

NEAGLE, Mr. M. In b.h. April 9, 1780. 8 p. 125. (Probably same as next).

NEAGLES, Richard. America's prize. Comm. M. March 22, 1779. Escaped. 3 p. 138. (Probably same as last).

NEAL, Alex. See KNELL.

NEAL, Archibald. Mariner. Franklin. Comm. M. Oct. 17, 1780. SP; HO.

NEAL, Charles. Reprisal's prize. Comm. M. August, 1777. Escaped. 3 p. 75. (Probably same as Neill).

NEAL, David. Mariner. General Nash or Ann. Comm. M. July 28, 1781. SP; HO.

NEAL, Henry. Mariner. Eliza, prize to the Grand Turk. Comm. M. Jan. 3, 1782. SP; HO; 3 p. 213.

NEAL, Robert of Portsmouth. Mariner. Aurora. Comm. M. July 27, 1780. SP; HO; HL; 3 p. 139.

NEAL, Wm. of Ireland.   Alliance's prize.   Comm. M. March 22, 1779. Escaped.   3 p. 138.

NEAZRO, Nath.   See NAZRO.

NE(A)GUS, NAGERS or NEIGORS, Bennet(t) of Bedford.   Captain.   Marquis de Morbec.   Comm. M. Oct. 2, 1781.   SP; HO; 3 p. 211; 10 v. 74 p. 142.

NEIL, Alexander.   See KNELL.

NEILL, Charles.   M.   Pard. for R. N. Jan. 4, 1779.   G.   (Probably same as Neal).

NELAND, James.   Seaman.   Wexford.   Sent from Kinsale to M. April 9, 1782.   HO.

NELSON, Joseph.   Seaman.   Confederacy.   Comm. F. Aug. 9, 1781.   SP.

NERO, Absalom of Dartmouth.   Charming Sally or Polly.   Captured Jan. 16, 1777.   Died.   3 p. 75; 7 p. 247.

NEVELL, James.   See NEWELL.

NEWCOMB, Bryant of Braintree.   Essex.   Comm. M. July 21, 1781.   Pard. for exchange Feb. 6, 1782.   G; SP; 3 p. 210; 10 v. 74 p. 34.

NEWCOMB, Ebenezer.   Reprisal.   P. M. Mate.   Comm. F. Aug. 9, 1777.   Pard. for exchange May 31, 1779.   G; 5A p. 37.

NEWCOMB(E), Jery. or Jeremiah of Boston.   Mariner.   Resolution.   Comm-M. Jan. 22, 1781.   SP; HO; HL; 3 p. 140; 10 v. 73 p. 316.

NEWCOMB, Thos.   Master.   Comm. F. Sept. 24, 1778.   5A p. 38.

NEWCOMBE, William.   Seaman.   Ranger.   Comm. M. Jan. 24, 1782.   HO.

NEWELL, James.   Master.   Black Prince or Princess.   Comm. M. Oct. 20, 1781.   Att. escape Nov. 18, 1781.   Out of b. h. Nov. 26.   SP; HO; 3 p. 212; 10 v. 74 pp. 153, 154, 156.

MARINERS OF THE AMERICAN REVOLUTION

NEWELL or NEWHALL, Timothy of Lynn. Mariner. Jack. Comm. M. Dec. 23 or 25, 1780. In hospital May 10, 1781. SP; HO; HL; 3 p. 139; 10 v. 73 p. 341.

NEWLAND, John. Mariner. Essex. Comm. M. Sept. 1, 1781. SP; HO.

NIAL or VIAL, Allen. Seaman. Thomas merchant ship. Captured but not comm. Oct. 23, 1781. HO.

NICHOLAS, John. Seaman. Bermuda. Comm. M. Jan. 22, 1782. HO.

NICHOLAS, Richard. M. Pard. for exchange Dec. 11, 1779. G.

NICHOLLS, Joseph of Scituate. Prize master. Black Prince or Princess. SP; 3 p. 212; 10 v. 74 p. 146.

NICHOLSON, Barcella. F. Pard. for R. N. Oct. 6, 1781. G.

NICHOLSON, Daniel. M. Pard. for exchange Dec. 11, 1779. G.

NICHOLSON, Daniel. M. Pard. for R. N. May 25, 1781. G. (See also D. NICKERSON).

NICHOLSON, John of Philadelphia. Captain. Brother of James and Samuel NICHOLSON. Hornet. Escaped. 5 v. 30 p. 346; 5A p. 37.

NICHOLSON, Robert of Marblehead. Boy. Franklin. Comm. F. Jan. 5, 1780. SP; HO; 10 v. 73 p. 340.

NICHOLSON, Thomas of Marblehead. Boy. Daniel or Rambler. Comm. F. Oct. 31, 1780. SP; HO.

NICKERSON, Danl. Alliance's prize. Comm. M. March 22, 1779. R. N. June 5, 1781. 3 p. 138; 10 v. 74 p. 22. (See also D. NICHOLSON).

NICKERSON, Mayo. Boy. Hercules. Captured but not comm. Oct. 15, 1781. HO.

NOLTON, John. See KNOWLTON.

NOONAM or NOONAN, John. Mariner. Essex. Comm. M. July 21, 1781. SP; HO; 3 p. 210; 10 v. 74 p. 34.

NORRIS, Jacob of Carolina. Charming Salley or Dalton. Captured Jan. 16, 1777. M. Still there Feb. 7, 1779. Escaped. 3 p. 74; 7 p. 248.

NORRIS or MORRIS, Malichi. Mariner. Betsey or Robertson. Comm. M. July 28, 1781. SP; HO; 3 p. 210; 10 v. 74 p. 36.

NORRIS, Roger. Seaman. Jason. Captured but not comm. Oct. 15, 1781. HO.

NORRISON, John. Essex. Taken at Eustatia. Comm. M. July 21, 1781. 10 v. 74 p. 34. (Probably same as Morrison).

NORTH, Joseph or Josiah of Bermuda. Mariner. Marmy or Mariana. Comm. M. July 3 or 28, 1779. SP; HL; 3 p. 138.

NORTH, Josh. M. Pard. for exchange Dec. 11, 1779. G.

NORTHLOP, Henry. Seaman. Mercury. Comm. F. Nov. 18, 1780. SP; HO.

NORTHUP, Harris. Seaman. General Mifflin. Comm. F. Aug. 9, 1781. SP; HO.

NORTHUP, Stephen. Seaman. General Mifflin. Comm. F. Aug. 9, 1781. SP; HO.

NORTON, Thos. Mariner. Lion. Comm. M. Aug. 31, 1781. SP; HO; 3 p. 211.

NORWOOD, Thomas of Bristol. Reprisal's prize. Comm. M. Aug. 1777. Escaped. 3 p. 75; 7 p. 251.

NOURSE, William. Midshipman. Confederacy. Comm. F. Aug. 9, 1781. Pard. for R. N. March 20, 1782. G; SP.

NOWLAND or NOWLING, James the elder, or Marblehead. Seaman. Jack. Comm. F. Feb. 3, 1781. SP; HO; 10 p. 340.

NOWLAND or NOWLING, James, the younger of Marblehead. Seaman or boy. Jack. Comm. F. Feb. 3, 1781. SP; HO; 10 v. 73 p. 340.

NOYES, NOYSE or NOYCE, Paul of Newburyport. Dalton. Comm. M. June, 1777. Pard. for exchange Dec. 20, 1778. Joined Alliance. G; 3 p. 74; 4 p. 187; 7 p. 244.

NUGENT, John. Seaman. Pomona. Comm. F. Aug. 7 or 9, 1779. Pard. for exchange Dec. 11, 1779. G; SP; HO.

NULTON, Benjamin. See MILTON.

NUTTER, Jacob of Portsmouth. Dalton or Charming Polly. Comm. M. June, 1777. Pard. for exchange Dec. 20, 1778. G; 3 p. 75; 7 p. 244.

NUTTON or NULTON, Benjamin of Milton. Boy. General Glover. Comm. F. Oct. 18, 1779. Pard. for exchange Dec. 11, 1779. G; SP; HO; 10 v. 73 p. 340.

NYE, Allen of Sandwich. Seaman. Adventure. Comm. M. Jan. 21, 1782. HO; 3 p. 213.

NYE, Thomas. Seaman. Bermuda. Comm. M. Jan. 22, 1782. HO.

O

OAKES, Jacob of Marblehead. Gunner. General Glover. Comm. F. Oct. 14 or 18, 1779. Pard. for exchange Dec. 11, 1779. SP; HO; 10 v. 73 p. 340; G.

OAKES, Joshua of Cohasset. Comm. Pembroke 1778 and M. Oct. 14, 1780. Pard. for R. N. Nov. 4, 1780. Entered or exchanged. G; 3 p. 139.

OAKES, Uriah. Imprisoned at Pembroke. Pardoned for R. N. May 18, 1781. Entered June 5, 1781. G; 3 p. 139; 10 v. 74 p. 22.

OAKMAN, Tobias. Captain. Comm. F. Jan. 23, 1778. Escaped. 5 v. 30 p. 348; 5A p. 37.

OATES, Benjamin. Rising States. Comm. F. June 14, 1777. Pard. for R. N. Dec. 3, 1778. R. N. Dec. 19, 1778. G; 5 v. 32 p. 282; 5A p. 36.

OBEN, Zebulon. Seaman. Diana. Comm. M. Jan. 24, 1782. HO.

OBER, Joseph. Seaman. Eagle. Comm. F. March 5, 1781. SP; HO.

O'BRION or O'BRYANT, Jas. of Philadelphia. Luzern of Philadelphia. Comm. M. July 6, 1781. Pard. for R. N. Aug. 8, 1781. G; 3 p. 209; 10 v. 74 p. 31.

ODDY, John. F. Pard. for R. N. Jan. 12, 1781. G.

ODELL, James. Mariner. Charming Polly. Comm. M. Sept. 19, 1780. SP; HO; 3 p. 139. See also ODLE and ODLBEY.

ODEN, Tim(oth)y Cutler. Master. Essex. Comm. M. Aug. 25, 1781. SP; HO; 3 p. 211.

ODEN, Wm. of Boston. Essex. Comm. M. Aug. 25, 1781. 10 v. 74 p. 44.

ODGER, ODGEN?, John. F. Pard. for exchange May 31, 1779. G.

MARINERS OF THE AMERICAN REVOLUTION

ODLE, Jas. M. In hospital May 10, 1781. 10 v. 73 p. 341. (See also ODELL and ODLBEY).

ODLBEY, James. M. HL. See also ODELL and ODLE.

OFFLING, Peter. F. Pard. for exchange Dec. 11, 1779. Pard. for R. N. Jan. 12, 1781. G.

OGDEN, John. Prize of the Sloop Independent. Comm. F. June 26, 1777. 5A p. 36.

O'HARA, John. Lion. Comm. M. Aug. 31, 1781. In b. h. May 22, 1782. 3 p. 211; 8 p. 139. (Probably same as next).

OHERE, George. Mariner. Lion. Comm. M. Aug. 31, 1781. SP; HO; (Probably same as previous).

O'NEILL, Charles. M. Pard. for R. N. July 13, 1779. G.

ORAM, Robert. Seaman. Susannah. Comm. F. June 27, 1781. SP; HO.

ORMSBEY, Browning or Brownell. M. In hospital May 10, 1781. Pard. for R. N. May 25, 1781. Entered June 5. G; 10 v. 73 p. 341; v. 74 p. 22.

ORR, William. Seaman. Pocahontas. Comm. F. Nov. 18, 1780. Pard. for R. N. March 27, 1781. G; SP; HO.

ORRICK or ORROCK, John of Marblehead. Mariner. James and Rebecca. or prize to the Franklin. Comm. M. Oct. 16 or 17, 1781. SP; HO; 3 p. 211; 10 v. 74 p. 145.

OSBORN, William. M. Pard. for R. N. Sept. 25, 1778. G.

OSGOOD, Nathl. Comm. Pembroke 1778 and M. Oct. 14, 1780. Pard. for R. N. May 11, 1781. Entered June 2, 1781. G; 10 v. 73 p. 347.

OSTIN, Daniel. See AUSTIN.

OWENS, Robert. Reprisal. Comm. F. Aug. 9, 1777. Escaped. 5A p. 37.

OWEN(S), Samuel. Mariner. Comet of Philadelphia. Comm. M. Jan. 6, 1781. Innoculated May 29, 1781. SP; HO; HL; 3 p. 140; 10 v. 73 pp. 312, 338, 346; 8 p. 130.

P

PAGE, Jacob.   F.   Pard. for exchange Dec. 11, 1779 and Nov. 9, 1781. G; 5A p. 39.

PAIN, John.   Seaman.   Terrible.   Comm. F. May 24, 1781.   SP; HO.

PAIN or PAYNE, Samuel of Cape Cod.   Mariner.   Chatham.   Comm. M. Aug. 23, 1781.   SP; HO; 3 p. 211; 10 v. 74 p. 43.

PALMER, John.   See PALMS.

PALMER, Reuben.   Seaman.   Fair American.   Comm. F. Nov. 18, 1780. SP.

PALMER, Robert.   F.   Pard. for R. N. May 28, 1781.   G.

PALMER or PALMS, John.   Prize of the Warren.   Comm. F. June 26, 1777. Pard. for exchange May 31, 1779.   G; 5A p. 36.

PARK, Humphrey.   See PORK.

PARKER, Bany or Barny of Yarmouth.   Seaman.   Adventure.   Comm. M. Jan. 21, 1782.   HO.   3 p. 213.

PARKER, Fortune of Boston.   Essex.   Comm. M. July 25, 1781.   Died. Aug. 16, 1781.   3 p. 210; 10 v. 74 pp. 36, 42.

PARKER, Walter of Rhode Island.   Seaman.   Twin Sisters.   Comm. M. Jan. 9, 1782.   HO; 3 p. 212.

PARKER, William.   Seaman.   Jack.   Comm. F. June 27, 1781.   SP; HO.

PARKINSON, Nich.   See PERKINSON.

PARISH or PARRISH, Aaron of Maryland.   Mariner.   Lively.   Comm. M. Dec. 27 or 30, 1780.   SP; HO; HL; 3 p. 140.

PARSONS, Andrew of Cape Ann.   Mariner.   Beaver.   Comm. M. July 23 or 27, 1781.   SP; HO; 3 p. 210.

PARSONS, Edmond. F. Pard. for exchange Dec. 11, 1779. G.

PARSONS, James. Seaman. Mercury. Comm. M. Feb. 6, 1782. HO.

PARSONS, John. Seaman. Neptune. Comm. F. July 20, 1781. SP; HO.

PARSONS, Josiah. Seaman. Hercules. Comm. M. Jan. 25, 1782. HO.

PARSONS, Nehemiah. Hercules. Captured but not comm. Oct. 15, 1781. HO.

PARSONS, Samuel. F. Pard. for R. N. Jan. 12, 1781,. G.

PARSONS or PERSONS, William of Marblehead. Seaman. Rhodes. Comm. F. Nov. 18, 1780. SP; HO; 10 p. 340.

PARSONS, Zachary. F. Pard. for exchange Dec. 11, 1779. G.

PARRY, Samuel. F. Pard. for exchange Dec. 11, 1779. G.

PATERSON, James. F. Pard. for R. N. Sept. 9, 1779. G.

PATEY or PATTE, Silvanus of Plymouth. Mariner. Chatham. Comm. M. Aug. 23, 1781. SP; HO; 3 p. 211; 10 v. 74 p. 43.

PATTANGILL, Joseph. Seaman. Phoenix. Comm. F. Nov. 18, 1780. SP; HO.

PATTEN, Mr. (Probably John PATTON). Comm. M. July 4, 1780. R. N. 8 p. 125.

PATTEN, Andrew. Prize master. Prize of the Independent. Comm. F, June 26, 1777. Escaped. 5A p. 36.

PATTERSON, Ephraim. Angelica. Comm. F. July 7, 1778. Escaped. 5A p. 38.

PATTERSON, James of Salem. Comm. M. July 20, 1781. Essex. 10 v. 74 p. 34.

PATTERSON, John. Satisfaction. Comm. F. July 27, 1778. 5A p. 38.

PATTERSON, Willm. Mariner. Essex. Comm. M. July 20, 1781. SP; HO; 3 p. 210.

PATTING, John. M. Pard. for exchange Dec. 11, 1779. G.

PATTON, John. Alliance's prize. Comm. M. March 22, 1779. Pard. for R.N. July 4, 1780. Entered or escaped. G; 3 p. 138. See also Mr. PATTEN.

PAUL, Mark. Boy. Sturdy Beggar. Comm. F. Jan. 27, 1778. Pard. for exchange May 31, 1779. Exchanged July 2, 1779. Joined Bonhomme Richard. G; 5 v. 32 p. 286; 5A p. 37.

PAUL, Samuel. Seaman. Hercules. Sent from Kinsale to M. April 9, 1782. HO.

PAYNE, Nathan. Seaman. Zephyr or Jack. Comm. F. June 27, 1781. SP; HO.

PEABODY or PEBODDY, Andrew. Black Prince. Comm. F. April 26, 1779. Pard. for exchange Dec. 11, 1779. G; 5A p. 39. (Probably same as next).

PEABODY, Andrew of Beverley. Mariner. Essex. Comm. M. July 27, 1781. SP; HO; 3 p. 210.

PEABODY, Jonathan. Seaman. Jason. Captured but not comm. Oct. 15, 1781. HO.

PEANE, James. Seaman. Thomas merchant ship. Captured but not comm. Oct. 23, 1781. HO.

PEARCE. See also PIERCE, PEIRCE.

PEARCE, Jeremiah. Seaman. Protector. Comm. F. Aug. 9, 1781. SP; HO.

PEARCE or PIERCE, John of Rhode Island. Gunner. General Washington. Comm. M. Sept. 7, 1781. SP; HO; 3 p. 211.

PEARCE, Robert. M. Pard. for exchange Dec. 11, 1779. G.

MARINERS OF THE AMERICAN REVOLUTION

PEARCEY or PIERCY, Joseph. Mariner. Resolution. Comm. M. Jan. 22, 1781. SP; HO.

PEARSE, Daniel F. Pard. for R. N. May 28, 1781. G.

PEARSE, William. Seaman. Wexford. Sent from Kinsale to M. April 9, 1782. HO.

PEARSON, Samuel. See PIERSON.

PEAS(E), George. Rising States. Comm. F. June 14, 1777. Escaped Feb. 16, 1778. 5 v. 30 p. 348; 5A p. 36.

PEASE, Timothy. Seaman. Daniel. Comm. F. Oct. 31, 1780. SP; HO.

PEASLEY or PEASLY, Amos. Seaman. Black Prince. Comm. F. April 26, 1779. Pard. for exchange Dec. 11, 1779. SP; 5A p. 39; G.

PECURE, Thomas. Seaman. Pocahontas. Comm. F. Nov. 18, 1780. Pard. for R. N. May 21, 1781. G; SP; HO.

PEDRICK, Joseph of Marblehead. Ascott and John. Comm. M. July 23, 1781. 3 p. 210; 10 v. 74 p. 35.

PEIRCE. See also PIERCE, PEARCE.

PEIRCE, John. Gunner or prizemaster. Angelica. Comm. F. July 7, 1778. Pard. for exchange Dec. 11, 1779. Exchanged July 2, 1779. Joined Bonhomme Richard. G; 5 v. 32 p. 286; 5A p. 38.

PELT, Joseph of Salem. Comm. Pembroke 1778 and M. Oct. 14, 1780. 3 p. 139.

PEMBERTON, Thomas or William. Mate. Revenge of Philadelphia. Comm. M. March 31, 1781. SP; HO; HL; 3 p. 140; 10 v. 73 p. 331.

PENDELL. See PINDLE.

PENGALLY, Jonathan. F. Pard. for exchange Dec. 11, 1779. G.

PENNY, Joseph. Mariner. L'Uzerne. Comm. M. July 7, 1781. SP; HO; 3 p. 209; 10 v. 74 p. 31.

MARINERS OF THE AMERICAN REVOLUTION

PEPPER, Michel. The Spy. Comm. F. Feb. 18, 1779. Pard. for exchange Dec. 11, 1779. G; 5A p. 39.

PERCEY, Richard. See PERRY.

PERKINS, Abijah. Doctor. The Swallow. Comm. F. Jan. 23, 1778. 5A p. 37. (Same as next?)

PERKINS, Elijah. F. Pard. for exchange May 31, 1779. G. (Same as last?)

PERKINS, John of Kittery. Dalton or Charming Polly. In hospital April, 1777. Comm. M. June, 1777. Pard. for exchange Dec. 11, 1779. G; 3 p. 75; 4 p. 184; 7 p. 245.

PERKINS, Joseph. Mariner. Essex. Comm. M. July 24, 1781. SP; HO; 3 p. 210; 10 v. 74 p. 35.

PERKINS, Thomas. General Sullivan. Comm. F. April 26, 1779. Pard. for exchange Dec. 11, 1779. and Nov. 9, 1781. G; 5A p. 39. (Probably same as next).

PERKINS, Thoms. of Wenham. Essex. Comm. M. July 21 or 24, 1781. Died. 3 p. 210; 10 v. 74 p. 35. (Probably same as last).

PERKINSON or PARKINSON, Nich. Mariner. Viper. Comm. M. Dec. 7, 1781. SP; HO; 3 p. 212.

PERO, John. Cook. Hercules. Captured but not comm. Oct. 15, 1781. HO.

PERRIGRIN, Mingo of Boston. Adventure. Comm. M. Jan. 21, 1782. 3 p. 213.

PERRY, George. Seaman. Fair American. Comm. F. Nov. 18, 1780. SP; HO.

PERRY, John. Franklin. Comm. F. Feb. 18, 1779. 5A p. 38.

PERRY, Ramond. Steward. Wexford. Captured but not comm. Oct. 2, 1781. HO.

PERRY or PERCEY, Richard of Kittery. Mariner. Susanna or prize to the Oliver Cromwell. Comm. M. July 3 or 28, 1779. Pard. for exchange Dec. 11, 1779. G; SP; HO; HL; 3 p. 138; 9 p. 80.

PERSONS, William. See PARSON.

PERSONS, Zacheus. Comm. F. April 19, 1779. 5A p. 39.

PETHERICK, Joseph. See POTHERICK.

PHARO or FARO(W), Isaac of North Carolina. Mariner. Lydia of North Carolina or Robertson. Comm. M. April 24, 1781. Innoculated May 28, 1781. SP; HO; HL; 3 p. 141; 10 v. 73 pp. 337, 346.

PHEZANTE, Stephen. F. Pard. for R. N. Dec. 16, 1778. G.

PHILLIPS or PHILIPS, Christopher. Angelica. Comm. F. July 7, 1778. Pard. for exchange May 31, 1779. G; 5A p. 38. (Probably same as next).

PHILIPS, Christian. Seaman. Wexford. Comm. M. Jan. 24, 1782. HO. (Probably same as last).

PHILIPS, James. Lieut. Angelica. Comm. F. July 7, 1778. Escaped. 5A p. 38.

PHILLIPS, John of Philadelphia. Warren. Comm. M. June, 1778. Escaped. 3 p. 137; 7 p. 255.

PHIPS or PHIPPS, George of Kittery. Aurora. Comm. M. July 25, 1780. Escaped July 31, 1781. HL; 10 v. 74 p. 37.

PICKERING, Charles. Seaman. Bermuda. Comm. M. Jan. 22, 1782. HO.

PICKERING, Levi. General Sullivan's prize. Comm. M. July 3, 1779. Pard. for exchange Dec. 11, 1779 and Nov. 9, 1781. G; HL; 3 p. 138.

PICKETT, William of Marblehead. Fancy. Comm. M. Aug. 7, 1777. Escaped. 3 p. 136; 7 p. 250.

PICKNALL, John of Salem. Hawk's prize. Comm. M. Oct. 1778. 7 p. 252.

PICKWORTH, John. Hawk. Comm. M. April 13, 1778. Escaped. 3 p. 137.

PIERCE. See also PEARCE and PEIRCE.

PIERCE, James. F. Pard. for exchange Dec. 11, 1779. G.

PIERCE, John. Commerce? Comm. F. Jan. 18, 1779. 5A p. 39.

PIERCE, John. F. Pard. for R. N. Nov. 6, 1780. G.

PIERCE, Joseph. Resolution. Comm. M. Jan. 22, 1781. In hospital May 10, 1781. 3 p. 140; 10 v. 73 pp. 316, 341.

PIERCE, Moses. Satisfaction. Comm. F. July 27, 1778. Pard. for exchange Dec. 11, 1779. Pard. for R. N. Nov. 6, 1780. G; 5A p. 38.

PIERCE, Robert of Marblehead. Fancy. Comm. M. Aug. 7, 1777. Exchanged. 3 p. 136; 7 p. 250.

PIERSON or PEARSON(S), Samuel of Ipswich. Mariner. James and Rebecca or prize to the Franklin. Comm. M. Oct. 2, 16 or 17, 1781. SP; HO; 3 p. 211; 10 v. 74 p. 145.

PIGON, Jacques. F. Pard. for exchange May 31, 1779. G.

PIKE, Mr. M. 8 p. 125-6.

PIKE, George. America's prize. Comm. M. March 22, 1779. Pard. for exchange Dec. 11, 1779. Pard. for R. N. Nov. 22, 1780. Entered or escaped. G; 3 p. 138.

PIKE, Hugh. Seaman. Diana. Comm. M. Jan. 23, 1782. HO.

PIKE, James of Boston. Master's mate. Alexander or prize to the South Carolina. Comm. M. Nov. 21, 1781. SP; HO; 3 p. 212; 10 v. 74 p. 155.

PIKE, Wm. General Sullivan. Comm. F. April 26, 1779. Pard. for exchange Dec. 11, 1779.and Nov. 9, 1781. G; 5A p. 39.

PIKETT, Wm. M. Pard. for exchange Dec. 11, 1779. G.

PINDAR, Joseph. Seaman. Newfoundland. Imprisoned at Edinburgh June 27, 1781. HO.

MARINERS OF THE AMERICAN REVOLUTION

PINDLE or PENDALL, Gasway or Gassaway. Mariner. Lively. Comm. M. Dec. 27, 1780. SP; HO; 3 p. 139.

PINE, John. Seaman. Marquis de la Fayette. Comm. M. Jan. 23, 1782. HO.

PINNINGTON George. F. Pard. for R. N. Nov. 22, 1780. G.

PIT or PITTS, Ebenezer of Dighton. Seaman. Twin Sisters. Comm. M. Jan. 9, 1782. HO; 3 p. 212.

PITCHER, John. Adventure. Comm. M. Jan. 21, 1782. 3 p. 213.

PITMAN, Thomas of Marblehead. Seaman. Harlequin. Comm. F. Feb. 3, 1781. SP; HO; 10 v. 73 p. 340.

PITT(S), William. Mariner. Comet of Philadelphia. Comm. M. Jan. 6, 1781. SP; HO; HL; 3 p. 140; 10 v. 73 p. 312.

PLATT, Ebenezer. F. 5 v. 31 p. 285.

PLUMMER, Joseph of Newburyport. Dalton. Comm. M. June, 1777. Pard. for exchange Dec. 20, 1778. Joined Alliance. G; 3 p. 74; 7 p. 244.

POLIN or POLAND, Abner. Hawk's prize. Comm. F. April 2, 1778. Pard. for exchange May 31, 1779. G; 5A p. 37.

POLLARD, Peter of Boston. 1st lieut. General Washington. Comm. M. Sept. 7, 1781. Att. escape Nov. 21, 1781. Out of b. h. Nov. 26, 1781. SP; HO; 3 p. 211; 10 v. 74 pp. 155, 156.

POLLING, William. Seaman. Jason. Captured but not comm. Oct. 15, 1781. HO.

POLLY, Elisha. Gunner. Confederacy. Comm. M. Sept. 7, 1781. SP; HO.

POOLE, George of Newbury. Little Porgy. Comm. M. Jan, 1782. 3 p. 213.

POOR, Joseph of Newburyport. Dalton. In hospital April, 1777. Comm. M. June, 1777. Pard. for exchange Feb. 2, 1779. Joined Alliance. G; 4 p. 184; 7 p. 244.

POOR, Nicho(las) of Boston. Essex. Comm. M. July 21, 1781. Pard. for R. N. Aug. 9, 1781. G; 3 p. 210; 10 v. 74 p. 34.

POOR(E), Philip of Ireland. General Sullivan's prize. Comm. M. July 3, 1779. Pard. for exchange Dec. 11, 1779. Pard. for R.N. Nov. 22, 1780. G; 3 p. 138.

POPE, Amherst or Ambrose. Boy. Twin Sisters. Comm. M. Jan. 9, 1782. HO; 3 p. 212.

POPE, Jacob. Surgeon. Twin Sisters. Comm. M. Jan. 9, 1782. HO; 3 p. 212.

POPE, Joseph of Marblehead. Mate. General Glover. Comm. F. Oct. 18, 1779. Pard. for exchange Dec. 11, 1779. G; SP; 10 v.73 p. 340.

PORK or PARK, Humphrey. Pard. for R.N. Sept. 25, 1778. G.

PORTER or POTTER, Burrel or Barrel of Lynn, Mass. Mariner. Ascot and John. Comm. M. July 7, 1781. SP; HO; 3 p. 209; 10 v. 74 p. 31.

PORTER, Edwd. of Philadelphia. Mariner. Betsey. Comm. M. July 23, 1781. In b.h. Oct. 17, 1781. Out of b.h. Nov. 19, SP; HO. 3 p. 210; 10 v. 74 pp. 35, 145, 154.

PORTER, Elias. Passenger. The Spy. Comm. F. Feb. 18, 1779. Pard. for exchange Dec. 11, 1779. G; 5A p. 39.

PORTER, Humphrey. Charming Polly. M. Escaped. 3 p. 75. (Probably same as POTTER).

PORTER, Nathaniel of Cape Pursue. Dalton. In hospital April, 1777. Comm. M. June, 1777. Pard. for exchange Dec. 20, 1778. G; 3 p. 74; 4 p. 184; 7 p. 246. (Probably same as next).

PORTER, Nathaniel. Seaman. Diana. Comm. M. Jan. 24, 1782. HO. (Probably same as last).

PORTER, William. Seaman. Morning Star. Comm. F. Oct. 16, 1781. SP; HO.

POST, Eldrad or Eldad. Commerce? Comm. F. Feb. 18, 1779. Pard. for exchange Dec. 11, 1779. G; 5A p. 39.

POTHERICK or PETHERICK, Joseph. Mariner. Ascot and John. Comm. M. July 23, 1781. SP; HO.

POTTER, Barrel. See PORTER

POTTER, Humphrey of Dartmouth. Charming Salley. Captured Jan. 16, 1777. Comm. M. Still there Feb. 7, 1779. R. N. 7 p. 247. (Probably same as PORTER).

POWELL, Eli or Eli(e)u. Mariner. Franklin. Comm. M. Nov. or Dec. 6, 1781. SP; HO; 3 p. 212.

POWELL, George. Seaman. Little Peggey. Comm. M. Jan. 9, 1782. HO.

POWERS, Benjamin of Millbury or Middleboro. Charming Sally. Comm. M. May 28, 1777. Still there Feb. 7, 1779. Pard. for exchange Dec. 20, 1778. G; 3 p. 75; 4 p. 185; 7 p. 247.

PRATT, James. Prize master. Comm. F. Feb. 18, 1779. 5A p. 39.

PRATT, James. Mariner. Lively. Comm. M. Dec. 27, 1780. Innoculated May 28, 1781. SP; HO; HL; 3 p. 140; 10 v. 73 p. 346.

PRATT, William. F. Pard. for R. N. Oct. 21, 1779. G.

PRESENTEE, Stephen. Angelica. Comm. F. July 7, 1778. R. N. 5A p. 38.

PRICE, Peter. F. Pard. for R. N. May 25, 1781. G.

PRICE, Richard of Maryland. Oliver Cromwell. Comm. M. Oct. 18, 1777. Pard. for exchange Dec. 11, 1779. G; 3 p. 75; 7 p. 255.

PRICE or PRI(E)ST of Virginia. Mariner. Viper. Comm. M. Dec. 7, 1781. SP; HO; 3 p. 212.

PRIOR, Daniel. Boy. Oliver Cromwell. Comm. F. Oct. 13, 1777. Pard. for exchange May 31, and Dec. 11, 1779. Exchanged July 2, 1779. Joined Bonhomme Richard. G; 5 v. 32 p. 386; 5A p. 37. (Probably same as next).

PRIOR or PRAYER, Daniel of Nantucket. 2nd lieut. Marquis de Morbec. Comm. M. Oct. 2, 1781. SP; HO; 3 p. 211; 10 v. 74 p. 142. (Probably same as last).

PRITCHARD, John. Seaman. Adventure. Comm. M. Jan. 21, 1782. HO.

PRITCHET, Sam'l. Lieut. marines. Rising States. Comm. F. June 14, 1777. Escaped. 5A p. 36.

PROCTOR, James of Boston. Seaman. Essex. Comm. M. July 21, 1781. Pard. for R. N. Oct. 24, 1781. Pard. for exchange Nov. 9, 1781. HO; G; 3 p. 210; 10 v. 74 pp. 34, 146.

PROCTOR, Thorndick. Seaman. Harlequin. Comm. F. May 16, 1781. SP; HO

PULSEVER, Samuel. Hercules. Captured but not comm. Oct. 15, 1781. HO.

PURCELL, Thoms. Seaman. Pocahontas. Comm. F. Nov. 18, 1780. Pard. for R. N. April 20, 1781. G; SP; HO.

PURNELL, Thos. Protector. Comm. M. July 21, 1781. Died. 3 p. 209.

PUTNAM, Elijah. Seaman. Jason. Captured but not comm. Oct. 15, 1781. HO.

Q

QUIGLY, Aaron. M. Pard. for R. N. Oct. 14, 1778. G. (Probably same as TWIGLEY).

QUIN, Patrick. Boy. Prize of the Independent. Comm. F. June 26, 1777. Pard. for exchange May 31, 1779. Exchanged July 2, 1779. Joined Bonhomme Richard. G; 5 v. 32 p. 286; 5A p. 36.

QUIN, Thomas of Virginia. Marquis de Morbec. Comm. M. Oct. 2, 1781. 3 p. 211. See Thoms. TANGLE.

QUINER, Abraham. Rambler. Comm. M. Feb. 16, 1780. Out of b. h. July 29, 1781. HL; 10 v. 74 p. 37; 3 p. 138.

R

RACE, William of Philadelphia.   Warren.   Comm. M. June, 1778.   R. N. 7 p. 255.

RACKLIEF, Joseph of Newburyport.   Dalton.   Comm. M. June, 1777. 7 p. 243.

RAGLAND, Benjamin.   M.   Pard. for R.N. Sept. 25, 1778.   G.

RALPH, Thomas of Harwick.   Seaman.   Adventure.   Comm. M. Jan. 21, 1782.   HO; 3 p. 213.

RAMENT, Robt. of Beverly.   Essex.   Comm. M. July 24, 1781.   10 v. 74 p. 35.

RAMSDELL, John.   Black Prince.   Comm. F. April 26, 1779.   Pard. for exchange Dec. 11, 1779.and Nov. 9, 1781.   G; 5A p. 39.

RAND, Wm. of Portsmouth.   Brig Thom.   Comm. M. Sept. 19, 1780. Pard. for exchange Nov. 9, 1781.   G; HL; 3 p. 139.

RANDEL(L), Archibald.   Reprisal.   Comm. F. Aug. 9, 1777.   Pard. for R.N. Dec. 19, 1778.   Pard. for exchange Dec. 11, 1779.   G; 5 v. 32 p. 282; 5A p. 37.

RAPHELL, Peter.   Angelica.   Comm. F. , July 7, 1778.   R. N.   5A p. 38.

RAPLEY, Paul.   See RIPLEY.

RARDON, Berth'w.   Rattlesnake.   Comm. F. Jan. 23, 1778.   5A p. 37.

RATFORD, Wm.   Hornet.   Comm. F. Oct. 13, 1777.   Escaped.   5A p. 37.

RATHBURN, John Peck.   Captain.   Wexford.   Comm. M. Feb. 7, 1782. HO.

RAVEL(L), John of Salem.   Captain.   Warren.   Comm. M. June 4, 1778. Escaped Oct. 1, 1778.   3 p. 137; 7 pp. 129, 170, 254.

MARINERS OF THE AMERICAN REVOLUTION

RAWORTH or RAYWORTH, John. Carpenter. Angelica. Comm. F. July 7, 1778. Pard. for exchange May 31, 1779. G; 5A p. 38.

RAYDON, Bartholomew. F. Pard. for R. N. June 17, 1779. G.

RAYLAND, Richard. F. Pard. for exchange May 31, 1779. G.

RAYWORTH, John. See RAWORTH.

READ or REED, Wm. of Virginia. Taken in a French vessel (Duc de Coigny?) M. Pard. for R. N. May 25, 1781. Entered June 5, 1781. G; 3 p. 139; 10 v. 74 p. 22.

READ. See also REED.

READING, John. Seaman. Jason. In M. but not comm. Oct. 15, 1781. HO.

READY, Stephen. The Spy. Comm. F. Feb. 18, 1779. Pard. for exchange Dec. 11, 1779. G; 5A p. 39.

REDINGTON, Daniel of Wenham. Mariner. Essex. Comm. M. July 21 or 24, 1781. SP; HO; 3 p. 210; 10 v. 74 p. 35.

REDMAN, Benjamin. Seaman. Ajax. Comm. F. Aug. 9, 1781. SP; HO.

REDMAN, James. Montgomery. Comm. F. Aug. 8, 1777. Escaped. 5A p. 36.

REDMAN, James. Revenge. Comm. F. Aug. 11, 1777. Escaped. 5A p. 37.

REDREW, Thos. Mariner. Lion or Franklin's prize. Comm. M. Nov. 21, 1781. SP; HO.

REED or READ, Ephraim. Reprisal. Comm. F. June 19, 1778. Pard. for exchange May 31, 1779. G; 5A p. 38.

REED or READ, George of Salem. Mariner. Eliza, prize to the Grand Turk. Comm. M. Jan. 3, 1782. Pard. for R. N. May 3, 1782. G; SP; HO; 3 p. 213.

REED, Patrick.   Montgomery of Philadelphia.   Comm. F. Aug. 8, 1777. Out of b.h. Oct. 11, 1778.   Pard. for exchange May 31, 1779.   G; 5 v. 32 p. 165; 5A p. 36.

REED.   See also READ.

REFFELL, Peter.   F.   Pard. for R. N. Dec. 16, 1778.   G.

REILAND, Richard.   The Swallow.   Comm. F. Jan. 23, 1778.   5A p. 37.

REILEY, Edw'd.   Master's mate.   Commerce?   Comm. F. Feb. 18, 1779. 5A p. 39.

REMICK, Jacob of Kittery.   Mariner.   Venus.   Comm. M. Nov. 21, 1781. SP; HO; 3 p. 212; 10 v. 74 p. 155.

REMINGTON, Robt. of Salem.   Ranger.   Comm. M. July 23, 1781.   3 p. 210; 10 v. 74 p. 35.

RENOLDS, Thomas of Baltimore.   Reprisal's prize.   Comm. M. Aug. 1777. Pard. for R. N. Sept. 25, 1778.   Entered or escaped.   G; 3 p. 75.

REPPLY, Paul.   See RIPLEY.

REYMOND, Robt.   Mariner.   Essex.   Comm. M. July 24, 1781.   SP; HO.

RHODES, Holden.   Prize master.   Satisfaction.   Comm. F. July 27, 1778. Pard. for exchange Dec. 11, 1779.   G; 5A p. 38.

RICE, Philip.   Seaman.   Mary and Elizabeth.   Comm. F. Dec. 30, 1779. SP; HO.

RICE, Samuel.   P. M. mate.   Satisfaction.   Comm. F. July 27, 1778. Pard. for exchange Dec. 11, 1779.   G; 5A p. 38.

RICH, Aquilla.   Mariner.   Resolution of Boston.   Comm. M. Jan. 22, 1781. SP; HO; HL; 3 p. 140; 10 v. 73 p. 316.

RICH, Ezekial of Cape Cod.   Resolution.   Comm. M. Jan. 22, 1781. Pard. for R. N. April 28, 1781.   Entered May 7, 1781.   G; 3 p. 140; 10 v. 73 pp. 316, 339.

RICH, James. Prize master. Essex. Comm. M. Aug. 25, 1781. SP; HO; 3 p. 211.

RICHARD, Jean or Jane. Revenge. Comm. F. Aug. 11, 1777. Pard. for exchange May 31, 1779. G; 5A p. 37.

RICHARDS or RICHARDSON, Benj. of England. Lexington. Comm. M. Sept. 19, 1777. R. N. or escaped. 3 p. 137; 7 p. 253.

RICHARDS, John. Mariner. General Nash, Betsey or Gatsey. Comm. M. July 28, 1781. SP; HO; 3 p. 211; 10 v. 74 p. 36.

RICHARDS, Peter. Lieut. The Alfred. Comm. F. July 18, 1778. Escaped. 5A p. 38.

RICHARDSON, Benj. See RICHARDS.

RICHARDSON, Gideon. Seaman. General Mifflin. Comm. F. July 20, 1781. SP; HO.

RICHARDSON, Icho'd. Prize of the Warren. Comm. F. Nov. 19, 1777. Escaped. 5A p. 36.

RICHARDSON, James of Marblehead or Woburn. Sturdy Beggar. Comm. M. June, 1777. Pard. for exchange Feb. 2, 1779. G; 3 p. 74; 7 p. 257.

RICHARDSON, Mourning. Seaman. Pocahontas. Comm. F. Nov. 18, 1780. Pard. for R. N. March 27, 1781. G; SP;

RICHARDSON, Wm. and his son. Passengers on the brig Talbot, a vessel from Maryland bound for France. Petitioned for release Nov. 10, 1780. Released on parole Nov. 11, 1780. G.

RICHET or RICKETS, Benjamin. Sturdy Beggar. Comm. F. Jan. 23, 1778. Pard. for exchange May 31, 1779. Exchanged July 2, 1779. G; 5 v. 32 p. 286; 5A p. 37.

RICHEY or RICHIE, James of Londonderry. Essex. Comm. M. July 25, 1781. 3 p. 210; 10 v. 74 p. 36. (See also RICKEY).

RICHEY or RICHIE, Robert of Scotland. Charming Sally. Captured Jan. 16, 1777. Pard. for R. N. Sept. 25, 1778. G; 7 p. 248. (See RICKEY).

RICHMOND, John of Virginia or Staten Island. Essex. Comm. M. July 20 or 21, 1781. R.N. Nov. 9, 1781. 3 p. 210; 10 v. 74 pp. 34, 151. (See Thomas RICHMOND).

RICHMOND, Thomas. F. Pard. for R.N. Jan. 27, 1781. G.

RICHMOND, Thomas. M. Pard. for R.N. Nov. 26, 1781. (Perhaps meant for John). G.

RICKETS, Benj. See RICHET.

RICKEY, James. M. Pard. for R.N. Aug. 9, 1781. G. (See also RICHIE).

RICKEY, Robert of Scotland. Charming Polly or Salley. M. Escaped. 3 p. 75. (Probably meant for RICHIE).

RIDDICK, Henry. Seaman. Fair American. Comm. F. Nov. 18, 1780. SP; HO.

RIDER, Bartholomew. F. Pard. for R.N. July 23, 1779. G.

RIDGWAY, Gore. Seaman. Jack. Sent sick Jan. 14, 1781 and not comm. F. HO.

RIGGINS, Eleazer. See HIGGANS.

RIGGS, Esau or Asa of Cape Ann. Mariner. Beaver. Comm. M. Sept. 1, 1781. SP; HO; 3 p. 211.

RIGHTINGTON, Henry. See WRIGHT(L)INGTON.

RILEY, William of Ireland. Lexington. Comm. M. Sept. 19, 1777. Pard. for exchange Dec. 11, 1779. G; 7 p. 252.

RINES, Thomas of Berwick, New Hampshire. Dalton. In hospital at Plymouth April, 1777. Died June 16, 1777. 3 p. 75; 4 p. 184; 7 pp. 51, 245.

RIPLEY, REPPLY or RAPLEY, Paul. Comet of Philadelphia. Comm. M. Jan. 6, 1781. SP; HO; HL; 3 p. 140; 10 v. 73 p. 312.

RISTEAU, George. F. Pard. for R.N. Jan. 9, 1782. G.

ROBERTS, John. C. Carpenter. General Sullivan. Comm. F. April 26, 1779. Pard. for exchange Dec. 11, 1779. G; 5A p. 39.

ROBERTSON, Robert. Master. Hornet. Comm. F. Oct. 13, 1777. Escaped. 5A p. 37.

ROBINS, Roger. F. Pard. for R. N. Oct. 6, 1781. G.

ROBINS, Rufus. Comm. M. Jan. 22, 1782. HO.

ROBINSON, George. F. Pard. for R. N. Aug. 9, 1781. G.

ROBINSON, James. Seaman. Polly. Comm. F. June 27, 1781. SP; HO.

ROBINSON, James. Seaman. Two Brothers. Comm. M. Jan. 23, 1782. HO.

ROBINSON, William. Jason. Captured but not comm. Oct. 15, 1781. HO.

ROCKFORD, George. Essex. Comm. M. July 24, 1781. Pard. for R. N. Aug. 9, 1781. G; 10 v. 74 p. 35.

ROGERS, Abista or Abisha of Martha's Vineyard. Charming Sally or Polly. Captured Jan. 16, 1777. M. Pard. for exchange Dec. 20, 1778. Still there Feb. 7, 1779. G; 3 p. 75; 7 p. 248.

ROGERS, Eliphalet or Lifelight of Martha's Vineyard. Seaman. Charming Sally or Polly. Captured Jan. 16, 1777. M. Pard. for exchange Dec. 20, 1778. Still there Feb. 7, 1779. Re-taken in Alliance, Feb. 9, 1780. G; SP; 3 p. 75; 7 p. 248.

ROGERS, Elisha. F. Escaped and re-captured Nov. 14, 1780. Pard. for exchange Dec. 11, 1779. G.

ROGERS, John. Rising States. Comm. F. June 14, 1777. Escaped. 5A p. 36.

ROGERS, Tho. P. M. mate. Comm. F. Jan. 23, 1778. Escaped. 5A p. 37.

ROLLS, Edward. Seaman. Harlequin. Comm. F. Feb. 3, 1781. SP; HO.

ROL(L)S, George. Captain. Janey. Comm. M. Aug. 19, 1778. Escaped. 3 p. 136; 7 pp. 163, 168, 256.

RONDEY, George. Seaman. Terrible. Comm. M. Feb. 6, 1782. HO.

ROSBACK, Samuel. Seaman. Dolphin. Comm. F. May 24, 1781. SP; HO.

ROSE, Thomas. Seaman. Twin Sisters. Comm. M. Jan. 9, 1782. HO; 3 p. 212.

ROSS, Alexander of Newburyport, Mass. Dalton. Comm. M. June, 1777. Escaped Dec. 19, 1778. Pard. for exchange Dec. 26, 1778. G; 3 p. 74; 4 p. 307; 7 pp. 49, 199, 243.

ROSS, Samuel of Bristol. Seaman. Susannah or Reprisal's prize. Comm. F. June 27, 1781. Pard. for exchange Dec. 11, 1779. G; SP; HO; 3 p. 75; 7 p. 251.

ROUNEY or ROWNEY, George. Mariner. Essex. Comm. M. July 27, 1781. SP; HO.

ROW, Soloman. Seaman. Hercules. Sent from Kinsale to M. April 9, 1782. HO.

ROWE, John. M. Pard. for R. N. Sept. 25, 1778. G.

ROWE, Joshua. Seaman. Jason. Captured but not comm. Oct. 15, 1781. HO.

ROWLEY, Benj. Mariner. Effingham. Comm. M. May 10, 1779. Pard. for exchange Dec. 11, 1779. G; SP; HO.

ROWNEY, George. See ROUNEY.

RUDDOCK, Boston. Rising States. Comm. F. June 14, 1777. Pard. for exchange May 31, 1779. G; 5A p. 36.

RUDROC, Thoms. of Waterford, N. J. Lion. Comm. M. Nov. 21, 1781. 10 v. 74 p. 155.

RUE, Israel. Seaman. Essex. Comm. M. Jan. 24, 1782. HO.

RUGER, John.   Seaman.   Fair American.   Comm. F. Nov. 18, 1780. SP; HO.

RUNNEL, John of Marblehead.   Grand Turk.   Comm. M. Jan. 1781. 3 p. 213.

RUNNELLS, Thomas of Baltimore.   Reprisal's prize.   Comm. M. June 29, 1777.   R. N.   7 p. 251.

RUSSELL, Daniel (Com.) of Carolina.   Prize master.   Black Prince or Princess.   Comm. M. Oct. 20, 1781.   SP; HO; 3 p. 212; 10 v. 74 p. 146.

RUSSELL, Thomas.   Seaman.   Fair American.   Comm. F. Nov. 30, 1780. Pard. for exchange April 20, 1781.   G; SP; HO.

RUSSELL, William.   Mariner.   Jason.   Comm. M. Dec. 16 or 19, 1779. Exchanged June 24, 1782.   Died March 7, 1784.   SP; HO; HL; 3 p. 138; 10 v. 73 p. 336.   See bibliography No. 8.

RUSSELL, William.   Seaman.   Monmouth.   Sally and Beckey.   Comm. F. Dec. 30, 1779.   SP; HO.

S

SACK, John. Mariner. Franklin. Comm. M. Dec. 6, 1781. SP; HO; 3 p. 212.

SADLER, Joshua. Cook. Hercules. Captured but not comm. Oct. 15, 1781. HO.

SALISBURY, Luther. Master. George. Comm. M. Sept. 7, 1781. SP; HO.

SALTER, Mr. (Probably Francis). M. Escaped Dec. 22, 1778. 7 p. 201.

SALTER, Francis of Marblehead. Fancy. Comm. M. Aug. 7, 1777. Escaped. 3 p. 136; 7 p. 249.

SALTER, Joseph of Marblehead. Prize master. Minerva or Brutus of Salem. Comm. M. Jan. 16, 1781. SP; HO; HL; 3 p. 140; 10 v. 73 p. 314.

SALTER, Thomas of Frenchman's Bay or Scotland. Fancy. Comm. M. Aug. 7, 1777. Pard. for exchange Dec. 11, 1779. G; 3 p. 136; 7 p. 251.

SAMPSON, Daniel. Mariner. Little Pegey or Porgy. Comm. M. Jan. 3, 1782. SP; HO; 3 p. 213.

SAN(D)FORD, Luscomb or Rescomb of Rhode Island. Minerva. Comm. M. Aug. 24, 1780. In Hospital May 10, 1781. SP; HO; HL; 3 p. 139; 10 v. 73 p. 341.

SATCHALL or SETCHELL, Isaak of Ipswich. Mariner. James and Rebecca, prize to the Franklin. Comm. M. Oct. 16, 1781. SP; HO; 10 v. 74 p. 145.

SAUL(S), Abraham. Seaman. Eagle or Randolph. Comm. F. Jan. 19, 1779. Pard. for exchange Dec. 11, 1779. G; SP; HO; 5A p. 39.

SAUNDERS, Joseph. Seaman. Hercules. Sent from Kinsale to M. April 9, 1782. HO.

MARINERS OF THE AMERICAN REVOLUTION

SA(U)NDERS, Wm. The Alfred. Comm. F. July 18, 1778. Pard. for exchange Dec. 11, 1779 and Nov. 9, 1781. G; 5A p. 38.

SAUNDERS, William of Boston. Mariner. St. Francis, or prize to the Franklin. Comm. M. Dec. 7, 1781. SP; HO; 3 p. 212.

SAVAGE or SAVIGE, John of Marblehead. Seaman. Comm. F. Feb. 3, 1781. Jack. SP; HO; 10 v. 73 p. 340.

SAVIL(L), Edwd. Mariner. Essex. Comm. M. July 21, 1781. Pard. for exchange Feb. 6, 1782. G; SP;

SAVOID, Thomas. Seaman. Monmouth. Comm. F. Dec. 21, 1779. SP; HO.

SAWLEY, Benj. of Falmouth. Effingham. Comm. M. May 10, 1779. 3 p. 138.

SAWYER, John. Seaman. General Wayne. Comm. F. Aug. 9, 1781. SP; HO.

SAWYER, Wm. Angelica. Comm. F. July 7, 1778. Pard. for exchange May 31, 1779. G; 5A p. 38.

SAYWARD, Jonathan. F. Pard. for exchange Dec. 11, 1779. G.

SAYWARD, Theodore. Seaman. Hercules. Comm. M. Jan. 24, 1782. HO.

SCHLATTER, Gerardus. Seaman. Fanny. Comm. F. Nov. 18, 1780. SP.

SCINNER, Wm. Montgomery. Comm. F. Aug. 8, 1777. Escaped. 5A p. 36. (Same as SKINNER?)

SCOTT, Cuff of Martha's Vineyard. Charming Sally or Polly. Captured Jan. 16, 1777. Pard. for R. N. Oct. 14, 1778. Entered or escaped. G; 3 p. 75; 7 p. 248.

SCOTT, Thomas. Seaman. Dolphin. Comm. F. May 24, 1781. SP; HO.

MARINERS OF THE AMERICAN REVOLUTION

SCRIGINS, John. General Sullivan. Comm. F. April 26, 1779. 5A p. 39.

SCRIGGINS, Saml. See SKRIGGINS.

SEAGERS, John. Seaman. Hercules. Captured but not comm. Oct. 15, 1781. HO.

SEAL, William. Mariner. Eliza, prize to the Grand Turk. Comm. M. Jan. 3, 1782. SP; HO; 3 p. 213.

SEARS, Jesse. Sturdy Beggar. Comm. F. Jan. 23, 1778. Died. 5A p. 37.

SEARS, Joshua. Comm. F. Feb. 18, 1779. Pard. for exchange Nov. 9, 1781. G; 5A p. 39.

SEAWARD, John. M. HL. (See SEWARD).

SECCOMBE, Joseph. See SICCOMBE.

SEGER, Geo. Doctor. Montgomery. Comm. F. Aug. 8, 1777. Escaped. 5A p. 36.

SELLERS, James of Old York. Dalton or Charming Polly. Comm. M. June 1777. In hospital April, 1777. Pard. for exchange Dec. 11, 1779. G; 3 p. 75; 4 p. 184; 7 p. 245.

SELLERS, Tobias of Old York, N. H. Dalton or Charming Polly. Comm. M. June, 1777. Pard. for exchange Dec. 20, 1778. G; 3 p. 75; 7 p. 245.

SEND, William. M. Pard. for exchange Dec. 11, 1779. G.

SERJANT, Daniel. Seaman. Hercules. Sent from Kinsale to M. April 9, 1782. HO.

SESSON, Preserved. M. Pard. for exchange Dec. 11, 1779. G. (See SISSAL)

SETCHEL, Isaac of Ipswich. See SATCHALL.

SEVER, Ebenezer. Angelica. Comm. F. July 7, 1778. Pard. for exchange May 31, 1779. G; 5A p. 38.

SEWARD, Emanuel. Seaman. Terrible. Comm. F. May 24, 1781. SP; HO.

SEWARD, John. Mate or mariner. Effingham, Weymouth or General Sullivan's prize. Comm. M. July 3, 1779. Pard. for exchange Dec. 11, 1779. G; SP; HO; 3 p. 138. See SEAWARD.

SEWARD, John. Captain. Portsmouth, N.H. M. 9 pp. 80, 99. See SEAWARD.

SEWELL, Ed. Essex. Comm. M. July 21, 1781. 3 p. 210.

SHACKFORD, Wm. of Newburyport. Dalton. Comm. M. June, 1777. Joined Alliance. 7 p. 243.

SHADWICK, Nathan. Seaman. Susannah. Comm. F. June 27, 1781. SP.

SHAHAGAN, James. Seaman. Retaliation. Comm. F. Oct. 31, 1780. Pard. for R.N. March 27, 1781. G; SP; HO.

SHAKLE or SHACKLES, Benjamin of England. Charming Sally or Polly. Captured Jan. 16, 1777. M. Died. 3 p. 75; 7 p. 248.

SHAREMAN, Saml. Mariner. Essex. Comm. M. July 24, 1781. SP; HO.

SHARRETT, Philip. F. Pard. for R.N. Jan. 1781. G.

SHAW, Ichabod of Hampton. Dalton. Comm. M. June, 1777. Pard. for exchange Dec. 20, 1778. G; 3 p. 74; 7 p. 246.

SHAW, John. Black Snake. Comm. F. Feb. 18, 1779. Pard. for exchange Dec. 11, 1779. Pard. for R.N. Jan. 12, 1781. G; 5A p. 39.

SHAW, John. Mariner. L'Uzerne. Comm. M. July 6, 1781. SP; HO; 3 p. 209; 10 v. 74 p. 31.

SHAW, Martin of Ireland or England. Fancy. Comm. M. Aug. 7, 1777. Pard. for exchange Dec. 11, 1779. G; 3 p. 136; 7 p. 251.

SHAW, Wm. Angelica. Comm. F. July 7, 1778. Pard. for exchange Dec. 11, 1779. G; 5A p. 38.

SHEAF, Henry of New York. Charming Salley or Dalton. Captured Jan. 16, 1777. Still there Feb. 7, 1779. Escaped. 3 p. 74; 7 p. 248.

SHEAFE, Samuel or Sampson. Seaman. McCleary. Comm. F. Aug. 28, 1778. Pard. for exchange Dec. 11, 1779. G; 5A p. 38; SP.

SHEALS, Nicholas. Lexington. Comm. M. Sept. 19, 1777. Escaped. 3 p. 137.

SHEARMAN, John of Rhode Island. Angelica. Comm. F. July 7, 1778. 5A p. 38.

SHEARS, Joshua. F. Pard. for exchange Dec. 11, 1779. G.

SHED, Joseph of Boston. Lyon. Comm. M. Aug. 31, 1781. Pard. for R. N. Sept. 10, 1781. G; 3 p. 211.

SHEERMAN, Charles Foster. See SHERMAN.

SHELDON, John. Adventurer. Comm. M. Jan. 21, 1782. 3 p. 213.

SHEPERD or SHEPARD, Michel of Boston. Jason. Comm. M. Sept. 15, 1781. 3 p. 138; 10 v. 74 p. 46.

SHEPHARD or SHEPPARD, Thos. of Baltimore. Mariner. Black Prince or Princess. Comm. M. Oct. 20, 1781. SP; HO; 3 p. 212; 10 v. 74 p. 146.

SHERBURNE, Andrew of Piscataqua (between Portsmouth and Kittery). Seaman. Greyhound. Comm. M. Jan. 25, 1782 at age of 16. See bibliography No. 9.

SHERMAN or SHEERMAN, Charles (Foster) of Rhode Island. Ranger. Comm. M. Aug. 23, 1778. Pard. for exchange Dec. 11, 1779 and Nov. 9, 1781. G; HL; 3 p. 137; 7 p. 256.

SHERMAN, John. F. Pard. for exchange May 31, 1779. G.

SHERMAN, Saml. of Plymouth. Essex. Comm. M. July 24, 1781. 3 p. 210; 10 v. 74 p. 35.

SHERRIN, John. Mariner. Viper. Comm. M. Dec. 7, 1781. SP; HO.

MARINERS OF THE AMERICAN REVOLUTION

SHERRY, John.   See SHURRY.

SHESTER, John.   Lexington.   Comm. M. Sept. 19, 1777.   Exchanged. 3 p. 137.   (Probably meant for CHESTER. q. v.)

SHEY, Nicholas.   M.   Pard. for R. N. Sept. 25, 1778.   G.

SHIELDS, James of Philadelphia.   Lexington.   Comm. M. Sept. 19, 1777. Pard. for R. N. Jan. 4, 1779.   Entered or escaped.   G; 3 p. 137; 7 p. 253.

SHILLABER, Benjamin.   Seaman.   Harlequin.   Comm. F. May 24, 1781. SP; HO.

SHILLABER, James.   M.   Pard. for exchange Dec. 20, 1778.   G.   (Probably same as Joseph).

SHILLABER or SHILABY, Joseph of Portsmouth.   Dalton.   In hospital April, 1777.   Comm. M. June, 1777.   Joined Alliance.   4 p. 184; 7 p. 245. (Probably same as James).

SHILLINGSFORTH, James.   Seaman.   Retaliation.   Comm. F. Oct. 31, 1780.   SP; HO.

SHOCKFORD, Wm.   M.   Pard. for exchange Dec. 20, 1778.   G.

SHOEMAKER, Capt.   M.   4 p. 396.

SHOMAKER, Anthony of Long Island.   Charming Sally or Polly.   Captured Jan. 16, 1777.   Escaped.   3 p. 75; 7 pp. 193, 247.

SHO(R)CKLEY or SHUCKLEY, Saml. of Bedford or Maryland.   Midshipman. Protector.   Comm. M. July 23, 1781.   SP; HO; 3 p. 140; 10 v. 74 p. 35.

SHORT, Thomas.   Seaman.   Pocahontas.   Comm. F. Nov. 18, 1780. SP.

SHRIGGINS, Saml.   See SKRIGINS.

SHRYM, John of Maryland.   Viper.   Comm. M. Sept. 12, 1781.   3 p. 212.

SHURREY or SHERRY, John.　　Mariner.　　Franklin.　　Comm. M. Dec. 6, 1781.　　SP; HO; 3 p. 212.

SIBSBURY, John.　　Seaman.　　Lively.　　Comm. F. after Oct. 16, 1781.　HO.

SICCOMBE or SECCOMBE, Joseph.　　Seaman.　　Harlequin.　　Comm. F. May 16, 1781.　　SP; HO.

SHULER, Exos.　　F.　　Pard. for exchange May 31, 1779.　　G.　(Possibly same as next).

SHULS, Evon.　　Sturdy Beggar.　　Comm F. Jan. 23, 1778.　　5A p. 37. (Possibly same as last).

SICK, William.　　Seaman.　　Bienfaisant, a French ship.　　Comm. Pembroke Jan. 17, 1782.　HO.

SIDERS, Martin.　　Seaman.　　Hercules.　　Sent from Kinsale to M. April 9, 1782.　HO.

SIMKINS, Nicholas.　　See SIMPKIN.

SIMMONDS, John.　　Seaman.　　Antibriton, a French ship.　　Imprisoned at Edinburgh Jan. 19, 1782.　HO.

SIM(M)ONS or SYMONDS, Nathl. or Nathan of Rhode Island.　1st lieut.　Adventure or prize to the Comet.　　Comm. M. March 31, 1781.　　SP; HO; HL; 3 p. 140; 10 v. 73 p. 331.

SIM(M)ON(S), Saml.　M.　In b. h. May 27, 1781.　　Escaped and re-captured July 6, 1781.　　Out of b. h. July 29, 1781.　　HL; 10 v. 73 p. 345; v. 74 pp. 31, 37.

SIMONDS, Harvey.　　Seaman.　　Wexford.　　Captured but not comm. Oct. 2, 1781.　HO.

SIM(M)S or SYMMS, Sampson of Bristol.　　Warren.　　Comm. M. June, 1778. Escaped May 15 and June 29, 1781.　　HL; 3 p. 137; 7 p. 255; 10 v.73 pp. 342, 345; v. 74 pp. 23, 29.　(Same as Samuel SIMS?)

SIMPER(S), Isaac.　　Sturdy Beggar.　　Comm. F. Jan. 23, 1778.　　Pard. for exchange May 31, 1779.　　G; 5A p. 37.

SIMPKIN or SIMKINS, Nicholas of Jersey. Lexington's prize. Comm. M. June, 1777. Escaped. 3 p. 74; 7 p. 249.

SIMPSON, John of Windham. Dalton or Charming Polly. Comm. M. June, 1777. Pard. for exchange Dec. 20, 1778. Joined Alliance. G; 3 p. 75; 7 p. 246.

SIMS, Samuel. M. Pard. for exchange Dec. 11, 1779. (Same as Sampson Simms?) G.

SINCLAIRE, John. Mate. Disdain. Comm. M. Jan. 3, 1782. SP; HO; 3 p. 213.

SINGLETORY, SINGLETON or SINGLETERRY, John of North or South Carolina. Medley. Comm. M. May 5 or 11, 1781. Innoculated May 28, 1781. SP; HO; HL (mark); 3 p. 209; 10 v. 73 pp. 340, 346.

SINGLETORY or SINGLETON, Josh. or Joseph of South Carolina. Medley. Comm. M. May 1 or 5, 1781. Innoculated May 28, 1781. SP; HO; 3 p. 209; 10 v. 73 pp. 339, 346.

SISAL, Edward of Rhode Island. Warren. Comm. M. June, 1778. 7 p. 255.

SISSAL, Preserved. Warren. Comm. M. June 4, 1778. Exchanged. 3 p. 137. (See SESSON.)

SKENETON, Thomas. Re-captured after escaping, Sept. 11, 1778. G.

SKINNER, Richard. Phoenix. Comm. M. May 10, 1779. Escaped. 3 p. 138. (Probably same as next).

SKINNER, Richard. Mate. Jason. Captured but not committed Oct. 15, 1781. HO. (Probably same as above).

SKINNER, Wm. of England or Philadelphia. Fancy. Comm. M. Aug. 7, 1777. Escaped. 3 p. 136; 7 p. 251. (Same as SCINNER?)

SKRIGINS, SHRIGGINGS, SCRIGGINS or SERRIGAN, Saml. of Kittery, N. H. Dalton.or Charming Polly. In hospital April, 1777. Died May 17, 1777. 3 p. 75; 4 p. 184; 7 pp. 38, 245.

SLACOM(B), Gabriel or Gabril. Prize master of Sturdy Beggar. Comm. F. Jan. 23, 1778. Escaped July 23, 1778. 5 v. 30 p. 348; v. 31 p. 287. 5A p. 37.

SLADE or SLATE, Edward. Angelica. Comm. F. July 7, 1777. Pard. for exchange May 31, 1779. G; 5A p. 38.

SLATER, Richd. Mariner. General Nash. Comm. M. May 4, 1781. Innoculated May 28, 1781. SP; HO; HL; 3 p. 141; 10 v. 73 p. 346.

SLOVER, James. Captain. Hector of Philadelphia. Comm. M. March 31, 1781. Pard. for R. N. May, 1781. G; 3 p. 141; 10 v. 73 p. 331. (Probably same as below).

SLOVER, Jno. Captain. R. N. June 5, 1781. M. 10 v. 74 p. 22. (Probably same as above).

SLYFIELD, Andrew of Marblehead. Fancy. Comm. M. Aug. 7, 1777. Escaped. 3 p. 136; 7 p. 250.

SMALL, William. Prize of the Independent. Comm. F. June 26, 1777. Pard. for R. N. Dec. 3, 1778. Entered Dec. 19, 1778. G; 5 v. 32 p. 282; 5A p. 36.

SMEDLEY, Saml. of Connecticut. Captain. Hibernia. Comm. M. March, 1781. Escaped Aug. 25, 1781. 3 p. 141; 10 v. 74 p. 44.

SMIL(E)Y, James. Angelica. Comm. F. July 7, 1778. Pard. for exchange May 31, 1779. G; 5A p. 38.

SMITH, Clemon. Doctor. Hornet. Comm. F. Oct. 13, 1777. Escaped. 5A p. 37.

SMITH, Daniel. Reprisal. Comm. F. Aug. 28, 1778. Pard. for exchange Dec. 11, 1779. G; 5A p. 38.

SMITH, Ephraim. Master. The Spy. Comm. F. Feb. 18, 1779. Escaped. 5A p. 39.

SMITH, George. Prize master. The Swallow. Comm. F. Jan. 23, 1778. 5A p. 37.

SMITH, George. Prize master. Swallow. Comm. F. Jan. 23, 1778. 5A p. 37.

SMITH, George. Prize master. Comm. F. Sept. 24, 1778. 5A p. 38.

SMITH, George. Steward. Disdain. Comm. M. Jan. 3, 1782. SP; HO; 3 p. 213.

SMITH, Henry of Newburyport. Dalton. In hospital May, 1777. Comm. M. June, 1777. Exchanged. 3 p. 74; 4 pp. 185, 306; 7 p. 244.

SMITH, Jacob. Mariner. Franklin. Comm. M. Dec. 6, 1781. SP; HO; 3 p. 212.

SMITH, Jesse. Seaman. Harlequin. Comm. F. May 16, 1781. SP; HO.

SMITH, John of Newburyport. Dalton. In hospital April 4, 1777. Comm. M. June, 1777. Pard. for exchange Dec. 20, 1778. G; 3 p. 74; 4 p. 184; 7 p. 244.

SMITH, John. Boatswain. Muscetor (Mosquito?) F. Pard. for R. N. Dec. 3, 1778. G; 5A p. 36.

SMITH, John. Seaman. Tom Lee. Comm. F. Aug. 9, 1781. SP; HO.

SMITH, John of Wilmington. Mariner. Black Prince or Princess. Comm. M. Oct. 20 or 28, 1781. SP; HO; 3 p. 212; 10 v. 74 pp. 146, 147.

SMITH, John of Marblehead. 2nd lieut. Black Prince or Princess. Comm. M. Oct. 16, 1781. SP; 3 p. 212.

SMITH, John. M. Pard. for R. N. March 20, 1782. G.

SMITH, Joseph. Montgomery. Comm. F. Aug. 8, 1777. Escaped. 5A p. 36.

SMITH, Josiah. Franklin. M. A passenger set free. Brother of surgeon from Dalton. 4 p. 185.

SMITH, Lier. Seaman. Newfoundland. Imprisoned at Edinburgh June 27, 1781. HO.

SMITH, Michael.   Comm. F. Aug. 8, 1777.   Pard. for exchange May 31, 1779.   G; 5A p. 36.

SMITH, Nathl. of Philadelphia.   Mariner.   Friendsgoodwill.   Comm. M. July 27, 1781.   SP; HO; 3 p. 210.

SMITH, Phineas of New York.   Charming Sally or Dalton.   Captured Jan. 16, 1777.   M.   Still there Feb. 7, 1779.   Escaped.   3 p. 74; 7 p. 248.

SMITH, Richard.   Seaman.   Harlequin.   Comm. F. May 24, 1781.   Pard. for exchange Dec. 11, 1779.   G; SP; HO.

SMITH, Richd. of Boston.   Protector.   Comm. M. July 23, 1781.   R. N. Aug. 8, 1781.   3 p. 209; 10 v. 74 pp. 35, 40.

SMITH, Richd.   Black Prince.   Comm. M. Oct. 20, 1781.   3 p. 212; 10 v. 74 p. 146.

SMITH, (Samuel) of Hampton.   Dalton.   Comm. M. June, 1777.   Escaped July 12, 1777.   4 pp. 305, 306; 7 p. 246.

SMITH, Samuel of Broad or Block Point.   Dalton or Charming Polly.   In hospital May, 1777.   Comm. M. Aug. 1777.   Pard. for exchange Dec. 11, 1779.   Escaped.   G; 3 pp. 74, 75; 4 p. 306; 7 p. 246. (Probably same as next).

SMITH, Samuel.   M.   Pard. for R. N. April 28, 1781.   (Probably same as last).   G.

SMITH, Silas of Salem.   Captain or prize master's mate.   Comm. F. Sept. 24, 1778.   Pard. for exchange Dec. 11, 1779 and Nov. 9, 1781.   G; 5 v. 32 p. 166; 5A p. 38.

SMITH, Solomon.   The Spy.   Comm. F. Feb. 18, 1779.   Pard. for exchange Dec. 11, 1779.   G; 5A p. 39.

SMITH, Capt. Thomas.   Comm. F. Feb. 18, 1779.   5A p. 39.

SMITH, Thomas.   F.   Pard. for exchange Dec. 11, 1779.   G.

SMITH, Thomas.   M.   Pard. for R. N. Aug. 24, 1781.   G.

MARINERS OF THE AMERICAN REVOLUTION

SMITH, Thos. of Spanish River. Mariner. Marquis de Morbec. Comm. M. Oct. 2, 1781. SP; HO; 3 p. 211; 10 v. 74 p. 142.

SMITH, William. Master. Salley. Sent to hospital March 23, 1777. Still in, April, 1777. Escaped from hospital July 2. Re-captured July 25. Taken out of b. h. Aug. 6. Escaped Sept. 20. Re-captured and put in b. h. Oct. 6, 1777. 4 pp. 184, 186, 305, 306, 307, 395, 396.

SMITH, Wm. Warren. Comm. M. June 4, 1778. Pard. for exchange Dec. 11, 1779. (Written twice). G; 3 p. 137.

SMITH, Wm. of Virginia. Betsey. Comm. M. July 23, 1781. Pard. for R. N. Aug. 30, 1781. G; 3 p. 210; 10 v. 74 p. 35.

SMITH, William of Ireland. Dalton. Comm. M. June, 1777. R. N. Aug. 18, 1781. 7 p. 246; 10 v. 74 p. 42.

SMITH, Zachariah. Seaman. Hercules. Captured but not committed Oct. 15, 1781. HO.

SMITH, Zoath. Cook. Hercules. Captured but not committed Oct. 15, 1781. HO.

SMITHERS, Benjamin. Seaman. Harlequin. Comm. F. May 24, 1781. SP; HO.

SMITHY, Richard. Prize master. Black Prince or Princess. Comm. M. Oct. 20, 1781. Escaped Nov. 15, 1781. Att. escape Nov. 18, 1781. Out of b. h. Nov. 26. SP; HO; 10 v. 74 pp. 153, 154, 156.

SMYTH, William. M. Pard. for R. N. Sept. 25, 1778. G.

SNEED, George. Fort Stanwin. Comm. F. June 3, 1780. SP; HO.

SNELL, Antoni. Seaman. Twin Sisters of R. I. Imprisoned in Security Prison Ship at Chatham, Dec. 18, 1781. HO.

SNOW. F. Escaped May 1, 1781. 10 v. 74 p. 26.

SNOW, Hemon, Hermon or Hayman of Cape Cod. Success. Comm. M. July, 1781. Pard. for exchange Dec. 11, 1779. Escaped Aug. 25, 1781. Out of b. h. Sept. 24, 1781. Pard. for R. N. Oct. 30, 1781. Entered Oct. 16, 1781. G; 10 v. 74 pp. 44, 45, 47, 145.

SNOW, Isaac. Mariner, Resolution of Boston. Comm. M. Jan. 22, 1781. SP; HO; HL; 3 p. 140; 10 v. 73 p. 316.

SNOW, Samuel of Marblehead. Still in F. May 8, 1781. Pard. for exchange Dec. 11, 1779. G; 10 v. 73 p. 340.

SNOW, Thomas. Phoenix. Comm. M. May 10, 1779. Pard. for exchange Dec. 11, 1779. Escaped. G; 3 p. 138.

SOMES or SOOMES, Jonathan. Comm. F. April 19, 1779. Pard. for exchange Dec. 11, 1779. Pard. for R. N. Nov. 6, 1780. G; 5A p. 39.

SOUTHWARD or SOUTHARD, George of Salem. Captain. Sturdy Beggar. Comm. M. June, 1777. Pard. for exchange Dec. 20, 1778. G; 3 p. 74; 4 pp. 185, 186; 7 p. 257.

SOWARDS, Jon'n. General Sullivan. Comm. F. April 26, 1779. 5A p. 39.

SOWARDS, Richard of Kittery. Dalton or Charming Polly. Comm. M. June, 1777. 3 p. 75; 7 p. 245.

SPADE, John or Jos. Mariner. Franklin. Comm. M. Dec. 6, 1781. SP; HO; 3 p. 212.

SPARROWHORN, Blake. Seaman. Wexford. Sent from Kinsale to M. April 9, 1782. HO.

SPEAR, Gersham of Boston. Comm. Pembroke 1778 and M. Oct. 14, 1780. Pard. for R. N. Nov. 4, 1780. G.

SPENCER, Samuel L'd. Doctor's mate. Angelica. Comm. F. July 7, 1778. Escaped. 5A p. 38.

SPLAND, Thomas. F. Pard. for R. N. Dec. 7, 1780. G.

SPOONER, David. Mariner. Industry. Comm. M. Nov. 18. 1780. SP; HO; 3 p. 139.

SPOONER, Eben. Charming Polly or Dalton. Comm. M. May, 1777. Escaped. 3 p. 75.

SPOONER, Edward of Newburyport. In hospital April, 1777. Comm. M. June, 1777. Pard. for R. N. Sept. 25, 1778. G; 4 p. 184; 7 p. 244.

SPOONER, Nathl. of Plymouth. Mariner. L'Uzerne of Philadelphia. Comm. M. July 7 or 9, 1781. Att. escape Aug. 25, 1781. Re-taken and in b.h. Out of b.h. Sept. 24, 1781. SP; HO; 3 p. 209; 10 v. 74 pp. 32, 44, 47.

SPRAGG, Stephen. Seaman. Thomas, Merchant ship. Captured but not comm. Oct. 23, 1781. HO.

SPRAGUE, Benj. See SPRIGGS.

SPRIGGINS, John. Seaman. General Sullivan. Comm. F. April 26, 1779. Pard. for exchange Dec. 11, 1779. G; SP; HO.

SPRIGGS or SPRAGUE, Benj. of Beverly. Mariner. Essex. Comm. M. Aug. 25 or 31, 1781. SP; HO; 3 p. 211.

SPRINGER or SPRINGES, Richard. Carpenter. Wexford. Captured but not comm. Oct. 21, 1781. HO.

SPRINGER, William. Seaman. Marquis de la Fayette. Comm. M. Jan. 22, 1782. HO.

STACEY or STATIA, Amb. of Marblehead. Mariner. John, prize to the Pilgrim. Comm. M. July 3, or 28, 1779. Pard. for exchange Dec. 11, 1779. SP; HO; HL; G.

STACEY or STATIA, John. Mariner. Monmouth. Comm. M. Dec. 16 or 18, 1779. In b.h. Jan. 7, 1780. SP; HO; HL; 3 p. 138; 8 p. 121.

STACEY, Moses of Marblehead. Hawk's prize. M. Pard. for exchange Dec. 11, 1779. G; 3 p. 137; 7 p. 252.

STACEY, Nathaniel of Marblehead. Freedom's prize. Captured April 27, 1777. M. Escaped. 3 p. 75; 7 p. 251.

STACEY, Samuel of Portsmouth or Kittery, N.H. Dalton or Charming Polly. Comm. M. June, 1777. Pard. for exchange Dec. 20, 1778. Went with Paul Jones. G; 3 p. 75; 7 p. 245.

STAKING or STARKINS, Benjamin of Long Island. Mariner. Gallsey, Gascon or Gatray. Comm. M. May 4, 1781. Innoculated May 28, 1781. SP; HO; HL; 3 p. 141; 10 v. 73 p. 346;

STALL, Jacob of Philadelphia. Luzerne. Comm. M. July 6 or 9, 1781. 3 p. 209; 10 v. 74 p. 32.

STANCHFIELD, John. Charming Polly or Salley. M. Escaped. 3 p. 75.

STANLY, James W. Angelica. Comm. F. July 7, 1778. 5A p. 38.

STANWOOD, Arans(i)e. Seaman. General Glover. Comm. F. Oct. 18, 1779. SP; HO.

STANWOOD, Joseph. 11 pp. 252-3.

STANWOOD, Joshua. Seaman. Hercules. Sent from Kinsale to M. April 9, 1782. HO.

STAPLES, Nath. of Kittery. Dalton or Charming Polly. In hospital April, 1777. Comm. M. June, 1777. Pard. for exchange May 31, 1779. G; 3 p. 75; 4 p. 184; 7 p. 245.

STARKINS, Benj. See STAKING.

STARKS, Israel. Comm. F. Feb. 18, 1779. Pard. for exchange Dec. 11, 1779. G; 5A p. 39.

STATEN, Willm. Mariner. Essex. Comm. M. July 20, 1781. SP; HO.

STATIA. See STACEY.

STEARNS, William of Maryland. Lexington's prize. Comm. M. June, 1777. Pard. for exchange Dec. 20, 1778. G; 7 p. 249. See STERNS.

STEDSON, Benjamin. Mariner. Mars. Comm. M. July 3, 1779. SP; HL.

STEEL, William. Soldier taken in South Carolina. Lion? Comm. M. Aug. 31, 1781. SP; HO; 3 p. 211. (He petitioned that he was free on parole at the time of the capitulation of Charlestown).

STENFELDT or STAMFIELD, Jan Jorg or John George of Holland. Charming Sally. Captured Jan. 16, 1777. M. Pard. for R. N. Sept. 25, 1778. G; 7 p. 248.

STEPHENS or STEVENS, John. M. Pard. for R. N. May 25, 1781. Entered June 5, 1781. G; 10 v. 74 p. 22.

STEPHENS, Luke.   Seaman.   Wexford.   Sent from Kinsale to M. April 9, 1782.   HO.

STEPHENS, Richard.   F.   Pard. for exchange Dec. 11, 1779.   G.

STEPHENS, Thomas.   F.   Pard. for R. N. Nov. 30, 1779.   G.

STEPHENS, Thomas.   See STEVENS.

STEPHENS, Wm.   Rising States.   Comm. F. June 14, 1777.   Pard. for exchange May 31, 1779.   G; 5A p. 36.

STEPHENSON or STEVENSON, Gilbert of Philadelphia.   Seaman.   Marquis de la Fayette.   Comm. M. Jan. 9, 1782.   HO; 3 p. 213.

STEPHENSON, John.   Mariner.   Hunter.   Comm. M. July 25, 1781.   SP; HO.

STEPHENSON, Stephen.   Seaman.   South Quay.   Comm. F. March 21, 1781.   SP; HO.

STERNS, Wm. of Maryland.   Lexington.   M.   Escaped.   3 p. 74.   See STEARNS.

STEVENS, George.   F.   Pard. for R. N. July 12, 1780.   G.

STEVENS, John.   Seaman.   Harlequin.   Comm. F. Feb. 3, 1781.   SP; HO; 10 v. 73 p. 340.

STEVENS, John from New Haven.   Two Sisters.   Comm. M. April 24, 1781.   3 p. 141; 10 v. 73 p. 337.

STEVENS, John.   Hunter.   Comm. M. July 25, 1781.   3 p. 210.

STEVENS, John.   See STEPHENS.

STEVENSON, Gilbert.   See STEPHENSON.

STEVENS, Sylvester of Marblehead.   Phoenix.   Comm. M. May 10, 1779.   Escaped.   3 p. 138.

STEVENS or STEPHENS, Thomas of Salem.   Warren.   Comm. M. June, 1778.   Pard. for exchange Dec. 11, 1779 and Nov. 9, 1781.   HL; 3 p. 137; 7 p. 254; G.

MARINERS OF THE AMERICAN REVOLUTION

STEVENSON, Mr. Lieut to Captain Lee. Escaped from M. Sept. 21, 1777, and arrived safe in Bilboa. 7 p. 74.

STEVENSON, Robert of Scotland. Fancy. Comm. M. Aug. 7, 1777. Escaped. 3 p. 136; 7 p. 251.

STEWARD or STUART, Daniel. Montgomery of Philadelphia. Comm. F. Aug. 8, 1777. In b.h. Sept. 4, 1778. Escaped. 5A p. 36; 5 v. 32 p. 73.

STEWARD, Richard. M. Pard. for exchange Dec. 20, 1778. G.

STEWART, John of Scotland or Ireland. Lexington. Comm. M. Sept. 19, 1777. Pard. for R. N. Oct. 14, 1778. Entered or escaped. G; 3 p. 137; 7 p. 254.

STEWART, John. Lion. Comm. M. Aug. 31, 1781. SP; HO; 3 p. 211.

STEWART, Michael. Seaman. Patty. Comm. M. Feb. 27, 1782. HO.

STICKNEY, John of Newburyport. Dalton. Comm. M. June, 1777. Exchanged. 3 p. 74; 7 p. 243.

STILL, George of England. Oliver Cromwell. Comm. M. Oct. 18, 1777. Escaped. 3 p. 75; 7 p. 255.

STILLWELL, John. Seaman. Confederacy. Comm. F. Aug. 9, 1781. SP; HO.

STIRING, George. Mariner. Newburn or General Nash. Comm. M. July 25 or 28, 1781. SP; HO. (Probably same as George STYREN).

STIRRY, Sipperan. Comm. F. Aug, 1778. Escaped. 5A p. 38.

STOBO, Jacob of South Carolina. 1st lieut. Eagle or General Washington. Comm. M. Sept. 7, 1781. SP; HO.

STODDARD, Saml. of Hingham. Mariner. Essex. Comm. M. July 21, 1781. SP; HO; 3 p. 210; 10 v. 74 p. 34.

STONE, Abner. Seaman. Eagle. Comm. F. March 5, 1781. SP; HO.

STONE, Benjamin. Seaman. Hercules. Sent from Kinsale to M. April 9, 1782. HO.

MARINERS OF THE AMERICAN REVOLUTION

STOPER, Benning of New Hampshire. The McClery. Comm. F. Aug. 1 1778. Died. 5A p. 38.

STRALON or STRATTON, Wm. of Boston or Cambridge. Phoenix of Boston. Comm. M. July 20, 1781. 3 p. 210; 10 v. 74 p. 34.

STRAWN, Jacob. Mariner. L'Uzerne. Comm. M. July 7, 1781. SP; HO.

STRIKER, Joseph of Marblehead. Freedom's prize. Captured April 27, 1777. Pard. for exchange Feb. 2, 1779. G; 3 p. 75; 7 p. 251.

STRINGER, Joseph. M. Pard. for R. N. Oct. 14, 1778. G.

STROUD, Elias. F. Pard. for R. N. Nov. 6, 1780. G.

STUART, Daniel. See STEWARD.

STUBBS, Benjamin Coffin of Portsmouth. Dalton. In hospital April, 1777. Comm. M. June, 1777. Pard. for exchange Dec. 20, 1778. G; 3 p. 75; 4 p. 184; 7 p. 244.

STUDLEY, or STUTILY, Guppy or Gulfry of Portsmouth, N. H. Dalton or Charming Polly. Comm. M. June 28, 1777. Pard. for exchange Dec. 20, 1778. G; 3 p. 75; 4 p. 188; 7 p. 245.

STUDSON, Elisha. Seaman. Wexford. Sent from Kinsale to M. April 9, 1782. HO.

STURGES, John. Mate. Venus. Comm. F. April 2, 1778. Escaped. 5A p. 37.

STURGIS, Daniel. F. Pard. for R. N. Nov. 22, 1780. G.

STUTSON, Benj. of Cohasset. Mart's or Mars's prize. Comm. M. July 3, 1779. 3 p. 138.

STYREN, George of North Carolina. General Nash. Comm. M. July 20, 1781. 3 p. 210; 10 v. 74 p. 36. (Probably same as George STIRLING).

SUMMER or SUMNER, Rufus or Raphes. Mariner. Protector. Comm. M. July 23, 1781. SP; HO; 3 p. 209; 10 v. 74 p. 35.

SUMMERS, Benjamin. Seaman. Hercules. Sent from Kinsale to M. April 9, 1782. HO.

SURRAN, Bernard. F. Pard. for R.N. Dec. 16, 1778. G. (Probably same as next).

SURRELL, Burnet. Angelica. Comm. F. July 7, 1778. R.N. 5A p. 38. (Probably same as last).

SUTHERLAND, John. Born Norfolk Co., Virginia. Lexington. Re-captured Feb. 18, 1778. G. (No other mention anywhere, so deduce he escaped again).

SUTTON, Uriah or Wm. of Virginia. Mariner. Franklin. Comm. M. Dec. 6, 1781. SP; HO; 3 p. 212.

SWAIN, Eliahim of Boston or Nantucket. Prize master. Essex. Comm. M. Aug. 25, 1781. SP; HO; 3 p. 211; 10 v. 74 p. 44.

SWAIN, John. Angelica. Comm. F. July 7, 1778. Escaped Dec. 27, 1778. 5 v. 32 pp. 283, 286; 5A p. 38.

SWAIN, John. Officer. Alliance. Comm. F. Oct. 3, 1779. 5 v. 32 p. 283.

SWAN, John. Fancy. Comm. M. Aug. 7, 1777. Escaped. 3 p. 136; 7 p. 249.

SWAN, Robert of Marblehead. Fancy. Comm. M. Aug. 7, 1777. Escaped. 3 p. 136; 7 p. 249.

SWASEY, Emanuel of Martha's Vineyard. Charming Sally or Polly. Captured Jan. 16, 1777. M. Still in M. Feb. 7, 1779. Pard. for exchange Dec. 11, 1779. G; 3 p. 75; 7 p. 248.

SWEET, Bernard. Seaman. Bermuda. Comm. M. Jan. 22, 1782. HO.

SWEET, Job. Seaman. Fair American. Comm. F. Nov. 18, 1780. SP; HO.

SWEET, John. Seaman. Flying Fish or Clinton. Comm. F. May 24, 1781. SP; HO.

SWEET, Thomas.   F.   Pard. for R. N. Nov. 6, 1780.   G.

SWEET, Virtue.   Mariner.   Lion.   Comm. M. Aug. 31, 1781.   SP; HO; 3 p. 211.

SWEETING, Richard.   Sturdy Beggar.   Comm. F. Jan. 23, 1778.   Pard. for exchange May 31, 1779.   G. 5A p. 37.

SWEETNALL, John.   F.   Pard. for exchange Dec. 11, 1779.   G.

SWET, Benjamin.   Seaman.   American.   Comm. F. June 27, 1781.   SP; HO.

SYMMONS, Abraham. of Rhode Island.   Alliance's prize.   M.   Pard. for R. N. July 23, 1779.   Entered or escaped.   G; 3 p. 138.

SYMMS, Sampson.   See SIMS.

SYMONDS, Nathl.   See SIM(M)ONS.

SYMONS, John.   Seaman.   Mary, prize to the Grand Turk.   Comm. M. Feb. 27, 1782.   HO.

SYMONS, Samuel of Rhode Island.   Polly.   Comm. M. Sept. 10, 1780.   Pard. for exchange Nov. 9, 1781.   G; 3 p. 139.   (Probably same as Saml. SIM(M)ON(S).

T

TABER or TABOR, Richard. Seaman. Sally and Becky. Comm. F. Dec. 30, 1779. SP; HO.

TALBOT, Silas. Captain. Washington of Providence. Comm. M. March 31, 1781. Escaped, re-captured and put in b.h. June 18, 1781. Out of b.h. June 26. Escaped July 5. In b.h. July 6. Out of b.h. July 23, Att. escape, put in b.h. Sept. 13. Out of b.h. Sept. 19, 1781. Pard. for exchange Oct. 16, 1781. (In spite of his attempts to escape he was exchanged in the place of one prisoner who was in hospital, together with seven other prisoners for Mr. Dillon and seven others). G; HL; 3 p. 140; 10 v. 73 p. 331; v. 74 pp. 26, 29, 30, 31, 35, 45, 46.

TALMAN, Peleg. Seaman. Wexford. Captured but not comm. Oct. 2, 1781. HO.

TANGLE or QUIN, Thos. Master. Marquis de Morbec. Comm. M. Oct. 2, 1781. SP; HO; 10 v. 74 p. 142.

TAPPAN or TAPPEN, Benj. Born in Boston. True Blue. Escaped and re-capt. Nov. or Dec. 1778 after being in F. about 14 mos. G. (See also TOPPIN).

TAPPIN, TAPPEN or TAPING, Lewin or Sewil. Mariner. Beaver or Essex. Comm. M. Aug. 25, 1781. SP; HO; 3 p. 211; 10 v. 74 p. 44.

TAPSCOTT, Ezekiel. Seaman. Pocahontas. Comm. F. Nov. 18, 1780. SP; HO.

TAPSCOTT, John. Pocahontas. Comm. F. Nov. 18, 1780. SP; HO.

TARR, Jacob of Cape Ann. Mariner. General Massey. Comm. M. Oct. 16, 1781. SP; HO; 3 p. 212; 10 v. 74 p. 145.

TARRANT, John. Seaman. Jack. Comm. F. Feb. 3, 1781. SP; HO.

TATE, Jesse. Seaman. Pocahontas. Comm. F. Nov. 18, 1780. SP; HO.

TAVINDER, Edwd. of West Falmouth, Cape Cod. Mariner. Essex. Comm. M. July 21, 1781. SP; HO; 3 p. 210; 10 v. 74 p. 34.

TAYLOR, Henry. Seaman. Centurion. Comm. F. March 21, 1781. SP; HO.

TAYLOR, James. F. Pard. for exchange Dec. 11, 1779. G.

TAYLOR, John. Captain. Fame. Comm. F. Aug. 9, 1781. SP; HO.

TAYLOR, Thomas. Carpenter. General Glover. Comm. F. Oct. 14 or 18, 1779. Pard. for exchange Dec. 11, 1779. G; SP; HO.

TEMPLE, Abraham. Seaman. Wexford. Sent from Kinsale to M. April 9, 1782. HO.

TEMPLETON, Andrew of Windham. Dalton or Charming Polly. In hospital April, 1777. Comm. M. June, 1777. Pard. for exchange Dec. 11, 1779. G; 3 p. 75; 4 p. 184; 7 p. 246.

TENIBLE, Anthony. See TINNABLE.

TENNANT or TENRANT, Jonathan. Black Snake. Comm. F. Feb. 18, 1779. Pard. for exchange Dec. 11, 1779 and Nov. 9, 1781. G; 5A p. 39.

TESHOW, John. See TISHAW.

TEW, James. Capt. marines. The Swallow. Comm. F. Jan. 23, 1778. Pard. for exchange May 31, 1779. G; 5A p. 37.

THAMSTONE, Geo. Prize master. Comm. F. June 19, 1778. 5A p. 38.

THAXTER, Seth. Seaman. Portsmouth. Comm. F. June 27, 1781. SP.

THAYER, George of Providence. Lexington. Comm. M. Sept. 19, 1777. Exchanged. 3 p. 137; 7 p. 253.

THELDEN, Jonathan. Seaman. Adventure. Comm. M. Jan. 21, 1782. HO.

THISTLE, Ezechia. Seaman. Diana. Comm. M. Jan. 23, 1782. HO.

THOM, Nicholas. See THORN.

THOMAS, English or Inglis of Boston.   Hawk's prize.   Comm. M. Oct. 1778.   Pard. for exchange Dec. 11, 1779 and Nov. 9, 1781.   G; HL; 7 p. 252; 10 v. 74 pp. 48, 148.

THOMAS, John.   Seaman.   Marquis de la Fayette.   Comm. M. Jan. 22, 1782.   HO.

THOMAS, Thomas.   Seaman.   Retaliation.   Comm. F. Oct. 31, 1780.   SP; HO.

THOMAS, Willm.   F.   Pard. for exchange Dec. 11, 1779.   G.

THOMPSON, Benjamin.   Seaman.   Terrible.   Comm. F. Aug. 9, 1781.   SP; HO.

THOMPSON, David of Ipswich.   Mariner.   Essex.   Comm. M. July 21 or 24, 1781.   SP; HO; 3 p. 210; 10 v. 74 p. 35.

THOMPSON, James.   Captain.   Rising States.   Comm. F. June 14, 1777.   Escaped June 19, 1777.   In France Oct. 25, 1777.   5 vol. 30 pp. 176 note, 177, 347, 350; 5A p. 36; 7 p. 75.

THOMPSON, James.   Oliver Cromwell.   Comm. F. Oct. 13, 1777.   Pard. for R. N. Dec. 3, 1778.   Entered or escaped.   G; 5 vol. 32 p. 71; 5A p. 37.

THOMPSON, John.   Seaman.   Venus of Philadelphia.   Comm. F. April 2, 1778.   Pard. for exchange May 31, 1779.   Exchanged July 2, 1779.   Joined Bonhomme Richard.   G; 5 v. 32 p. 286; 5A p. 37. (May be same as next).

THOMPSON, John of Philadelphia.   2nd lieut.   Alliance, a French prize.   Comm. M. Nov. 21, 1781.   SP; HO; 3 p. 212; 10 v. 74 p. 155. (May be same as last).

THOMPSON, John.   Seaman.   Bunker's Hill.   Comm. F. April 7, 1780.   SP; HO; 10 v. 73 p. 340.

THORN or THOM, Nicholas.   Fancy.   Comm. M. Aug., 1777.   Pard. for exchange Dec. 11, 1779.   G; 3 p. 136; 7 p. 249.

THRASH, Philip.   M.   Pard. for R. N. Nov. 22, 1780.   G.

THRASHER or THRESHER, Wm. Gunner. General Sullivan. Comm. F. April 26, 1779. Pard. for exchange Dec. 11, 1779 and pard. for R. N. Nov. 6, 1780. G; 5A p. 39.

THROOP, William. Mariner. Nancy. Comm. M. July 21, 1781. SP; HO. (Probably same as TROOP(S).

TIBBE or TIBBITS, Nathaniel. Comm. F. Feb. 18, 1779. Pard. for exchange Dec. 11, 1779. G; 5A p. 39.

TIBBITS, Richd. (Salter) of Portsmouth, N. H. Mariner. Aurora. Comm. M. July 25, 1780. SP; HO; HL; 3 p. 139; 9 pp. 80, 81; 10 v, 74 p. 151.

TIBBOTT, Nicholas. Seaman. Mercury. Comm. M. Feb. 6, 1782. HO.

TILESTON, Capt. M. Made his escape two days after he was brought in. 4 p. 185.

TILLE(E), Henry. Revenge. Comm. F. Aug. 11, 1777. Pard. for exchange May 31, 1779. G; 5A p. 37.

TILLOIS, Alexander. Revenge. Comm. F. Aug. 11, 1777. Pard. for exchange May 31, 1779. G; 5A p. 37.

TILLOIS, Aimable or Ameble. Revenge. Comm. F. Aug. 11, 1777. Pard. for exchange May 31, 1779. G; 5A p. 37.

TINDALL, Alex of Philadelphia. Greyhound. Mariner. Comm. M. July 9, 1781. Escaped Aug. 25, 1781. out of b. h. Sept. 24. Attempted escape Nov. 14, 1781. Out of b. h. Nov. 28. SP; HO; 10 v. 74 pp. 28, 44, 45, 47, 142, 152, 156.

TINNABLE or TENIBLE, Anthony. Mariner. Two Sisters. Comm. M. May 11, 1781. Innoculated May 28, 1781. SP; HO; HL; 3 p. 141; 10 v. 73 pp. 340, 346.

TISHEW, TISHAW, TESHOW or FISHOW, John. Mariner. Hannable of Newbury. Comm. M. Jan. 6 or 18, 1781. SP; HO; HL; 3 p. 140; 10 v. 73 pp. 312, 315.

TISSOCKS or TISSICK, Joseph of Charlestown. Essex. Comm. M. July 21, 1781. 3 p. 210; 10 v. 74 p. 34.

TOBY, Peter of Kittery. Charming Polly or Dalton. In hospital April, 1777. Comm. M. June, 1777. Pard. for exchange Dec. 20, 1778. G; 3 p. 75; 4 p. 184; 7 p. 245.

TOB(E)Y, William. Mariner. Little Pegey or Porgy. Comm. M. Jan. 3, 1782. SP; HO; 3 p. 213.

TOOMS, Andrew of Portsmouth, N.H. Mariner. Venus. Comm. M. Nov. 21, 1781. SP; HO; 3 p. 212; 9 p. 80; 10 v. 74 p. 155.

TOPHAM, Francis. Mariner. Viper. Comm. M. Dec. 7, 1781. SP; HO.

TOPHAM, John. Seaman. Harlequin. Comm. F. May 16, 1781. SP; HO.

TOPPIN, Benjamin Hall. Prize master the T(rue) Blue. Comm. F. June 19, 1778. Pard. for R.N. June 17, 1779. G; 5A p. 38. (Probably same as TAPPAN).

TOWEL, Thomas. F. Pard. for R.N. Oct. 6, 1781. G.

TOWNSEN, James. Seaman. Patty. Comm. M. Feb. 27, 1782. HO.

TOWNSEND or TOWNSHEND, Daniel. Reprisal. Comm. F. Aug. 9, 1777. Pard. for R.N. Jan. 25, 1779. G; 5A p. 37.

TOWNSEND, Jonah. Boy. Hercules. Captured but not comm. Oct. 15, 1781. HO.

TOWNSEND, Moses. Mariner. William. Comm. Pembroke 1778 and M. Oct. 14 or 17, 1780. SP; HO; HL; 3 p. 139.

TOWNS(HEND), Samuel of Salem. Warren. Comm. M. June, 1778. Pard. for exchange Dec. 11, 1779 and Nov. 9, 1781. G; HL; 3 p. 137; 7 p. 254.

TOWNSEND, Uriah. Sailmaker. Rising States. Comm. F. June 14, 1777. Escaped. 5A p. 36.

TOYE, John. M. Pard. for exchange Dec. 11, 1779. (Perhaps same as FOYE). G.

TRASK, Philip.   America's prize.   Comm. M. March 22, 1779.   Pard. for exchange Dec. 11, 1779.   G; 3 p. 138.

TREADWELL, Samuel of Ipswich.   Fancy.   Comm. M. Aug. 7, 1777. Escaped Feb. 1, 1778.   Re-captured March 14, 1778.   Pard. for exchange Dec. 11, 1779.   G; 3 p. 136; 7 pp. 94, 105, 250.

TREFATHAN, TRIFFERING or TRIFFENDO, George of Portsmouth.   Dalton or Charming Polly.   Comm. M. June, 1777.   Pard. for exchange Dec. 20, 1778.   G; 3 p. 75; 7 p. 244.

TREFFREY, Michael.   See TRIFTY.

TREFY, John.   Seaman.   Terrible.   Comm. F. May 24, 1781.   SP; HO.

TREFY, William.   Seaman.   Terrible.   Comm. F. May 24, 1781.   SP; HO.   (See also TRIFFEY and TREVER).

TREVER or TRIFFEY, William.   Mariner.   Phoenix.   Comm. M. May 10, 1779.   Pard. for exchange Dec. 11, 1779.   G; SP; HO; 3 p. 138.

TRIFFENDO, George.   See TREFATHAN.

TRIFFERING, George.   See TREFATHAN.

TRIFFEY, Wm.   HL.   (See also TREFY and TREVER).

TRIFTY? or TREFFREY, Michael of Marblehead.   Fancy.   Comm. M. Aug. 7, 1777.   Pard. for exchange Dec. 11, 1779.   G; 7 p. 250.   (See also FREFICE).

TRIGLONG or TRIGLOHER, Philip.   Pilot.   Comm. F. Feb. 18, 1779. Pard. for exchange Dec. 11, 1779.   G; 5A p. 39.

TRION or TRYON, Jacob.   Luzerne of Philadelphia.   Comm. M. July 6, 1781.   3 p. 209; 10 v. 74 p. 31.

TRION, John.   Prize Master.   Comm. F. July 15, 1777.   Escaped.   5 vol. 30, p. 344; 5A p. 36.

TROOP(S), Wm. of South Carolina.   Essex.   Comm. M. July 21, 1781. 3 p. 210; 10 v. 74 p. 34.   (Probably same as THROOP).

TROP, Eddy. Prize master. Wexford. Captured but not comm. Oct. 2, 1781. HO.

TROTT, Captain. Prisoner in Bristol April 25, 1778. 7 p. 115.

TRUE, Jacob. Dalton. Captured Dec. 24, 1776. M. 3 p. 74.

TRUE, Joseph of Newburyport. Dalton. Comm. M. June, 1777. Went with Paul Jones. 7 p. 244.

TRUSKE, Samuel. Seaman. Hope. Comm. M. Feb. 6, 1782. HO.

TRYALL, Isaac. Mariner. L'Uzerne. Comm. M. July 6, 1781. SP; HO.

TRYON, Jacob. See TRION.

TRYON, William. Lieut. Notre Dame. Comm. F. July 15, 1777. Escaped and in b. h. July 30, 1777. Escaped and re-taken March 7, 1778. Escaped July 23, 1778. G; 5 vol. 30 pp. 344, 348; vol. 31 p. 287. (The only official mention is a petition to be released from b. h. March 25, 1778 in G.)

TUCK, John. Seaman. Diana. Comm. M. Jan 23, 1782. HO.

TUCK, Sewel. Capt. Marines. Montgomery. Comm. F. Aug. 8, 1777. Escaped. 5A p. 36.

TUCKER. (Probably Nicholas). F. Escaped May 1, 1781. 10 v. 74 p. 26.

TUCKER, Jacob. Prize master's mate. Comm. F. Aug. 28, 1778. Pard. for exchange Dec. 11, 1779. G; 5A p. 38.

TUCKER, Nathaniel. Hawk's prize. Comm. F. April 2, 1778. Pard. for exchange May 31, 1779. G; 5A p. 37.

TUCKER, Nicholas of Marblehead. Still in F. May 8, 1781. Pard. for exchange Dec. 11, 1779 and Oct. 16, 1781. Escaped. G; 10 v. 73 p. 340. When his pardon came through on Oct. 16, 1781, he had escaped and Capt. John Manley was exchanged in his stead.

TUCKER, Reuben, of Newburyport. Dalton. Sent to hospital Feb. 15, 1777. Comm. M. June, 1777. Pard. for exchange Dec. 11, 1779. G; 3 p. 74; 4 pp. 44, 185; 7 p. 244.

MARINERS OF THE AMERICAN REVOLUTION

TUCKER, Richard. Mate. Phoenix. Comm. M. May 10, 1779. Pard. for exchange Dec. 11, 1779. G; SP; HO; HL; 3 p. 138; 10 v. 73 p. 326.

TUCKER, William. Seaman. Susannah. Comm. F. June 27, 1781. SP; HO.

TUCKER, William. Seaman. Jason. Comm. M. Jan. 25, 1782. HO.

TUCKER, William. Seaman. Wexford. Sent from Kinsale to M. April 9, 1782. HO.

TUCKERMAN, Francis. Viper. Comm. M. Dec. 7, 1781. 3 p. 212.

TUFTS, Aaron of Medford. Essex. Comm. M. Aug. 25, 1781. Died Sept. 18, 1781. 3 p. 211.

TUNDY or FUNDY, John. Mariner. Eliza, prize to the Grand Turk. Comm. M. Jan. 3, 1782. SP; HO; 3 p. 213.

TURNER, Gideon. Soldier, taken on shore. Comm. M. Feb. 7, 1782. HO.

TURNER, Isaac. Seaman. Susannah. Comm. F. June 27, 1781. SP; HO.

TURNER, William of Charleston. Mariner. Essex. Comm. M. July 21, 1781. SP; HO; 3 p. 210; 10 v. 74 p. 34.

TURNER, Willm. of North Carolina. Mariner. General Nash or Newburn. Comm. M. July 28, 1781. SP; HO; 3 p. 210; 10 v. 74 p. 36.

TURPIN, John. Seaman. Sturdy Beggar. Comm. F. Jan. 23, 1778. Pard. for exchange May 31, 1779. Joined Bonhomme Richard. G; 5 v. 32 p. 286; 5A p. 37.

TURPIN, Richard. Gunner. Comm. F. Feb. 18, 1779. 5A p. 39.

TWIGLEY, Aaron of New Jersey. Lexington. Comm. M. Sept. 19, 1777. R. N. 7 p. 254. (Probably same as QUIGLEY).

TWINEMAN, John. Seaman. Antibriton. Imprisoned at Edinburgh Jan. 19, 1782. HO.

TWOMBLEY, William. Seaman. Hydra or American. Comm. F. Feb. 3, 1781. SP; HO.

TYLER, Isaac. Seaman. Hercules. Sent from Kinsale to M. April 9, 1782. HO.

TYLER, James. Master's mate. Angelica. Comm. F. July 7, 1778. 5A p. 38.

TYSICK, Joseph. Mariner. Essex. Comm. M. July 21, 1781. SP; HO.

U

UNDERWOOD, John of Salem. Warren. Comm. M. June, 1778. Pard. for exchange Dec. 11, 1779. Pard. for R. N. Aug. 9, 1781. Escaped. G; HL; 3 p. 137; 7 p. 254.

UNGLEY, Wm. Comm. F. Feb. 18, 1779. 5A p. 39.

UNION, Elias of Marblehead. Seaman. General Glover. Comm. F. Oct. 18, 1779. Pard. for exchange Dec. 11, 1779. Still in F. May 8, 1781. G; SP; HO; 10 v. 73 p. 340.

UNION, John. F. Pard. for exchange Dec. 11, 1779. G.

UPHAM, Robert. Boy. Swallow of R. I. Comm. F. Jan. 23, 1778. Pard. for exchange May 31, 1779. Joined Bonhomme Richard. G; 5 v. 31 p. 286; 5A p. 37.

UPTON, John. Prize master. Newfoundland. Imprisoned at Edinburgh June 27, 1781. HO.

V

VAIL, David. See VEAL.

VALENTINE, James of Marblehead. Fancy. Comm. M. Aug. 7, 1777. Died March 4, 1779. Colburn says he escaped. 3 p. 136; 7 pp. 226, 250.

VALLET(T), David. Mariner. Protector. Comm. M. July 23, 1781. SP; HO. 3 p. 209; 10 v. 74 p. 35.

VANDERFORD, Benj. Mariner. Harlequin. Comm. M. Dec. 23 or 24, 1780. In hospital May 10, 1781. SP; HO; HL; 3 p. 139; 10 v. 73 p. 341.

VANDERFORD, Jno. Harlequin. Comm. M. Dec. 24, 1780. Pard. for R. N. May 11, 1781. Entered June 5, 1781. G; 3 p. 139; 10 v. 73 p. 341; v. 74 p. 22.

VANDERSON, William of New York. Charming Sally. Captured Jan. 16, 1777. M. Still in M. Feb. 7, 1779. R. N. 7 p. 248. (May be same as next). See also VENDISON.

VAN DUERSON, William. M. Pard. for exchange Dec. 20, 1778. (May be same as last). See also VENDISON. G.

VANOSTEN, James. Seaman. Ajax. Comm. F. Aug. 9, 1781. SP; HO.

VARBLE or VARBALL, Joseph. Revenge. Comm. F. Aug. 11, 1777. Pard. for exchange May 31, 1779. G; 5A p. 37.

VARNEY, John. F. Pard. for exchange Dec. 11, 1779. G.

VARNIEL or VARNEAL, Francis. Revenge. Comm. F. Aug. 11, 1777. Pard. for exchange May 31, 1779. G; 5A p. 37.

VARNUMS, Nathl. See VENUS.

VASSALS, James. See VESSELL.

VEAL or VAIL, David. Ann. Comm. M. July 28, 1781. 3 p. 210; 10 v. 74 p. 36.

VELSON, John. Seaman. Terrible. Comm. F. May 24, 1781. SP; HO.

VENDISON, Wm. Dalton. Comm. M. June, 1777. Escaped. 3 p. 74. (Possibly same as VANDERSON and VAN DUERSON).

VENTEOR, VENTON or VINTON, Thos. Mariner. Essex. Comm. M. July 21 or 27, 1781. SP; HO; 3 p. 210.

VENTON, Thos. See VENTEOR

VENUS, VENUNS, VENOM or VARNUMS, Nathl. of Maryland. Mariner. Two Sisters. Comm. M. April 24, 1781. Innoculated May 29, 1781. SP; HO; 3 p. 141; 10 v. 73 pp. 337, 346.

VESSELL or VASSALS, James. Soldier taken in South Carolina. Comm. M. Oct. 2, 1781. SP; HO; 3 p. 211; 10 v. 74 p. 142.

VEVER, Henry. Seaman. Betsey. Comm. M. Feb. 27, 1782. HO.

VIAL, Allen. See NIAL.

VIAL, Donnely. Seaman. Wexford. Sent from Kinsale to M. April 9, 1782. HO.

VICAR, VICKERS or VICTORY, William of Maryland. Mariner. L'Uzerne Comm. M. July 7, 1781. SP; HO; 3 p. 209; 10 v. 74 p. 31.

VICKERY, Elias of Marblehead. Freedom's prize. Captured April 27, 1777. M. Died Feb. 3, 1779. 3 p. 75; 7 pp. 221, 251. (See also Elisha WICKERY).

VICKERY, Jacob 1st of Marblehead. Fancy. Comm. M. Aug. 7, 1777. Pard. for exchange Dec. 11, 1779. G; 3 p. 136; 7 p. 249; 8 p. 121; 10 v. 73 p. 328.

VICKERY, Jacob 2nd of Marblehead. Fancy. Comm. M. Aug. 7, 1777. Pard. for exchange Dec. 11, 1779. G; 7 pp. 249, 250.

VICKERY, William senior. Seaman. Jason. Comm. M. Jan. 25, 1782. HO.

VICKERY, William Junior. Seaman. Jason. Comm. M. Jan. 25, 1782. HO.

VICTORY, Wm. See VICAR.

VIDDEAN, John of England. Lexington. Comm. M. Sept. 19, 1777. R. N. 7 p. 253.

VILLES, Danl. See WILLET.

VILLET, Daniel. See WILLETT.

VINROE, Thos. Lieut. Angelica. Comm. F. July 7, 1778. Escaped. 5A p. 38.

VINTON, Thos. See VENTEOR.

VOKES, James. Seaman. Bermuda. Comm. M. Jan. 22, 1782. HO.

VOLLAM, John. M. Pard. for R. N. April 28, 1781. G.

VOS(E), Elisha. Mariner. Essex. Comm. M. July 27, 1781. SP; HO; 3 p. 210.

VOX, Samuel. Mariner. Essex. Comm. M. July 28, 1781. SP; HO.

W

WADDLE, Joseph of Dartmouth. Adventurer. Comm. M. Jan. 21, 1782. 3 p. 213.

WADLEY, William. Seaman. Wexford. Sent from Kinsale to M. April 9, 1782. HO.

WAILLAND or WHALAND, Benj. or Mr. Sturdy Beggar. Comm. F. Jan. 23, 1778. Escaped July 23, 1778. 5 v. 31 p. 287; 5A p. 37.

WAISTCOAT, Jabez. See WESTCOTT.

WAITE, Aaron of Ipswich. Thom. Comm. M. Sept. 19, 1780. Exchanged. 3 p. 139. (Probably meant to be WHITE).

WAITE or WEIGHT, Amhurst of Marblehead or Newbury. Hawk's prize. Comm. M. Oct. 16, 1777. Pard. for exchange Dec. 11, 1779. G; 3 p. 137; 7 p. 252.

WAITE or WAITT, Jacob of Marblehead. Seaman. Rambler. Comm. F. Dec. 30, 1779. SP; HO; 10 v. 73 p. 340.

WALBER, James. F. Pard. for exchange Dec. 11, 1779. G.

WELCH, Mr. Lieut. of Lexington. M. Escaped May 20, 1778. 7 p. 123.

WALKER. Captured March 16, 1777. In hospital at Plymouth March 23, 4 pp. 44, 184.

WALKER, David. Seaman. General Wayne. Comm. F. Aug. 9, 1781. SP.

WALKER, Edwd. General Sullivan. Comm. F. April 26, 1779. Pard. for exchange Dec. 11, and Nov. 9, 1781. G; 5A p. 39.

WALKER, Newell, Nevill, Noble or Nables of Maryland. Mariner. L'Uzerne. Comm. M. July 7 or 9, 1781. SP; HO; 3 p. 209; 10 v. 74 p. 32.

WALKER, Richard or Richmond. Seaman. Twin Sisters. Comm. M. Jan. 9, 1782. HO; 3 p. 212.

WALKER, Robert. Prize master. The Alfred. Comm. F. July 18, 1778. Escaped. 5A p. 38.

WALKINSON. See WILKINSON.

WALL, John. Seaman. Susannah. Comm. F. June 27, 1781. SP; HO.

WALL, Richard. Mate. Richard. Comm. F. Oct. 14, 1779. Pard. for exchange Dec. 11, 1779. G; SP; HO.

WALLACE or WALLIS, John. Mariner. Essex. Comm. M. Aug. 31, 1781. SP; HO; 3 p. 211.

WALLS, Ephraim. Comm. F. Oct. 13, 1777. Pard. for exchange Dec. 11, 1779. G; 5A p. 37

WALTON, Thomas. Seaman. Susannah. Comm. F. June 27, 1781. SP; HO.

WALTON, William. See WATSON.

WARD, Nathaniel. Warren. Comm. M. June, 1778. Pard. for exchange Dec. 11, 1779 and Nov. 9, 1781. G; HL; 3 p. 137; 7 p. 254.

WARD(E), Thoms. of Boston. Protector. Comm. M. July 23, 1781. Died Aug. 3, 1781. 10 v. 74 pp. 35, 38.

WARD, William. Seaman. Harlequin. Comm. F. May 16, 1781. SP; HO.

WARDEN, John. F. Pard. for R. N. Jan. 12, 1781. G.

WARDLE, John. Lieut L. M. Comm. F. June 19, 1778. 5A p. 38.

WARNER, Nathaniel of Newburyport. Dalton. Comm. M. June, 1777. Pard. for exchange Dec. 20, 1778. Escaped. G; 3 p. 74; 7 p. 244. (Probably same as next).

WARNER, Nathl. Mariner. Jason. Comm. M. Dec. 16 or 18, 1779. In b. h. Oct. 17, 1781. SP; HO; HL; 3 p. 138; 10 v. 74 pp. 145, 154. (Probably same as last).

MARINERS OF THE AMERICAN REVOLUTION

WARREN, Gideon of Berwick, N. H.   Dalton or Charming Polly.   Comm. M. June, 1777. Died Sept. 3, 1777.   3 p. 75; 4 p. 395; 7 pp. 60, 245.

WASHBURN.   M.   10 v. 74 p. 33.

WASHBURN(E), Abiel.   Seaman.   Sally and Becky.   Comm. F. Dec. 30, 1779.   SP; HO.

WASHBURN or WASHBOROUGH, John of Plymouth.   Mariner.   Duc de Coigne.   Comm. M. July 18, 1780.   SP; HO; HL; 3 p. 139.

WATERS, Stephen of Salem.   Warren.   Comm. M. June, 1778.   Pard. for exchange Dec. 11, 1779.   G; 3 p. 137; 7 p. 254.

WATKINS, George of Virginia.   Janey.   Comm. M. Aug. 19, 1778.   Pard. for exchange Dec. 11, 1779.   G; 3 p. 136; 7 p. 256.

WATKIN(G)S, Stepn.   Mariner.   Lively.   Comm. M. Dec. 27, 1780.   Innoculated May 29, 1781.   Pard. for R. N. May 11, 1781.   G; SP; HO; 3 p. 139; 10 v. 73 p. 346.

WATKINS, Thos. of Maryland.   Booty (Betsey?)   Comm. M. March 22, 1779.   Escaped.   3 p. 137.

WATSON, John.   Swallow.   Comm. F. Jan. 23, 1778.   Escaped Dec. 27, 1778.   5 v. 32 p. 283; 5A p. 37.

WATSON or WALTON, William.   Mariner.   Hunter.   Comm. M. July 25, 1781.   SP; HO.

WATTS, John.   Seaman.   Jason.   Sent from Kinsale to M. April 9, 1782.   HO.

WAYMOUTH or WEYMOUTH, Nehemiah.   M.   9 p. 99.

WAYMOUTH or WEYMOUTH, Tobias of Berwick, N. H.   Dalton or Charming Polly.   Comm. M. June, 1777.   Pard. for exchange Dec. 20, 1778.   G; 3 p. 75; 7 p. 245.   (Probably same as next).

WAYMOUTH or WEYMOUTH, Tobias of Berwick.   Mariner.   Jolly Tar.   Comm. M. Oct. 17, 1780.   SP; HO; HL; 3 p. 139; (Probably same as last).

MARINERS OF THE AMERICAN REVOLUTION

WEADON, Eleazer. Angelica. Comm. F. July 7, 1778. 5A p. 38.

WEATHEREL. See WETHERALL.

WEBB, John. Seaman. Betsey, merchant ship. Captured but not comm. Oct. 23, 1781. HO.

WEBB, Moses. F. Pard. for R.N. Oct. 6, 1781. G.

WEBB, Robert. The Swallow. Comm. F. Jan. 23, 1778. Pard. for exchange May 31, 1779. G;; 5A p. 37.

WEBB, Saml. of Scituate. Essex or Phoenix of Boston. Comm. M. July 20, 1781. SP; HO; 3 p. 210; 10 v. 74 p. 34.

WEBB, Seth. Seaman. Hydra. Comm. F. Feb. 3, 1781. Escaped Aug. 24 or 25. Described in SP 42/57 as "about 28 yrs., 5'9", middle size, pale complexion, sandy hair, usually wore light blue jacket and waistcoat. SP. (Can be deduced that he was re-captured as he appears in SP but escaped again as he does not appear in HO).

WEBBER, George. Seaman. Thorn. Comm. M. Feb. 6, 1782. HO.

WEBBER, John. Commerce? Comm. F. Feb. 18, 1779. Pard. for exchange Dec. 11, 1779.and Nov. 9, 1781. G; 5A p. 39.

WEBSTER, Stephen. F. Pard. for exchange Dec. 11, 1779.

WEIBERT, Lt. Col. Comm. F. Aug. 26, 1777. Exchanged Dec. 10, 1778. Joined Bonhomme Richard. 5 v. 32 p. 286.

WEIGHT, Amhurst. See WAITE.

WELCH. Comm. M. March 16, 1777. 4 p. 44.

WELCH or WELSH, David of Ireland. Lexington. Comm. M. Sept. 19, 1777. Escaped. 3 p. 137; 7 p. 252.

WELCH or WELTCH, John. Captain. Hornet. Comm. F. Oct. 13, 1777. Escaped. 5 p. 346; 5A p. 37.

WELCH, John. Capt. Marines. The Alfred. Comm. F. July 18, 1778. Escaped. 5A p. 38.

WELCH or WELSH, Patrick.   Seaman.   Adventure.   Comm. M. Jan. 21, 1782.   HO;   3 p. 213.

WELCH, Peter.   Seaman.   Nancy or Larravie.   Comm. F. March 21, 1781.   SP; HO.

WELCH, Thos.   Dalton.   M.   Escaped.   3 p. 74.

WELCH, Thomas of Ireland.   Charming Sally.   Captured Jan. 16, 1777.   M.   Still there Feb. 7, 1779.   Pard. for R. N. Sept. 25, 1778.   G;   7 p. 248.

WELCH, Thomas of Ireland.   Lexington.   Comm. M. Sept. 19, 1777.   R. N. or escaped.   3 p. 137;   7 p. 253.   (See below).

WELCH or WELSH, Thomas.   M.   Pard. for R. N. Jan. 4, 1779.   G;   (Probably same as last).

WELDON, James.   Seaman.   Pocahontas.   Comm. F. Nov. 18, 1780.   SP; HO.

WELKENS, Hezekiah.   Seaman.   Newfoundland.   Imprisoned at Edinburgh June 27, 1781.   HO.

WELKINS, Reuben.   Seaman.   Newfoundland.   Imprisoned at Edinburgh June 27, 1781.   HO.

WELLS, Andrew.   Soldier taken in South Carolina.   Lion?   Comm. M. Aug. 31, 1781.   SP; HO;   3 p. 211.

WELLS, Eusah or Enoch.   Mariner.   Little Pegey.   Comm. M. Jan. 3, 1782.   SP; HO;   3 p. 213.

WELLS, John.   Seaman.   Harlequin.   Comm. F. May 16, 1781.   SP; HO.

WELSH.   See WELCH.

WESTCOTT or WAISTCOAT.   Jabez of Providence or Newbury.   Hannible of Newbury.   Comm. M. March 31, 1781.   Pard. for R. N. Oct. 1781.   Entered Aug. 23, 1781.   G; HL;   3 p. 141;   10 v. 73 p. 331;   v. 74 p. 43.

WESTON, Joseph.   Seaman.   Mercury.   Comm. F. March 21, 1781.   SP; HO.

WETHERALL or WEATHEREL, Job. Prize master. Comm. F. Feb. 18, 1779. Pard. for exchange Dec. 11, 1779. G; 5A p. 39.

WEYMAN, Jacob. M. Pard. for exchange Dec. 11, 1779. G.

WEYMOUTH. See WAYMOUTH.

WHALAND, Benj. See WAILLAND.

WHARF, John. Seaman. General Glover. Comm. F. Oct. 18, 1779. Pard. for exchange Dec. 11, 1779. G; SP.

WHEATON, Ebenezer. Seaman. Angelica. Comm. F. July 6, 1778. Pard. for exchange Dec. 11, 1779. G; SP.

WHEATON, Louis or Levi. Angelica. Comm. F. July 7, 1778. Pard. for exchange May 31, 1779. G; 5A p. 38.

WHEELER, John of Rhode Island. Black Snake. Comm. M. March 12, 1778. 3 p. 137; 7 p. 255. (Same as Jonathan?)

WHEELER, Jonathan. M. Pard. for exchange Dec. 11, 1779. (Same as John?) G.

WHEELER, Joseph. Mariner. Lively. Comm. M. Dec. 27, 1780. SP; HO.

WHEELER, Joshua. Reprisal. Comm. F. Aug. 9, 1777. Pard. for R. N. Dec. 3, 1778. Pard. for exchange May 31, 1779. G; 5A p. 37. (Probably same as below).

WHEELER, Joshua. Lively. Comm. M. Dec. 27, 1780. Innoculated May 28, 1781. HL; 3 p. 139; 10 v. 73 p. 346. (Probably same as above).

WHEELWRIGHT, Robt. Mariner. Beaver. Comm. M. July 23 or 27, 1781. SP; HO; 3 p. 210.

WHILEY, Isaac. Seaman. Hercules. Comm. M. Jan. 25, 1782. HO.

WHILLET, Daniel. See WILLET.

WHIPPLE, David. Seaman. Jason. Captured but not comm. Oct. 15, 1781. HO.

WHIPPLE, Robert. Seaman. Portsmouth. Comm. F. July 20, 1781. SP; HO.

WHITE. M. 10 v. 74 p. 151.

WHITE, Aaron. M. Pard. for exchange Nov. 9, 1780. G; HL; (See WAITE).

WHITE, Bartholomew. Montgomery. Comm. F. Aug. 8, 1777. Accidentally shot dead in prison March 25, 1779. 5A p. 36.

WHITE, Benj'n or Bengian of Marblehead. Franklin. Comm. F. Feb. 18, 1779. Still there May 8, 1781. Pard. for exchange Dec. 11, 1779 and Nov. 9, 1781. G; 5A p. 38; 10 v. 73 p. 340.

WHITE, John. F. Pard. for exchange Dec. 11, 1779. G.

WHITE, John. Seaman. Centurion. Comm. F. May 24, 1781. SP.

WHITE, Leven or Seven. Mariner. Marmy or Mariana. Comm. M. July 3 or 28, 1779. Pard. for exchange Dec. 11, 1779. In b. h. Feb. 1, 1781. Out of b. h. Feb. 2, G; SP; HO; HL; 3 p. 138; 10 v. 73 p. 319.

WHITE, Robert. Seaman. Jack. Comm. F. March 5, 1781. SP; HO.

WHITE, Thomas. Lieut. Montgomery of Philadelphia. Comm. F. Aug. 8, 1777. Pard. for exchange May 31, 1779 or Dec. 11, 1779. G; 5 v. 32 p. 286; 5A p. 36.

WHITE, Thomas of North Carolina. Mariner. Robinson. Comm. M. April 24, 1781. Innoculated May 28, 1781. SP; HO; 10 v. 73 pp. 337, 346.

WHITE, Thos, of Marshfield. Mariner. Marquis de Morbec. Comm. M. Oct. 2, 1781. SP; HO; 3 p. 211.

WHITE, Thomas. M. HL.

WHITE, William of Newburyport. Fancy. Comm. M. Aug. 7, 1777. Pard. for exchange Dec. 11, 1779. G; 3 p. 136; 4 p. 307; 7 p. 249.

WHITE, William. Seaman. Wexford. Sent from Kinsale to M. April 9, 1782. HO.

WHIT(E)PAIN, Willm. Mariner. Revenge of Philadelphia. Comm. M. Jan. 11, 1781. SP; HO; HL; 3 p. 140; 10 v. 73 p. 313.

WHITFIELD, John. Seaman. Pocahontas. Comm. F. Nov. 18, 1780. SP; HO.

WHITLER, William. Seaman. Diana. Comm. M. Jan. 24, 1782. HO.

WHITMAN, Asa. See WITHAM.

WHITMORE, Jonathan of Newburyport. Dalton or Charming Polly. Sent to hospital Feb. 15, 1777. Comm. M. June, 1777. Pard. for R. N. no date. G; 3 p. 75; 4 pp. 44, 184, 187, 306; 7 p. 244.

WHITSHAND, Andrew. Charming Polly. Captured May, 1777. M. Exchanged. 3 p. 75. (Possibly meant for WITHAM).

WHITTAM. See WITHAM.

WHITTEMORE, Jacob. Boy. Fair American. Comm. F. Nov. 18, 1780. SP; HO.

W(H)IT(W)RONG, Samuel of Marblehead. Fancy. Comm. M. Aug. 7, 1777. Pard. for exchange Dec. 11, 1779. G; 3 p. 136; 7 p. 250.

WIBERT, Antoine Felix. F. Discharged Dec. 4, 1778. G.

WICKERY, Elisha. M. Pard. for exchange Feb. 2, 1779. (See Elias VICKERY). G.

WIDGER or WIGGER, Thomas of Marblehead. Hawk's prize. Comm. M. Oct. 16, 1777. Pard. for exchange Dec. 11, 1779. G; 3 p. 137; 7 p. 252; 10 v. 73 p. 329.

* WIDGER, William. Born Marblehead Sept. 18, 1748. Phoenix. Comm. M. May 10, 1779. Pard. for exchange Dec. 11, 1779 but remained until general exchange. G; SP; HO; HL; 3 p. 138. See bibliography No. 10. (After his release he became captain of the Increase and died October 10, 1823).

MARINERS OF THE AMERICAN REVOLUTION

WIDOW, John. Lexington. Comm. M. Sept. 19, 1777. Escaped. 3 p. 137.

WILD, Samuel. Seaman. English schooner. Comm. M. Jan. 25, 1782. HO.

WILDS, Elisha of Boston. Mariner. Jolly Tar. Comm. M. Oct. 17, 1780. SP; HO; 3 p. 139.

WILE, Thoms. of Mashfield. Marquis de Morbec. Comm. M. Oct. 2, 1781. 10 v. 74 p. 142.

WILKINSON, Frederick. Seaman. South Quay. Comm. F. March 21, 1781. SP; HO.

WILKINSON, Joseph. M. HL. (Probably same as next).

WILKINSON or WALKINSON, Josh. of Rhode Island. Mariner. Robinson or Robertson. Comm. M. April 24, 1781. SP; HO; 10 v. 73 p. 337. (Probably same as last).

WILK(E)S, Hardy. Soldier taken in South Carolina. Two Brothers? Comm. M. July 20, 1781. SP; HO; 3 p. 211; 10 v. 74 p. 34.

WIL(L)COCKS, Isaac. Seaman. General Wayne. Comm. F. Aug. 9, 1781. SP; HO.

WILCOCKS, Robert. Master. The Swallow. Comm. F. Jan. 23, 1778. Pard. for exchange May 31, 1779. G; 5A p. 37.

WILLETT or VILLET, Daniel of Newbury or Newburyport. Revenge. Comm. M. May, 1778. Pard. for exchange Dec. 11, 1779. G; 3 p. 139; 7 p. 257. (Probably same as next).

WILLET, WHILLET or VILLES, Daniel of Newbury. Mariner. Marquis de Morbec. Comm. M. Oct. 2, 1781. SP; HO; 3 p. 211; 10 v. 74 p. 142. (Probably same as last).

WILLIAMS, Abraham. Boatswain's mate. Hercules. Captured but not comm. Oct. 15, 1781. HO.

WILLIAMS, Benja. M. R. N. July 29, 1781. Pard. for exchange Oct. 1781. G; 10 v. 74 p. 37.

WILLIAMS, Ebenezer. Seaman. Daniel. Comm. F. Oct. 31, 1780. SP.

WILLIAMS, John. Friends Good Will. Comm. M. July 23, 1781. 3 p. 210; 10 v. 74 p. 35.

WILLIAMS, John. F. Pard. for R. N. Aug. 9, 1781. G.

WILLIAMS, John. F. Pard. for R. N. Oct. 6, 1781. G.

WILLIAMS, John Foster. Captain. Protector. Comm. M. July 21, 1781. Pard. for exchange Nov. 9, 1781. G; 10 v. 74 pp. 34, 156.

WILLIAMS, Malichi. See WILLIAMSON.

WILLIAMS, Samuel of England. Lexington. Comm. M. Sept. 19, 1777. Pard. for R. N. Oct. 14, 1778. Entered or escaped. G; 3 p. 137; 7 p. 253.

WILLIAMS, Thos. of Lynn, Mass. Mariner. Ascot and John. Comm. M. July 7, 1781. SP; HO; 3 p. 209; 10 v. 74 p. 31.

WILLIAMS, Wm. Master. Montgomery. Comm. F. Aug. 8, 1777. Escaped. 5A p. 36.

WILLIAMS, Wm. of Cape Ann. Beaver. Comm. M. July 23, 1781. R. N. Aug. 20, 1781. 10 v. 74 pp. 35, 43.

WILLIAMSON, John. Lieut. Comm. F. Sept. 24, 1778. Escaped. 5A p. 38.

WILLIAMS(ON), Malichi or Malichy of Virginia. Mariner. Betsey or Robertson. Comm. M. July 28, 1781. SP; HO; 3 p. 210; 10 v. 74 p. 36.

WILLIE or WILLEY, Winthrop. See WILLS.

WILLIS. M. 9 p. 69-70.

WILLIS, Ebenezer of Dartmouth. Charming Sally or Polly. Died at Plymouth May 17, 1777. 3 p. 75; 7 pp. 38, 247.

WILLS, John. Mariner. Phoenix. Comm. M. May 10, 1779. Pard. for exchange Dec. 11, 1779. G; SP; HO; HL; 3 p. 138.

MARINERS OF THE AMERICAN REVOLUTION

WILLS, WILLIE or WILLEY, Winthrop of Kittery, N. H. Dalton. Comm. M. June, 1777. Pard. for exchange Dec. 20, 1778. G; 3 p. 74; 4 p. 184; 7 p. 245.

WILLSON, James. Seaman. Portsmouth. Comm. F. June 27, 1781. SP; HO.

WILSON, Andrew. Seaman. Aurora. Comm. F. Nov. 18, 1780. SP; HO.

WILSON, Barney or Barry. Mariner. Essex. Comm. M. July 20, 1781. SP; HO; 3 p. 210; 10 v. 74 p. 34.

WILSON, Ephraim of Northboro'. Mariner. Essex. Comm. M. Aug. 25 or Sept. 1, 1781. SP; HO; 3 p. 211.

WIL(L)SON, George of Philadelphia. Montgomery of Philadelphia. Comm. F. Aug. 8, 1777. Died Dec. 9, 1778. 5 v. 32 p. 281; 5A p. 36.

WILSON, John. F. Pard. for R. N. Nov. 22, 1780. G.

WILSON, Robert of Pennsylvania. Mariner. Viper. Comm. M. Dec. 7, 1781. SP; HO; 3 p. 212.

WILSON, Willm. of Philadelphia. Mariner. L'Uzerne. Comm. M July 6, 7 or 9, 1781. SP; HO; 3 p. 209; 10 v. 74 p. 32.

WINSTANLEY, James. F. Pard. for exchange Dec. 11, 1779. G.

WITHAM, Aaron. Seaman. Ranger. Comm. M. Jan. 24, 1782. HO.

WHITHAM or WHITTAM, Andrew of Berwick, N. H. Dalton. In hospital April, 1777. Comm. M. June, 1777. Pard. for exchange Dec. 20, 1778. G; 4 p. 184; 7 p. 245. (Probably same as next) See also WHITSAND).

WITHAM, Andrew. Seaman. Fort Stanwin. Comm. F. Aug. 4, 1780. Escaped and re-captured Nov. 14, 1780. G; SP; HO. (Probably same as last).

WITHAM or WHITMAN, Asa of New Gloucester. Dalton or Charming Polly. In hospital April, 1777. Comm. M. June, 1777. Put in b. h. Aug. 9, 1777. Died Feb. 3, 1779. 3 p. 75; 4 p. 184, 306, 307; 7 pp. 221, 244.

WOLT, Joseph of England. Lexington. Comm. M. Sept. 19, 1777. R.N. 7 p. 253.

WOOD, Allen of Virginia. Lively of Baltimore. Comm. M. Dec. 27, 1780. or Jan. 16, 1781. In hospital May 10, 1781. Pard. for R.N. May 11, 1781. Entered June 5, 1781. G; 3 p. 140; 10 v. 73 pp. 314, 341; v. 74 p. 22.

WOOD, Champion. Seaman. Hetty. Comm. F. March 21, 1781. SP.

WOOD, Esra. Soldier taken on shore. Comm. M. Feb. 7, 1782. HO.

WOOD, Israel. Black Prince. Comm. F. April 26, 1779. Pard. for exchange Dec. 11, 1779 and Nov. 9, 1781. G; 5A p. 39.

WOOD, Thomas. Mariner. Little Pegey or Porgy. Comm. M. Jan. 3, 1782. SP; HO; 3 p. 213.

WOODARD, David. Seaman. Jason. Captured but not comm. Oct. 15, 1781. HO.

WOODBRIDGE, Saml. of Newburyport. Dalton. In hospital April, 1777. Comm. M. June, 1777. Pard. for exchange May 31, 1779. G; 3 p. 74; 4 p. 184; 7 p. 244.

WOODBRIDGE, Thomas. Seaman. Harlequin. Comm. M. Feb. 6, 1782. HO.

WOODBURY, Joshua. Seaman. Two Brothers. Comm. M. Jan. 23, 1782. HO.

WOODBURY, Levi of Beverly. Essex. Comm. M. July 24, 1781. 10 v. 74 p. 35.

WOODBURY, Nathl. Mariner. Harlequin. Comm. M. Dec. 23 or 24, 1780. In hospital May 10, 1781. SP; HL; 3 p. 139; 10 v. 73 p. 341.

WOODBURY, Nathaniel. Seaman. Diana. Comm. M. Jan. 23, 1782. HO.

WOODHOUSE or WOODPRUCE, Clement of England or Virginia. Dalton. Comm. M. June, 1777. Escaped. 3 p. 74; 7 p. 246.

MARINERS OF THE AMERICAN REVOLUTION

WOODMAN, James. Seaman. Harlequin. Comm. F. May 16, 1781. SP; HO.

WOODMAN, Joshua. F. Pard. for exchange Dec. 11, 1779. G.

WOODMAN, Nathaniel. Seaman. Protector. Imprisoned at Deal Aug. 24, 1781. HO.

WOODMAN, William. See WOODWARD.

WOODPRUCE, Clement. See WOODHOUSE.

WOODROW, James of Ireland. Tracey of Boston. Comm. M. Jan. 6, 1781. Pard. for R.N. Feb. 20, 1781. Entered March 7, 1781. G; 3 p. 140; 10 v. 73 pp. 312, 324.

WOODS, John of Boston. General Mifflin. Comm. M. October 17, 1781. 3 p. 212.

WOODWARD, Daniel. Comm. F. Aug. 28, 1778. Pard. for exchange Dec. 11, 1779 and Nov. 9, 1781. G; 5A p. 38.

WOODWARD, James. Gunner. Rising States. Comm. F. June 14, 1777. Escaped June 19. Re-captured and in b.h. June 23. 5 v. 30 p. 344. 5A p. 36.

WOOD(W)ARD, Thomas. Mariner. Little Porgy or Pegey. Comm. M. Jan. 3, 1782. SP; HO; 3 p. 213.

WOODWARD or WOODMAN, William of New Haven. Charming Sally or Polly. Captured Jan. 16, 1777. M. Escaped. 3 p. 75; 7 p. 247.

WOODWELL, Gideon. 11 pp. 252-3.

WORDSWORTH, Thomas. Seaman. Harlequin. Comm. F. May 24, 1781. SP; HO.

WORTH, Theophiels. Comet of Philadelphia. Comm. M. Jan. 11, 1781. 10 v. 73 p. 313.

WRIGHT(L)INGTON or RIGHTINGTON, Henry of Dartmouth. Charming Salley. Captured Jan. 16, 1777. M. Still in M. Feb. 7, 1779. Pard. for exchange Dec. 20, 1778. G; 7 p. 247.

WYATT, Standfast. Seaman. General Wayne. Comm. F. Aug. 9, 1781. SP; HO.

WYATT, Stephen. Seaman. Phoenix. Comm. F. Nov. 18, 1780. SP; HO.

WYER, Nathaniel of Newburyport. Dalton. Comm. M. June, 1777. Pard. for exchange Dec. 20, 1778. Escaped. G; 3 p. 74; 7 p. 243.

WYLER, Barnet Lewers. Boatswain or seaman. Active. Comm. F. March 5, 1781. SP; HO.

WYMAN or WYMOND, Jacob of Cape Pursue. Dalton. In hospital April, 1777. Comm. M. June, 1777. Exchanged. 3 p. 75; 4 p. 184; 7 p. 246.

Y

YAGGER, Henry. See JAGER.

YARD, Edw. Venus of Philadelphia. Comm. F. April 2, 1778. Pard. for exchange Dec. 11, 1779. G; 5A p. 37.

YATES, John. Comm. F. Oct. 20, 1778. Pard. for exchange Dec. 11, 1779. G; 5A p. 38.

YOLING, Edward of Salem. Warren. Comm. M. June, 1778. Exchanged. Returned to M. June 13, 1780 as he had been found as Prize master on a ship taken by the French and now re-taken. G; 7 p. 254.

YONGUE, Geo. Comm. F. Feb. 18, 1779. Escaped. 5A p. 39.

YOULING, YOLIN or EULIN, Benjamin of New Gloucester. Dalton or Charming Polly. Comm. M. June, 1777. Pard. for exchange Dec. 20, 1778. Joined Alliance. G; 3 p. 75; 7 p. 244.

YOUNG, Nathn. or Nath'l. of Cape Cod. Mariner. Essex. Comm. M. July 24 or 25, 1781. SP; HO; 3 p. 210; 10 v. 74 p. 36.

YOUNG, Stephen. Mariner. Resolution of Boston. Comm. M. Jan. 22, 1781. In hospital May 10, 1781. SP; HO; HL; 10 v. 73 p. 316, 341.

YOUNGER, Levy or Levi. Seaman. General Glover. Comm. F. Oct. 18, 1779. Pard. for exchange Dec. 11, 1779. G; SP.

ADDITIONS AND CORRECTIONS

ASPEN, George. Should read ASPEN or ANSPIN, George.

BASE, William. Add: See also BASTES.

FREDERICK, James. M. Pard. for exchange Dec. 20, 1778. G.

GREEN, John. Mariner. Little Pegey or Porgy. Comm. M. Jan. 3, 1782. SP; HO; 3 p. 213.

HACKETT, John. See HOCKETT.

HAMMOND, William. Imprisoned at Pembroke. Pard. for R. N. June 17, 1779. G.

HUNT, Abijah. Add Comm. M. July 7, 1781.

McCOFFREY. See McCRAFFEE.

MICHELL, William. Seaman. Hercules. Sent from Kinsale to M. April 9, 1781. HO.

SMITH, George. Omit first item on p. 175 as listed on previous page.

SMITH, Gilbert. Black Prince. Comm. F. April 26, 1779. Pard. for exchange Dec. 11, 1779 and Nov. 9, 1781. G; 5A p. 39.

STACEY, Samuel. Boy. General Glover. Comm. F. Oct. 18, 1779. SP; HO.

TAPPAN or TAPPEN. Add 7 p. 149.

THORN or THOM, Nicholas. Add of Marblehead.

NOTES ON THE PRISONS

The two buildings which the British government decided upon to confine the American rebels who were brought to England during the Revolutionary War were Old Mill Prison at Plymouth and Forten Prison at Gosport near Portsmouth.

The most detailed description of Mill Prison comes from Andrew Sherburne's diary: "This prison was situated on a promontary, projecting into the sound, between Plymouth and Plymouth Dock, two considerable towns; it lies on the right hand, as you go from Dock to Plymouth, and about an equal distance from either. Formerly there stood wind mills on this eminence, which circumstance gave it the name of "Mill Hill;" hence the prison was called "Mill Prison".

There is a great deal more about the layout and fortifications but the above description should suffice in locating the site. However, the maps of the last century show a location of Mill Prison which it is hard to reconcile with this description, so that it would appear that if the description is accurate, the prison was either torn down or put to another use soon after the American prisoners were re-patriated.

Of the location of Forten prison, a little more is known. Originally this building was erected as a naval hospital by a private entrepreneur by the name of Nathaniel Jackson, who contracted with the government to receive a certain sum for every naval officer and rating who occupied a bed there. Its name at that time was Fortune Hospital. When the government built its own Naval Hospitals, Fortune was no longer required but later, under the name of Forten, which was also adopted by the surrounding neighborhood, it became a place of confinement for prisoners of war, although it must have been enlarged and modified to perform this service.

The site of Fortune Hospital can be located from an old map in Gosport Public Library. It would appear to be on the exact site now occupied by a hospital for Sea Cadets, which is part of the H. M. S. St. Vincent Naval Training school.

No contemporary picture of either prison has been discovered. There is a panoramic lithograph view by H. Worsely, dated 1826, of which there is a print in the Plymouth Public Library, a portion of which shows Millbay prison, but whether this is the building which concerns us it is hard to say. It certainly does not accord with Sherburne's description of the two high walls twenty feet apart, etc.

It is possible that diaries or sketches made by the French and Dutch prisoners, who were confined in these places in far greater numbers than the Americans, may one day come to light.

APPENDIX I

LIST OF AMERICAN SHIPS CAPTURED BY THE BRITISH DURING THE REVOLUTIONARY WAR

This list of ships does not claim to be exhaustive as very extensive research would be needed to compile a complete list from all possible sources. Complete lists will probably appear over the years in *Naval Documents of the American Revolution*, which is being published in stages by the Naval History Division.

In addition to the ships listed in the sources used to compile the list of mariners, an analysis has also been made of the records of the High Court of Admiralty in the Public Record Office in London, which contain minutes of the sessions held by the court over various captured ships, or prizes. It was expected that in the records of the prize courts would be found data for all the ships mentioned in the list of mariners but instead it was found that very few of these ships ever came before the prize court, while numerous others, not mentioned in the list, were found. From this it is deduced that most of the ships from which the prisoners came were sunk or re-captured by the Americans or dealt with by a vice-admiralty court elsewhere. The crews of the ships from which no prisoners were brought to England were either all lost or imprisoned elsewhere.

Those ships for which a PRO Reference Number is given are to be found in the High Court of Admiralty Prize Court Records Class 28, but unless there is an asterisk, there is no mention of them in the prisoner list. Those without a reference number are to be found only in the sources used to compile the list of mariners.

The dates of capture in this table are usually the dates on which the prisoners were committed, but where an asterisk appears beside the date, this is the actual date of capture. Where the record has been extracted from the prize court the word ante appears, meaning that the ship was captured before this date, which is the date on which the case came up in court.

It is believed that many more names of captured American ships can be found in the Admirals' despatches in the Public Record Office and elsewhere and also in the records of the Vice-Admiralty courts in North America and the West Indies, also in the Public Record Office.

217

APPENDIX I

Ship's name	Captain's name	By what ship captured	Date of capture	Notes and comments	PRO Ref. HCA/28
Active	Richard Bishop		Oct. 18, 1778	Bound from Ostend to St. Eustatia. Taken by William Arnold, a customs official at Cowes, Isle of Wight.	1/296
Active	John Craig	Stag	Mar. 5, 1781	A re-capture	4/230 *
Adventure		Comet	March, 1781	Could have been a re-capture previously captured by American ship named Comet.	
Adventurer			Dec. 1781 *		
Ajax			Aug. 1781		
Alexander			Nov. 1781	Re-capture, previously captured by American ship S. Carolina.	
Alfred			July, 1778		
Alliance			March 1779		
Alliance			Dec. 1779		
Alliance			June, 1781 *		
America			Feb. 1781		
American			June 1781		
American Union			Sept. 1780*		
Angelica	William Davis		May, 1778*		
Ann			March, 1781*		
Antibriton			Jan. 1782	A French ship	

219

Ship's name	Captain's name	By what ship captured	Date of capture	Notes and Comments	PRO Ref. HCA/28
Ascott and John			May, 1781 *		
Aurora	Samuel Gerrish	Cerberus	July 25, 1780*		3/224 *
Beaver			March, 1781*		
Behmus	Nathaniel Harris	Achilles	ante Apr. 80.	Appeared to be a re-capture	2/398
Bellona			July, 1781		
Bermuda			Jan. 1782		
Betsey		Savage	Aug. 1778*	Originally French. Re-captured by the American ship Oliver Cromwell, Thomas Simmons master Sept. 1, 1778 to Salem with John Foster as Prizemaster. Re-taken by HMS Squirrell Sept. 6, 1778.	1/170 *
Betsey	Offin Boardman	Union	ante June, 80.	Was going from Nantes to Va.	3/45
Betsey			March, 1781*		
Betsey	Jesse Harding	Enterprise	Oct. 1781	A merchant ship	5/319
Betsey	George West	Surprize	ante Nov. 81		
Bienfaisant			ante Oct. 81	A re-capture	5/324
Black Prince			Jan. 1782		
Black Prince			April, 1779		
Black Princess	Edwd. M'Carty		July, 1779*		
			Oct. 1781*	French privateer	

APPENDIX I

Ship's name	Captain's name	By what ship captured	Date of capture	Notes and comments	PRO Ref. HCA/28
Black Snake	Wm. Lucran or Le Craw		Aug. 1777*		
Blossom			Oct. 1781		
Brune			Oct. 1781		
Bunkers Hill			April, 1780		
Cabot					
Centurion			Nov. 1780		
Chance	Wm. Almy	Admiral Edwards	May, 1781	Taken by Americans to Va. Re-taken by British to N.Y. Re-taken by Americans to Boston. Re-taken by British.	3/45*
Charming Polly			May, 1777*		
Charming Polly	Francis Brown		Sept. 1780		
Charming Sally			Jan. 1777		
Chatham			June, 1781*		
Civil Usage	Giddson		Feb. 1782		
Collection	Wyatt St. Barbe		ante July, 79		
Comet			Oct. 1781*		2/8
Commerce			Feb. 1779		
Confederacy			April 1781*		
Confederacy			Feb. 1782		
Count D'Estaign	John Kenrick	Brutus and Little Brutus	ante Nov. 79	Amer. privateer, crew of 76.	2/121
Countess of Marlboro			May, 1781*		

221

Ship's name	Captain's name	By what ship captured	Date of capture	Notes and comments	PRO ref. H CA/28
Dalton	Eleazer Johnston	Reasonable	Dec. 1776*		
Daniel			Oct. 1780		
Diana	John Miller	Levant Bonetta Griffin	ante Dec. 79		2/200
Diana	Joy Castle	Alert	ante May, 80	A re-capture	3/8
Diana	William Down		Feb. 81*		
Delaware	Adam Wellman	Hyena	ante Dec. 79		2/200
Dennis			March, 1781*		
Desire	George Smith	Rippon	Jan. 1777	Taken to Cape of Good Hope. Re-captured from the Black Princess	5/416
Diligence			July, 1780		
Disdain			Jan. 1782		
Dolphin	Israel Turner	Peace & Plenty	ante Aug. 79		2/12
Dolphin	Wm. Middleton		May, 1781		
Dove	Wm. M'Collock	Bridgett	ante Aug. 82	Captured by a "refugee boat" from the Virginians and carried into N. Y. where she was.... sent as a privateer under name of Resolution and c. Xmas 1780 taken by Saratoga, rebel frigate to Phila. and now re-taken by British.	7/165

APPENDIX I

Ship's name	Captain's name	By what ship captured	Date of capture	Notes and comments	PRO Ref. HCA/28
Duc de Coigny			July, 1780		
Duke of Leinster			May, 1781		
Eagle			March, 1781		
Eagle			Feb. 1782		
Eagle	John Fitzhenry		ante July, 80	Originally of Bristol. Taken by Amer. privateer the Bennington on way from Newfoundland. Re-taken by Atalanta.	3/87
Elie or Elia					
Elijah or Eliza	Hamilton Foster		Nov. 81 *	On voyage from Jamaica to Glasgow taken by Grand Turk Nov. 15, 1781. Re-captured by British Nov. 21.	
Elizabeth	William Pritchard	Quebec	ante Sept. 79	Originally British.	2/89
English			July, 1781		
Essex			Dec. 1780		
Essex	Timothy C. Oden		June, 1781		
Fair American	John Smith	Vestale	Nov. 1780		3/451 *
Fame			March, 1781		
Fame	John Taylor		Aug. 81		
Fame			Feb. 1782		
Fancy	John Lee		Aug. 1777*		
Fanny			Jan. 1782		

Ship's name	Captain's name	By what ship captured	Date of capture	Notes and comments	PRO Ref. HCA/28
Favourite	Jeremiah Morgan	Flora?	ante Dec. 80		3/436
Favourite	Elias Davis	Shaftesbury	June, 1782*	Taken on voyage Port au Prince to Amsterdam.	7/238
Fearnought	Wm. Patten or Patton		March, 1782 ante Dec. 79		2/205
Five Brothers					
Flying Fish			May, 1781		
Fort Stanwin			April, 1780		
Fox	Alexr. Ross	Alert	ante Jan. 81		4/3
Fox	Stephen Hills			Captured by Americans ante Jan. 1779. Re-taken by British ships Flora and Rainbow ante Jan. 1781. Later captured by French.	5/416
Fox	Israel Johnson	Jenny	ante Oct. 82	A re-capture.	7/214
Franklyn			Oct. 1780		
Franklin		New Adventure	Oct. 1781*		5/426 *
Franklin	Thos. Cox	Latona	ante Sept. 82		7/180
French Bermuda			Jan. 1782		
Friends	John Norcombe	Venus	ante Aug. 82		7/164
Friends Adventure	Stephen Pightling	Vulture	Dec. 4, 1780		4/3 *
Friends Adventure	Thos. Fossey	Adml. Bonnington	ante Aug. 82		7/164

APPENDIX I

Ship's name	Captain's name	By what ship captured	Date of capture	Notes and comments	PRO Ref. HCA/28
Friends Good Will	Geo. Mitchel		May, 1781*	Taken by William Hill the mate and others of the crew and brought to Bristol.	1/292
Friendship	William Coombes		ante July, 79		
Gascon			Mar. 1781*		2/20
Gatray	Robert Spears		May, 1781		2/126*
General Dalling	Nicholas Bartlett		ante Nov. 79		
General Glover			Oct. 1779	Crew of 66	
General Massey			Oct. 1781		
General Mercer			Dec. 1780*		
General Mifflin			June, 1780*		
General Mifflin			July, 1781		
General Nash			March, 1781*		
General Sinclair			Oct. 1780*		
General Sullivan			April, 1779		
General Washington			May, 1781*		
General Washington			June, 1781*		
General Wayne			Aug. 1781		
George	Gregory Cozzens		ante May 77	Brought to North Britain by part of the crew of the ship.	2/349
George					
Governor Johnson	Michael Barder	Ceres	Sept. 1781		
Grand Turk			ante July, 80		3/70

225

Ship's name	Captain's name	By what ship captured	Date of capture	Notes and comments	PRO Ref. HCA/28
Greyhound	Jacob Willis		Oct. 1780 *	Capt. also given as Jno. Kemp	
Hambden			Jan. 1779		
Hampton	George Stewart	Alert	ante Nov. 82		7/236
Hannable			Sept. 1780 *		
Hannah	Thomas Parker	Lydia	ante Nov. 81	A re-capture	5/353
Happy Return			June, 1781		
Harlequin			June, 1780 *		
Hawke	Hibbart		April, 1778*		
Hawke	George West	Vulture	ante Mar. 83		8/129
Hector	James Slover		Sept. 1780 *		
Hercules	Thos. Dismore	Minerva	Oct. 1781	Crew of 116	5/427 *
Hercules	Thos. Elkins	Lady Howe	Jan. 1782		6/238 *
Hero	Wm. Shillins or Skillins	York	ante Nov. 82		7/236
Hero			Jan. 1781		
Hetty			March, 1781		
Hibernia	Saml. Smedly		Oct. 1780 *		
Hiram	Burton Hathaway	Botetourt	ante Sept. 79		
Hope	James Gillis	Griffin and Speedwell	ante Sept. 78	Claimed by Sir Edmund Head, Wm. Hest, Geo. Kincard of N. Amer. passengers, who were forced from Amer. on account of allegiance to His Majesty.	1/4D

APPENDIX I

Ship's name	Captain's name	By what ship captured	Date of capture	Notes and comments	PRO Ref. HCA/28
Hope	Thos. Munro	Jupiter	ante Apr. 82		6/285
Hornet	John Welch		July, 1778	Capt. also given as Jno. Nicholson	
Hunter			Mar. 1781*		
Huntingdon			May, 1781		
Independence	Stephen Hopkin	Byron	ante Aug. 79		2/11
Independent					
Industry	Benjamin Atkins	Wm. Altham	ante May, 80	Also called Union	2/418
Industry			July, 1780*		
Jack			July, 1780*		
Jack			Feb. or June, 1781		
James and Rebecca	Wm. Harding	Endymion	Oct. 1781	Taken by Franklin, John Turner master, and now re-taken by British ship Endymion.	5/285*
Janey	George Rolls				
Jason	John Manley		Sept. 1779*		
Jason	Chas. Hambleton	Monsieur	Oct. 81	Crew of 76 men	5/426*
John	Don McNiven	Grantham Packet	ante Dec. 80	British ship originally taken by Amer. ship Pilgrim and now re-taken	3/427
John			Mar. 1781*		
Johns			May, 1781		
Jolly Tar			July, 1780*		

Ship's name	Captain's name	By what ship captured	Date of capture	Notes and comments	PRO Ref. HCA/28
Jupiter	Chris. Bassett	Emperor	ante Nov. 80	A re-capture	3/386
Lady Washington	John Oliver	Alderny	ante Jan. 81	French privateer	4/1
Lark			May, 1781		
Larravie			Mar. 1781		
Le Dauphin de Baltimore	Nicholas Martin	Genl. Conway	ante Jan. 83		8/4
Lexington	Henry Johns(t)on		Sept. 1777*		
Lion or Lyon	John Green		June, 1781*		
Little Purgey or Porgy	John Brown		ante Dec. 79	Stated to be an English ship captured by the Oliver Cromwell and later set free to return to England	2/217
Little Purgey or Porgy	Wm. Armstrong	Guernsey	Nov. 1781*		6/4*
Lively	Jas. Belt	Jupiter	Dec. 1780*		3/233*
Lively	Henry Stoughton	Surprize Vestal	Oct. 1780		4/3
Lord Camden			ante Jan. 81	Previously captured by Franklin John Turner Commr. and now re-taken	
Lucee	Wm. Randall	York	ante Sep. 82		7/181
Lucretia	Seth Cleaveland and Danl. Rhodes	Thynne	July, 1778*	From S. Carolina. Re-taken by Americans July, 78 and re-taken by British July 18, 78 by	1/3C*

APPENDIX I

Ship's name	Captain's name	By what ship captured	Date of capture	Notes and comments	PRO Ref. HCA/28
Luke	Jos. Clark	Farmer	ante Dec. 80	Grasshopper, Cygnet and Seaford.	3/426
Lurana	Jas. Heydon	Alemena and Kite	ante Aug. 82	A re-capture	7/165
Luzerne			May, 1781*		
Lydia			April, 1781		
McClenachan	Thos. Houston	Guernsey	ante Sep. 82		7/180
McClery			Oct. 1780*		
Marboys			ante Nov. 79		
Maria	Francis Rival		June, 1779*		2/122
Mariana			June, 1780*		
Marlborough			July, 1779		
Marmy	Joshua Swain	Milford	June, 1781*		
Marquis de la Fayette	Bennet Neagus		Sept. 1781*	Of Dunkirk	2/11*
Marquis of Mole-bank or De Morbec				Believed to be the Martha. British ship taken by the Black Prince off Scotland.	
Martha	Alexr. Thompson		ante Jan. 80		2/249
Mary			Feb. 1782	Re-capture previously captured by American ship Grand Turk	
Mary and Elizabeth	Benjamin Weekes	Hussar	Dec. 79		2/83*

Ship's name	Captain's name	By what ship captured	Date of capture	Notes and comments	PRO Ref. HCA/28
Maryland			Sept. 1780 *	Captured by Disdain, an American ship and now re-captured.	
Mathew			Dec. 1781		
Medly			May, 1781		
Mercury			Nov. 1780		
Mercury			Feb. 1782		
Minerva			June, 1780 *		
Montgomery			Aug. 1781 *		
Monmouth			Oct. 1779 *		
Morning Star	Wm. McCleuer		Aug. 1781		
Mosquito or Muscetor	John Harris or John Martin		Aug. 1777	May have been two different ships. No date for J. Martin	
Mulbury			Aug. 1780		
Nancy	Briamond	Offer	ante July 79		2/8
Nancy	Samuel Hanway	Watt	ante Nov. 79		2/121
Nancy	John Dean	Neptune	ante June, 80	Taken by Americans May 24, 1780 and re-taken May 29	3/62
Nancy			Nov. 1780		
Nancy			Jan. 1781 *	Captured by American ship Saratoga and now re-captured	
Nantz	William Williams	Shaftesbury	ante July 79		1/181
Neptune	Ignatius Webber	Dragon	Dec. 1779	British ship captured by the Providence, a rebel sloop of Boston and now re-taken.	2/270

APPENDIX I

Ship's name	Captain's name	By what ship captured	Date of capture	Notes and comments	PRO Ref. HCA/28
Nesbitt	John Green	Liberty	ante July 79		1/270
Newburn			July, 1781		
Newbury	John Allen	Alarm	ante Nov. 82	Part of cargo French	7/236
Newfoundland			June, 1781		
North Star	Francis Fawston	Surprize	ante Feb. 80	A re-capture	2/279
Notre Dame			May, 1777 *		
Oliver Cromwell	Hammon Corter		Aug. 1779		
Oliver Cromwell	Edward Febour		ante Dec. 79	A Re-capture	2/171
Orange Free			Feb. 1782		
Patty			Feb. 1782		
Peggy					
Petomme					
Phoenix	Eli Vickery		Feb. 1779 *		1/226
Phoenix			Nov. 1780		
Phoenix	Jos. Cunningham		April, 1781 *		
Pilgrim	Jas. Harr	Lightning	ante Nov. 82		7/236
Pocahontas			Nov. 1780		
Polly	Thos. Lang		March 1780 *	Formerly a British ship called Neptune of Glasgow, taken by the Americans. Freighted by persons who had been captured by the rebels she returned to	2/241

231

MARINERS OF THE AMERICAN REVOLUTION

Ship' name	Captain's name	By what ship captured	Date of capture	Notes and comments	PRO Ref. HCA/28
Polly	Jas. Edwin or Erwin	Conqueror	June 27, 81*	Bristol under the same captain. Taken by Americans to Philadelphia and now re-taken. Crew of 35	6/18*
Polonick			March, 1781		
Pomona	John Robertson	Diana	July, 79		2/15*
Portsmouth			June, 1781		
Protector	John F. Williams		May, 1781*		2/120
Providence			ante Nov. 79		
Rambler			Oct. 1779*		
Randolph			Jan. 1779		
Ranger	John Holmes	Richard	Aug. 79		2/11
Ranger			July, 1781		
Rattlesnake	Edw'd. McCullock	Surprize	ante Feb. 83		8/82
Raven	Danl. Needham	Triumph and Duchess of Kingston	ante Oct. 78		1/5E
Rebecca	Joseph Chase			From Charles Town. Claimed by passengers John Moncrieff, Robert Ray and Wm. Creighton leaving America on account of their allegiance to His Majesty.	
Rebecca	John Gale	Aolus	Oct. 1780*		7/180
Rebel	Zachariah Sairs	Brune	ante Sept.82	Capt. by Viper and now re-capt	4/191
Resolution					

APPENDIX I

Ship's name	Captain's name	By what ship captured	Date of capture	Notes and comments	PRO Ref. HCA/28
Resolution	Saml. Rice	Intrepid	Nov. 1780		7/218
Retaliation		Sandwich Pomona Russell	ante Oct. 82		
Reprisal	Weeks		Aug. 1778		
Robertson			Jan. 1781*		
Robinson			April, 1781		
Royal Louis			Nov. 1778*		
St. Francis			Dec. 1781	Captured by the Franklin and now re-captured.	
St. George	Gilbert Falconer	Winchelsea	ante Sep. 79	Originally British, taken by Americans. Re-captured by Winchelsea, then Bristol, Porpoise and Niger appeared.	2/18
St. John	John Riggin	Terrible	ante Sep. 79		2/83
Salley (Brigantine)	Thomas Tracy	Sarah Goulburn	ante Oct. 77		1/1
Sally	Edward Bowen		ante Nov. 79		2/122
Sally	Nathnl. Phillips	Aolus	ante Sep. 82		7/181
Sally	Nathnl. Harding	Pacifick	ante July, 83		8/327
Salley and Becky			Dec. 79		
Samuel and Elizabeth	Jacques Clementbeen		ante Nov. 79	A re-capture	2/121

Ship's name	Captain's name	By what ship captured	Date of capture	Notes and comments	PRO Ref. HCA/28
Saratoga			Jan. 1780		
Satisfaction			July, 1778		
Somerset			Feb. 1782		
South Quay			March, 1781		
Spy			Feb. 1779		
Sturdy Beggar	George Southward		Oct. 1776		
Success	James Wilkinson		ante Apr. 80	This vessel belonged to American Loyalists, John Stoughton and Henry Nash of N. Y. and Johns Joaquim Netto of N. Y. and Portugal. It was taken by both British and French.	2/391
Success	Wm. White	Preston James Mary	ante May 81	Was French. Captured by British. Captured by Americans. Re-captured by British.	4/419*
Susannah			March, 1781*		
Susannah	John Murphey		July, 1779	Previously captured by American ship Oliver Cromwell	
Swallow					
Sweet Lucretia					
Talbot	Soloman Frazier	Cerberus	ante Oct. 80		3/383
Terrible			Sept. 1780*		
Thom			July, 1780*	Prob. meant for Thorn or Thos.	

APPENDIX I

Ship's name	Captain's name	By what ship captured	Date of capture	Notes and comments	PRO Ref. HCA/28
Thomas	Isaac Smith	Enterprise	Oct. 1781	A merchant ship	5/319 *
Thorn	Phil Aubin	Grantham	Feb. 1782		3/224
Thorne	John Martin	Surprize	ante Sep. 80		3/382
Tom Johnson	William Coward		ante Oct. 80		
Tom Lee			March, 81 *		
Tracey			Sept. 1780 *		
True Blue			Jan. 1778 *		
Twin Sisters			June, 1781 *		
Two Brothers	Wm. MacBride	Duke of Portland and Barbary	Jan. 1782		1/210
Two Sisters			March, 1781		
Ulysses			June, 1781		
Union	William Jenkins or Francis Brown	Diana	ante Aug. 79	Formerly the British ship Perkins, now re-taken.	1/183
Union			March, 1781		
Venus	Jas. Ward	Terror	ante May 81		4/334
Venus			Dec. 1779		
Venus			June 1781 *		
Viper	John Hanson	General Conway	Sept. 81 *		5/319 *
Virginia	Peter Hodgkinson	New Adventure	ante Mar. 82	Taken by Americans to Philadelphia and now re-taken	6/145
Warren	John Ravel(1)		Dec. 1777 *		

Ship's name	Captain's name	By what ship captured	Date of capture	Notes and comments	PRO Ref. HCA/28
Washington	Daniel M'Neil	Stag	Oct. 1780 *		7/238
Wasp	John Rathbone	Recovery	ante Nov. 82		5/427 *
Wexford	or John Peck Rathburn		Oct. 1781	Formerly the Mars of Guernsey captured by American frigate Alliance and taken to Boston. Now re-taken as a privateer with crew of 120.	
Weymouth			July, 1779		
Wild Cat			July 1779 *		
William			Oct. 1780		
William	Burns			This ship sailed Dec. 1782 from Jamaica under convoy of HMS Ardant, Vaughan and Hydra. On Jan. 23 at 6 a.m. was taken by American privateer Dolphin and at 8 p.m. re-taken by Vaughan.	5/382
William and Mary	Phil. Marriet or Marriot	Santa Margaritta	ante Nov. 81		5/352
Wolf	Nathnl. Nowell	Planter, Lydia, James, Northumberland	ante July 82		7/114
Yankee					

APPENDIX I

Ship's name	Captain's name	By what ship captured	Date of capture	Notes and comments	PRO Ref. HCA/28
Yorke Packet	Stephen Weekes	Farmer	Jan. 1776	Sole property of Walter Franklin of N.Y. Taken at Savannah River.	4/21
Zephyr Zephyr	John Howland	Stagg	ante April, 80 June, 1781		2/369

ADDITIONS TO LIST OF SHIPS

Ship's name	Captain's name	By what ship captured	Date of capture	Notes and comments	PRO Ref. HCA/28
Betsey	Jas. Robb	Hornet	ante Jan. 83	Taken on voyage Guadaloupe to Boston.	8/14
Eagle	Wm. Smith	Fly	ante Dec. 80	A re-capture.	3/451
Montgomery	Benj. Hill		Aug. 1777		
Neptune		Pilgrim	June, 1781		
Polly	Reuben Folger	Jupiter	ante Apr. 82		6/285
Retaliation			Oct. 1780		
Revenge	Alex Murray	Enterprize	ante Oct. 80		3/227
Revenge			Jan. 1781		
Rhodes			Nov. 1780		
Richmond	George Ford	Byron and four others	ante Apr. 80		2/370
Rising States	Saml. Mansfield	Genl. Conway	ante Sept. 82		7/181
Rising States	James Thompson	Terrible	June, 1777		
Roebuck	Jonathan Felt	Unity	ante Mar. 80		2/364
Roebuck			Jan. 1781		
Union	Gideon Henfield			See Independence.	

238

APPENDIX II

An Act to impower His Majesty to secure and detain Persons charged with, or suspected of, the Crime of High Treason, committed in any of His Majesty's Colonies or Plantations in *America*, or on the High Seas, or the Crime of Piracy.

WHEREAS a Rebellion and War have been openly and traiterously levied and carried on in certain of His Majesty's Colonies and Plantations in America, and Acts of Treason and Piracy have been committed on the High Seas, and upon the Ships and Goods of His Majesty's Subjects, and many Persons have been seised and taken, who are expresly charged or strongly suspected of such Treasons and Felonies, and many more such Persons may be hereafter so seised and taken: And whereas such Persons have been, or may be brought into this Kingdom, and into other Parts of His Majesty's Dominions, and it may be inconvenient in many such Cases to proceed forthwith to the Trial of such Criminals, and at the same Time of evil Example to suffer them to go at large; be it therefore enacted by the King's most Excellent Majesty, by and with the Advice and Consent of the Lords Spiritual and Temporal, and Commons, in this present Parliament assembled, and by the Authority of the same, That all and every Person or Persons who have been, or shall hereafter be seised or taken in the Act of High Treason committed in any of His Majesty's Colonies or Plantations in America, or on the High Seas, or in the Act of Piracy, or who are or shall be charged with or suspected of the Crime of High Treason,

Treason, committed in any of the said Colonies, or on the High Seas, or of Piracy, and who have been, or shall be committed, in any Part of His Majesty's Dominions, for such Crimes, or any of them, or for Suspicion of such Crimes, or any of them, by any Magistrate having competent Authority in that Behalf, to the Common Gaol, or other Place of Confinement as is herein-after provided for that Purpose, shall and may be thereupon secured and detained in safe Custody, without Bail or Mainprize, until the First Day of January, One thousand seven hundred and seventy-eight; and that no Judge or Justice of Peace shall bail or try any such Person or Persons without Order from His Majesty's most Honourable Privy Council, signed by Six of the said Privy Council, until the said First Day of January, One thousand seven hundred and seventy-eight, any Law, Statute, or Usage, to the contrary in anywise notwithstanding.

And whereas it may be necessary to provide for such Prisoners within this Realm some other Places of Confinement besides the Common Gaols; be it enacted by the Authority aforesaid, That it shall and may be lawful for His Majesty, by Warrant under His Sign Manual, to appoint One or more Place or Places of Confinement within the Realm, for the Custody of such Prisoners; and all and every Magistrate and Magistrates, having competent Authority in that Behalf, are hereby authorised to commit such Persons as aforesaid to such Place or Places of Confinement, so to be appointed, instead of the Common Gaol.

Provided always, and be it enacted, That no Offences shall be construed to be Piracy within the Meaning of this Act, except Acts of Felony committed on the Ships and Goods of His Majesty's Subjects by Persons on the High Seas.

Provided also, and it is hereby declared, That nothing herein contained is intended, or shall be construed to extend to the Case of any other Prisoner or Prisoners than such as shall have been out of the Realm at the Time or Times of the Offence or Offences wherewith he or they shall be charged, or of which he or they shall be suspected.

And be it further enacted by the Authority aforesaid, That this Act shall continue and be in Force until the said First Day of January, One thousand seven hundred and seventy-eight, and no longer.

F I N I S.

APPENDIX III

An Act for the better detaining, and more easy Exchange, of *American* Prisoners brought into *Great Britain*.

WHEREAS, since the Commencement of the present War, Exchanges of Prisoners taken in America, or conveyed to America, have been there regularly made, with Advantage to His Majesty's Service: And whereas it may be likewise convenient for the said Service, that American Prisoners brought into Great Britain should be detained, and exchanged, in the same Manner; may it therefore please Your Majesty that it may be enacted; and be it enacted by the King's most Excellent Majesty, by and with the Advice and Consent of the Lords Spiritual and Temporal, and Commons, in this present Parliament assembled, and by the Authority of the same, That, from and after the passing of this Act, it may and shall be lawful for His Majesty, during the Continuance of the present Hostilities, to hold and detain in such Prisons or Places within Great Britain, as to His Wisdom shall seem fit, as Prisoners of War, all Natives or other Inhabitants of the Thirteen revolted Colonies not at His Majesty's Peace, who have been, or shall be, taken by Sea or Land, and brought into Great Britain: And it shall be lawful for His Majesty to discharge any Person or Persons so taken and detained as Prisoner or Prisoners of War, either absolutely, or upon such Conditions, and with such Limitations, or for such a Time, as His Majesty shall deem proper; as also to authorise any Commissioner or Commissioners to discharge or exchange all and every Person or Persons as aforesaid, according to the Custom and Usage of War, and the Law of Nations; Regard being had in the said Exchanges relative to Officers in His Majesty's Service, whether the said Officers have been made Prisoners in America or elsewhere, to the Rank of the said Prisoners, and the Length of Time since they have been taken: And the Detention, Enlargement, or Exchange aforesaid, shall be good and valid, any Warrant of Commitment, or Cause therein expressed, or any Law, Custom, or Usage, to the contrary notwithstanding.

BIBLIOGRAPHY

PRINTED SOURCES

DIARIES, NARRATIVES AND BIOGRAPHIES

1 Barney, Mrs. Mary (Chase). A Biographical Memoir of the late Commodore Joshua Barney. Boston. 1832.

2 Carpenter, Jonathan, Diary of. In *Vermont Historical Society Proceedings*, 1872 pp. vii-xi.

3 Colburn, Jeremiah. A List of the Americans Committed to Old Mill Prison since the American War. *New England Historical and Genealogical Register*, vol. 19, pp. 74-5; 136-141; 209-213.

4 Cutler, Samuel. Prison Ships and the "Old Mill Prison", Plymouth, England, 1777. Communicated by the Rev. Samuel Cutler of Boston. (Being the Journal of Mr. Samuel Cutler). *New England Historical and Genealogical Register*, vol. 32 pp. 42-44; 184-188; 305-308; 395-398.

5 Connor, Timothy. A Yankee Privateersman in Prison in England, 1777-1779. Communicated by William Richard Cutter of Lexington, Mass., with Notes. (Being the Journal of Timothy Connor). *New England Historical and Genealogical Register*, Vol. 30 pp. 174-177; 343-352; vol. 31 pp. 18-20; 212-3; 284-8; vol. 32 pp. 70-73; 165-168; 280-286.

5A Roll Appended to Journal of a Forton Prisoner. A Roll of Men's Names, Ships and Stations, from what State, Run, Dead. etc. A continuation of No. 5. *New England Historical and Genealogical Register*, vol. 33 pp. 36-41.

6 Fanning's Narrative. Being the Memoirs of Nathaniel Fanning, an Officer of the Revolutionary Navy, 1778 - 1783. Ed. and annotated by John S. Barnes. Printed for the Naval Historical Society 1912.

MARINERS OF THE AMERICAN REVOLUTION

7   Herbert, Charles. A Relic of the Revolution, Containing a Full and Particular Account of the Sufferings and Privations of all the American Prisoners Captured on the High Seas, and carried into Plymouth, England, etc. By Charles Herbert of Newburyport, Mass. Boston, 1847.

8   Russell, William, the Journal of (1776-1782). In *Ships and Sailor of Old Salem*. By Ralph D. Paine. Chapter VII. N.Y. 1909. About 50 pages.

9   Sherburne, Andrew, A Pensioner of the Revolution, Memoirs of. Written by himself. Utica, 1828.

10   Widger, William, Diary of, kept at Mill Prison, England, 1781. With an Introduction by William Hammond Bowden. *Essex Institute Collections*. Vol. 73 pp. 311-347; vol. 74 pp. 22-48; 142-158. 1937-8.

11   Coffin, Joshua. A Sketch of the History of Newbury, Newburyport and West Newbury. Boston 1845.

12   Matthewman, Lieut. Luke of the Revolutionary Navy, Narrative of. Taken from the New York Packet, 1787 and printed in *Magazine of American History*, vol. 2 pp. 175-184. 1878.

13   Conyngham, Gustavus, a Captain of the Continental Navy, 1777-1779, Letters and Papers Relating to the Cruises of. Ed. by Robert W. Neeser. Published by the Naval Historical Society, Vol. 6. 1915.

14   Blatchford, John, the Narrative of, detailing his sufferings in the Revolutionary War, while a prisoner with the British. As related by himself. With Introduction and notes by Charles I. Bushnell. N.Y. 1865. (He sailed on the Hancock under Manley. Captured by the Rainbow and sent to England for trial but not imprisoned).

15   Potter, Israel Ralph, 1744-1826, Life and Adventures of. Pub. 1824. Re-printed 19 pp. in *Magazine of History*, extra number 16. (Escaped before being imprisoned and lived in London thirty years before returning to America).

16   Talbot, Silas, a Commodore in the Navy of the United States, The Life of. By Henry T. Tuckerman. Pub. 1850. Reprinted in *Magazine of History*, extra number 120.

BIBLIOGRAPHY

17   Manley, Captain John, Second in Rank in the United States Navy, 1776-1783. By Isaac Greenwood. Boston, 1915.

18   Hinman, Royal R. Catalogue of Names of the First Puritan Settlers in the Colony of Connecticut. 1846.

RECORDS OF SERVICE

19   Jonston, Henry P. Records of Connecticut Men in the Military and Naval Service during the Revolution. 1889.

20   Massachusetts Soldiers and Sailors of the Revolutionary War. 13 vols. 1896.

21   Remick, Oliver P. A Record of the Services of the Commissioned Officers and Enlisted Men of Kittery and Eliot, Maine, 1775-1783. 1901. (Some of the names of this present book are mentioned with genealogical notes).

22   Pennsylvania Archives 2nd series vol. I pp. 227-405. 5th series vol. I pp. 417-609.

23   Middlebrook, Louis F. Maritime Connecticut during the American Revolution. Essex Institute. 2 vols. 1925.

24   Morgan, Wm. James. Captains to the Northward. The New England Captains in the Continental Navy. Barre, Mass. 1959. (Has bibliography).

RECORDS OF SHIPS

25   Lincoln, Charles H. Naval Records of the American Revolution, 1775-1788. Printed from the Originals in the Library of Congress. 1906.

26   Allen, Gardner Weld. Massachusetts Privateers of the Revolution. (Mass. Historical Society). 1927.

HISTORICAL BACKGROUND

27 Abbott, Willis J. Blue Jackets of 76. A History of the Naval Battles of the American Revolution. N. Y. 1888.

28 Abell, Francis. Prisoners of War in Britain, 1756-1815. 1914.

29 Allen, Gardiner Weld. A Naval History of the American Revolution. 2 vols. 1913. Reprinted 1962.

30 Clark, William Bell. Ben Franklin's Privateers. Baton Rouge, 1956.

31 Maclay, Edgar Stanton. A History of American Privateers. 1899.

22 Maclay, Edgar Stanton. A History of the United States Navy, 1775-1894. Pub. 1895.

MANUSCRIPT SOURCES

33 National Maritime Museum, Greenwich, England. Correspondence between the Commissioners for taking care of sick and hurt seamen and the Admiralty, relating to American prisoners of war. 2 bundles. ADM/M/404, 405.

34 Public Record Office, London, England. State Papers, Domestic: Naval. Letters to the Secretaries of State relating to Naval affairs. S. P. 42/57.

35 Public Record Office, London. England. Home Office, Correspondence and Papers, Departmental: Admiralty. Original In-letters. H. O. 28/1.

36 House of Lords Record Office. Petition of Upwards of two hundred American prisoners confined in Mill Prison at Plymouth. 19 June, 1781.

www.ingramcontent.com/pod-product-compliance
Lightning Source LLC
Chambersburg PA
CBHW050343230426
43663CB00010B/1970